CW01236711

Changing Families, Changing Food

Palgrave Macmillan Studies in Family and Intimate Life

Titles include:

Harriet Becher
FAMILY PRACTICES IN SOUTH ASIAN MUSLIM FAMILIES
Parenting in a Multi-Faith Britain

Jacqui Gabb
RESEARCHING INTIMACY AND SEXUALITY IN FAMILIES

Peter Jackson (*editor*)
CHANGING FAMILIES, CHANGING FOOD

David Morgan
RETHINKING FAMILY PRACTICES

Eriikka Oinonen
FAMILIES IN CONVERGING EUROPE
A Comparison of Forms, Structures and Ideas

Róisín Ryan-Flood
LESBIAN MOTHERHOOD
Gender, Families and Sexual Citizenship

Palgrave Macmillan Studies in Family and Intimate Life
Series Standing Order ISBN 978-0-230-51748-6 hardback
(*outside North America only*)

You can receive future titles in this series as they are published by placing a standing order. Please contact your bookseller or, in case of difficulty, write to us at the address below with your name and address, the title of the series and the ISBN quoted above.

Customer Services Department, Macmillan Distribution Ltd, Houndmills, Basingstoke, Hampshire RG21 6XS, England

Changing Families, Changing Food

Edited By

Peter Jackson
University of Sheffield, UK

palgrave
macmillan

Selection and editorial matter © Peter Jackson 2009
Individual chapters © their respective authors 2009

All rights reserved. No reproduction, copy or transmission of this publication may be made without written permission.

No portion of this publication may be reproduced, copied or transmitted save with written permission or in accordance with the provisions of the Copyright, Designs and Patents Act 1988, or under the terms of any licence permitting limited copying issued by the Copyright Licensing Agency, Saffron House, 6–10 Kirby Street, London EC1N 8TS.

Any person who does any unauthorized act in relation to this publication may be liable to criminal prosecution and civil claims for damages.

The authors have asserted their rights to be identified as the authors of this work in accordance with the Copyright, Designs and Patents Act 1988.

First published 2009 by
PALGRAVE MACMILLAN

Palgrave Macmillan in the UK is an imprint of Macmillan Publishers Limited, registered in England, company number 785998, of Houndmills, Basingstoke, Hampshire RG21 6XS.

Palgrave Macmillan in the US is a division of St Martin's Press LLC, 175 Fifth Avenue, New York, NY 10010.

Palgrave Macmillan is the global academic imprint of the above companies and has companies and representatives throughout the world.

Palgrave® and Macmillan® are registered trademarks in the United States, the United Kingdom, Europe and other countries

ISBN-13: 978-0-230-22398-1   hardback
ISBN-10: 0-230-22398-2   hardback

This book is printed on paper suitable for recycling and made from fully managed and sustained forest sources. Logging, pulping and manufacturing processes are expected to conform to the environmental regulations of the country of origin.

A catalogue record for this book is available from the British Library.

Library of Congress Cataloging-in-Publication Data
Changing families, changing food / edited by Peter Jackson.
    p. cm.
  Includes bibliographical references and index.
  ISBN 978-0-230-22398-1 (alk. paper)
    1. Family–Great Britain. 2. Food–Social aspects–Great Britain.
3. Diet–Great Britain. I. Jackson, Peter, 1955–
HQ613.C42 2009
394.1'20941–dc22   2009013629

10 9 8 7 6 5 4 3 2 1
18 17 16 15 14 13 12 11 10 09

Printed and bound in Great Britain by
CPI Antony Rowe, Chippenham and Eastbourne

To our families

Contents

List of Figures and Tables	ix
List of Contributors	x
Series Preface	xiii
Introduction: Food as a Lens on Family Life *Peter Jackson*	1

Part I Pregnancy and Motherhood — 17

1. Off to a Healthy Start: Food Support Benefits of Low-Income Women in Pregnancy — 19
   Fiona Ford and Robert Fraser

2. (New) Family Formation and the Organisation of Food in Households: Who Does What and Why? — 35
   Helen Stapleton and Julia Keenan

3. Pregnancy Police? Maternal Bodies, Surveillance and Food — 57
   Rebekah Fox, Paula Nicolson and Kristin Heffernan

Part II Childhood and Family Life — 75

4. 'She's got a really good attitude to healthy food...Nannan's drilled it into her': Inter-generational Relations within Families — 77
   Penny Curtis, Allison James and Katie Ellis

5. Fathers, Food and Family Life — 93
   Alan Metcalfe, Caroline Dryden, Maxine Johnson, Jenny Owen and Geraldine Shipton

6. 'I don't go in for all that scaremongering': Parental Attitudes to Food Safety Risk — 118
   Lindsay Blank, Paul Bissell, Elizabeth Goyder and Heather Clark

Part III Family Meals — 129

7 Myths of the Family Meal: Re-reading Edwardian Life Histories — 131
   Peter Jackson, Sarah Olive and Graham Smith

8 Food as a Medium for Emotional Management of the Family: Avoiding Complaint and Producing Love — 146
   Joseph Burridge and Margo Barker

9 The Governing of Family Meals in the UK and Japan — 165
   Takeda Hiroko

Part IV Family and Community — 185

10 Eating In Time, Eating Up Time — 187
    Megan Blake, Jody Mellor, Lucy Crane and Brigitta Osz

11 Making Healthy Families? — 205
    Trish Green, Jenny Owen, Penny Curtis, Graham Smith, Paul Ward and Pamela Fisher

12 Institutional Dining Rooms: Food Ideologies and the Making of a Person — 226
    Oscar Forero, Katie Ellis, Alan Metcalfe and Rebecca Brown

Conclusion — 246
   Peter Jackson

Notes — 251

References — 257

Index — 276

List of Figures and Tables

Figures

I.1	The *Changing Families, Changing Food* research programme	9
1.1	Recruitment timeline	29
7.1	Changing mealtimes, 1961–2001	136
8.1	Advert for 'Heinz Ravioli'	155
8.2	Advert for 'Bird's Custard'	158
8.3	Percentage of material featuring feedback in *Woman and Home* by decade	159
8.4	Percentage of material featuring feedback in *Woman's Own* by decade	160

Table

5.1	Household composition and demographics	100

List of Contributors

Margo Barker is a Lecturer in Nutritional Epidemiology in the School of Medicine, University of Sheffield.

Paul Bissell is a Senior Lecturer in Public Health at the School of Health and Related Research (ScHARR), University of Sheffield.

Megan Blake is a Lecturer in Geography at the University of Sheffield.

Lindsay Blank is a Research Associate in Public Health at ScHARR, University of Sheffield.

Rebecca Brown is a Research Associate at the Centre for Child and Family Research, Loughborough University.

Joseph Burridge is a part-time teacher in the School of Sociology and Social Policy at the University of Nottingham, a university teacher in the Department of Social Sciences at the University of Loughborough, and a Research Associate in the School of Nursing and Midwifery at the University of Sheffield.

Heather Clark is a Research Associate in Public Health at ScHARR, University of Sheffield.

Lucy Crane is a PhD student in the Department of Geography, University of Sheffield.

Penny Curtis is a Senior Lecturer in Research in the School of Nursing and Midwifery, University of Sheffield.

Caroline Dryden is a Lecturer in Health Studies in ScHARR, University of Sheffield.

Katie Ellis is a PhD student in the Department of Sociological Studies, University of Sheffield.

Pamela Fisher is a Senior Lecturer in Sociology, University of Huddersfield.

Fiona Ford is a Research Dietician in Reproductive and Developmental Medicine, University of Sheffield.

Oscar Forero is a Senior Research Associate at ESRC's Centre for Economic and Social Aspects of Genomics, Lancaster University and a

Consultant Tutor at the Centre for Development, Environment and Policy at the School of Oriental and African Studies, University of London.

Rebekah Fox is a Research Associate in the Department of Health and Social Care at Royal Holloway, University of London.

Robert Fraser is a Reader in Reproductive and Developmental Medicine, University of Sheffield.

Elizabeth Goyder is a Reader in Public Health Medicine at ScHARR, University of Sheffield.

Trish Green is a Research Associate in the Department of Landscape, University of Sheffield.

Kristin Heffernan is a Lecturer in Social Work at the State University of New York at Brockport.

Takeda Hiroko is a Lecturer in Japanese Studies in the School of East Asian Studies, University of Sheffield.

Peter Jackson is Professor of Human Geography at the University of Sheffield.

Allison James is Professor of Sociology at the University of Sheffield and Director of the Centre for the Study of Childhood and Youth.

Maxine Johnson is a Research Associate in Public Health at ScHARR, University of Sheffield.

Julia Keenan is a Research Assistant at the Leeds Social Science Institute, University of Leeds.

Jody Mellor is a Research Assistant in the School of Religious and Theological Studies at Cardiff University.

Alan Metcalfe is a Research Associate in the Department of Geography, University of Sheffield.

Paula Nicolson is Professor of Critical Social and Health Psychology in the Department of Health and Social Care at Royal Holloway, University of London.

Sarah Olive is a PhD student at the Shakespeare Institute, University of Birmingham.

Brigitta Osz is a PhD student in Anthropology at the University of Szeged, Hungary.

Jenny Owen is a Senior Lecturer in Health Studies at ScHARR, University of Sheffield.

Geraldine Shipton is a psychoanalyst in private practice and an honorary Senior Research Fellow in ScHARR, University of Sheffield.

Graham Smith is a Senior Lecturer in Social Science in the Department of Health and Social Care, Royal Holloway, University of London.

Helen Stapleton is a Lecturer in the School of Nursing and Midwifery, University of Sheffield.

Paul Ward is Associate Professor of Public Health Research at Flinders University in Adelaide.

Series Preface

The remit of the *Palgrave Macmillan Studies in Family and Intimate Life* series is to publish major texts, monographs and edited collections focusing broadly on the sociological exploration of intimate relationships and family organisation. As editors we think such a series is timely. Expectations, commitments and practices have changed significantly in intimate relationship and family life in recent decades. This is very apparent in patterns of family formation and dissolution, demonstrated by trends in cohabitation, marriage and divorce. Changes in household living patterns over the last 20 years have also been marked, with more people living alone, adult children living longer in the parental home, and more 'non-family' households being formed. Furthermore, there have been important shifts in the ways people construct intimate relationships. There are few comfortable certainties about the best ways of being a family man or woman, with once conventional gender roles no longer being widely accepted. The normative connection between sexual relationships and marriage or marriage-like relationships is also less powerful than it once was. Not only is greater sexual experimentation accepted, but it is now accepted at an earlier age. Moreover heterosexuality is no longer the only mode of sexual relationship given legitimacy. In Britain as elsewhere, gay male and lesbian partnerships are now socially and legally endorsed to a degree hardly imaginable in the mid-twentieth century. Increases in lone-parent families, the rapid growth of different types of step-family, the de-stigmatisation of births outside marriage, and the rise in couples 'living-apart-together' (LATs) all provide further examples of the ways that 'being a couple', 'being a parent' and 'being a family' have diversified in recent years.

The fact that change in family life and intimate relationships has been so pervasive has resulted in renewed research interest from sociologists and other scholars. Increasing amounts of public funding have been directed to family research in recent years, in terms of both individual projects and the creation of family research centres of different hues. This research activity has been accompanied by the publication of some very important and influential books exploring different aspects of shifting family experience, in Britain and elsewhere. The *Palgrave Macmillan Studies in Family and Intimate Life* series hopes to add to this list of influential research-based texts, thereby contributing to existing knowledge and informing current debates. Our main audience consists of academics and advanced students, though we intend that the books in the series will be accessible to a more general readership who wish to understand better the changing nature of contemporary family life and personal relationships.

We see the remit of the series as wide. The concept of 'family and intimate life' will be interpreted in a broad fashion. While the focus of the series will clearly be sociological, we take family and intimacy as being inclusive rather than exclusive. The series will cover a range of topics concerned with family practices and experiences, including, for example, partnership; marriage; parenting; domestic arrangements; kinship; demographic change; inter-generational ties; life-course transitions; step-families; gay and lesbian relationships; lone-parent households; and also non-familial intimate relationships such as friendships. We also wish to foster comparative research, as well as research on under-studied populations. The series will include different forms of book. Most will be theoretical or empirical monographs on particular substantive topics, though some may also have a strong methodological focus. In addition, we see edited collections as also falling within the series' remit, as well as translations of significant publications in other languages. Finally we intend that the series has an international appeal, in terms of both topics covered and authorship. Our goal is for the series to provide a forum for family sociologists conducting research in various societies, and not solely in Britain.

In this volume, Peter Jackson and his colleagues explore the intimate but complex relationships between food and family practices. This set of closely inter-related papers, arising out of a research programme funded by the Leverhulme Trust, leave the reader in no doubt as to the centrality of these relationships and how explorations of the way in which food is chosen, prepared and consumed provide a lens for the exploration of the continuities and changes in modern family life. To ask 'who cooks what for whom and on what occasions?' is to raise a whole series of questions about notions of family responsibilities and solidarities and about the relationships between families and wider communities and sets of relationships.

Much of the analysis within this set of papers revolves around the familiar axes of gender and generation. Readers will find that in many ways the familiar gender division of labour within the household applies as much to the buying and preparation of food as it does to other areas of domestic labour. Yet, at the same time, it is not the case that fathers are minor players in these key domestic activities; certainly gender needs to be seen in relational terms in order to explore the complexities of these divisions in daily family life. Similarly, generation continues to constitute a major strand within family life influencing some of the continuities in food practices and shaping the deeper meanings of food in everyday life.

The reader will also be quickly reminded that the relationships between food and family exist within wider political and cultural contexts. Widely reported discussions and initiatives around healthy, and especially unhealthy eating seem to convey the message that food is too serious a matter to be left to individual family members and decisions. A variety of public campaigns and professional interventions, together with more commercially-based campaigns, provide the context within which the relationships between food and family are played out. In these exchanges between public and private, between state, market and families, issues of social class emerge as key divisions. Several of the articles included here provide a useful corrective to some of the strident claims within the public debates. On the one hand, the 'family meal' of the past is shown to have strong mythical elements while, on the other, family members in the present are shown to be aware, caring and resourceful even when operating within constrained circumstances.

Readers of this collection will find considerable diversity in terms of methodology, subject matter and location. But running through all these papers is a strong sense of the importance of food as a major strand in understanding contemporary family practices and of the moral and emotional significance of meals in everyday life. It is likely that public debates about the relationships between food, health and family life will continue, especially within the context of the present global economic crisis. There is much here that can contribute to these debates and to stimulate further research into this vital area of family and intimate life.

Graham Allan, Lynn Jameson and David Morgan
Series Editors

Introduction: Food as a Lens on Family Life

Peter Jackson

When 'celebrity chef' Jamie Oliver launched an attack on the Turkey Twizzler in January 2005 as part of his high-profile campaign to improve the quality of British school meals, he tapped into a rich vein of public concern.[1] For his campaign touched on one of the most highly charged issues in contemporary Britain: the relationship between families and food. This book seeks to address these complex and contested issues by viewing family life through the lens of food. To summarise our argument in a sentence, we propose that charting the nation's changing dietary practices – what we eat, how, when and where – provides a powerful way of observing changes in family life (and *vice versa*).

At the time we began the research for this book, Jamie Oliver was campaigning to raise the nutritional standard of school meals in Britain, promoting the cause of 'healthy eating' as part of a wider programme of changes, aimed at combating the rapid growth of childhood obesity. A few years earlier, the Food Standards Agency (FSA) had introduced a new national '5-a-day' target for the consumption of fresh fruit and vegetables, with subsequent campaigns to reduce the amount of salt and saturated fats in the national diet. Following these campaigns and initiatives, cookery lessons are being reintroduced as a compulsory element of the school curriculum, with all 11–14 year olds in English schools having to learn to cook for a minimum of one hour a week (Department for Children, Schools and Families: press notice 2008/0015). But these nutritional initiatives have not gone unchallenged. The proportion of children taking school meals dropped significantly in the wake of the changes, with around 250,000 fewer meals being served in secondary schools in the year after the changes were introduced (according to a survey from the Schools Food Trust and the Local Authority Caterers' Association reported in *The Times On-line* 10 July 2008). Many parents switched to providing packed lunches for their children and, in some cases, the reaction was more extreme. For a short while in 2006, Julie Critchlow, Sam Walker and Marie Hamshaw from Rawmarsh in South Yorkshire became a *cause célèbre* in the 'food wars' that raged in British schools and playgrounds. Vilified in the press as 'sinner ladies' and 'junk food mums', the Rawmarsh mothers (as they were dubbed) resorted to passing take-away food to their children through the school railings, protesting at not being properly consulted before the local school introduced new rules, banning children from leaving the school premises at lunchtimes (*Education Guardian* 20 March 2006).

Jamie Oliver's campaign took a new turn in 2008 as our research was coming to an end, culminating in a television series called 'Jamie's Ministry of Food'. The series set out to revive Britain's war-time effort to improve the nation's diet by teaching basic cooking skills and giving sound, government-backed, dietary advice. Jamie set up a Food Centre in Rotherham, providing free food advice and cooking demonstrations and managed to recruit one of the 'Rawmarsh mothers' (Julie Critchlow) to join the campaign. While cooking skills used to be passed down through the generations, Jamie claimed, several generations of children had now left school without learning to cook at school or at home.[2] He insisted that cooking lessons should be compulsory at primary as well as secondary schools and that the government should invest more in home economics teaching, mobile food centres and adult cookery classes. During the TV series, Jamie taught local people to cook a handful of simple recipes and urged them to 'Pass It On' to their neighbours and workmates. The series caught the public imagination and was described as one of the most powerful political documentary series in years (*The Guardian* 1 October 2008), revealing the persistent social divisions that continue to haunt British society, with dire consequences in terms of public health. Successive programmes showed that it was possible to change people's cooking and eating habits, albeit often only in the short-term and with the encouragement of a TV celebrity.

As all these examples suggest, the relationship between families and food is socially significant, personally engaging, emotionally charged and politically contested. This book explores these issues by looking along the life-course, from pregnancy and motherhood, through childhood and family life, examining the social significance of 'family meals' before moving out into the wider community. While our focus is mostly on contemporary Britain, we highlight the specificity of the

British situation with some carefully chosen historical and international comparisons. By approaching the family through the lens of food, we aim to offer a new perspective on family life, challenging received ideas about the alleged decline of the 'family meal', the individualisation of 'food choice' and the relationship between professional advice on 'healthy eating' and the everyday practices of family living. We begin, though, by describing some of the basic contours of change in contemporary British families.

Changing families

References to 'the family' as a singular, monolithic and unchanging social institution are clearly misplaced. Families in contemporary Britain take many forms, with increasing numbers of people living on their own, beyond the boundaries of the nuclear family.[3] Of the 16.5 million families in Britain in 2001, nearly 12 million (around 70%) were married couples; another two million were cohabiting couples; and 2.7 million were lone parent families. Married couples with dependent children living under the same roof – the archetypal 'nuclear family' – represented less than a third (27.5%) of all families, with fewer than a quarter of individuals now living in such households (National Statistics 2007). And yet the image of the nuclear family remains a powerful, normative social ideal, underpinned by strong institutional forces and capable of exerting considerable moral force. The strength of the family as an ideal is shown in our research on homeless men who sought to (re)create family-like relations through networks of fictive kin and through their attempts to foster a homely, familial atmosphere in hostels and similar institutional settings. It is also demonstrated within the 'chosen' families of same-sex partnerships, described by Weeks *et al.* (2001), where many non-heterosexual couples employed the metaphor of 'family' to emphasise the strength of their kin-like social networks and their commitment to their partners. Same-sex couples may be 'doing family' in a different way from conventional heterosexual families but many of them also sought legitimacy for their chosen relationships through linking them with positive family images (*ibid.*: 11).[4]

The statistics also show that British people are marrying later and in fewer numbers than in previous generations. Increasing numbers of people are separating and divorcing, and increasing numbers are cohabiting and having children outside marriage. The 2001 Census was the first to ask questions about step-families and revealed that there were 700,000 step-families with dependent children and a further

200,000 with non-dependent children, together comprising more than 5% of all families in the UK.[5] As well as providing a snapshot of contemporary family life, the figures also suggest that individuals are experiencing a greater diversity of family structures during their lifetime as they move from their 'family of birth' through various 'families of choice' (Allan and Crow 2001). The number of households is increasing as the average household size declines, with a 3.9% increase in the proportion of one-person households between 1991 and 2001. Gay and lesbian couples appear to be growing in number and social acceptability, too, with increasing numbers of people living in same-sex households (though such data have only been recorded since 1994–5 in the General Household Survey and are probably subject to significant under-reporting).[6]

While families and households have always taken a variety of forms, their diversity appears to have increased further since the Second World War. The diversity of contemporary family life is further amplified when the statistics are broken down by ethnicity and geographical region (National Statistics 2007). It is widely acknowledged, for example, that British-Asian households are generally larger than households headed by members of other ethnic groups and that they are more likely to include individuals from multiple generations living in households consisting of 'extended families' (including those to whom one is related beyond the members of any one nuclear family). Likewise, there are significantly fewer co-habiting households in Northern Ireland than in the rest of the UK; a higher proportion of single-parent families (both male- and female-headed) in London than elsewhere in the UK; and a higher proportion of married stepfamilies in Yorkshire and Humberside than elsewhere in the UK (where much of the research for this book was based).

There is, then, no such thing as 'the family' in the sense of a single, homogeneous and timeless entity. Recent research insists, instead, on the diversity of family composition and the fluidity of family relationships (Williams 2004). In the case of divorced or separated families, parents and children may be stretched out across several different households (Smart and Neale 1999). In other cases, the members of transnational families may be stretched out across several continents (Bauer and Thompson 2006). As Marjorie DeVault observed in *Feeding the Family*, the family is a 'falsely monolithic' concept (1991: 15). She goes on to argue that 'a "family" is not a naturally occurring collection of individuals; its reality is constructed from day to day, through activities like eating together' (*ibid.*: 39). We share DeVault's emphasis on the practical work involved in 'doing family' as a way of avoiding ideological references to 'the family' as a social institution or as a timeless, natural unit of society.

Much recent sociological work on consumption has taken a practice-based approach (Warde 2005). Inspired by theorists such as Reckwitz, De Certeau and Bourdieu, this work has focused on the practice of everyday life, where social structures like 'the family' are reproduced through the endless repetition of routine activities, like cleaning and cooking, taking the children to school and meeting up with friends. Recent work on the family has taken a similar approach. David Morgan (1996) emphasises the significance of 'family practices' (the dynamic processes through which families are created) rather than the conventional approach to family as a structure to which people belong. For Morgan, 'family' is better understood as an adjective rather than as a noun. Building on Morgan's work, Janet Finch (2007: 66) talks about the practice of 'displaying families' (where the meaning of one's actions has to be conveyed to and understood by relevant others if those actions are to be effective as constituting 'family' practices). There is often, of course, a significant gap between idealised notions of family life and how family is performed in practice, a point which John Gillis (1997) alluded to in his useful distinction between the families we live by and the families we live with. Morgan insists that we should open up the 'black box' of family life to examine the relationships that occur within families and the wider social networks of which they form a part.[7] For family life is composed of multiple roles and relationships: between parents and children, mothers and fathers, husbands and wives, brothers and sisters, uncles, aunts and cousins (among many other roles and relationships). Morgan suggests that an analysis of the social practices involved in 'feeding the family' (who prepares food for whom, on what occasions, where and when, and under what circumstances) is likely to reveal the fluidity of contemporary family relations as well as the durability of some family practices and structures.[8]

In what follows, we seek to understand the social practices which constitute contemporary family life and the many different ways of 'doing family'. Like kinship, in Finch and Mason's (2000) work, 'family' should not be understood as a structure or system, but as constituted in relational practices, involving a wide range of participants, both kin and non-kin. We argue that food practices offer a particularly powerful lens through which to view recent changes in family life and a valuable way of addressing the diversity of contemporary families including variations *between* families (in terms of class, ethnicity and place), the social dynamics *within* families (by gender and generation, for example), different family *types* (including single-person households, nuclear, extended and step families) and changing family *contexts* (including historical and geographical variations, for example). The book sets out to offer a new perspective on family life, transcending disciplinary boundaries and challenging received ideas about 'the family'.

Changing food

As family living arrangements have changed significantly since the Second World War, so too have the farming and food industries. Underlying trends including the intensification of agricultural production, the globalisation of food supply chains and changes to national and international regulatory regimes and modes of governance (Morgan et al. 2006). Accompanying these global shifts has been a series of counter-tendencies including the rise of organic farming, opposition to the introduction of genetically modified foods and the growth of 'alternative' food networks such as farmers' markets and other forms of direct selling, designed to reduce 'food miles' and cut out the middlemen (Maye et al. 2007). As power within the food retailing industry has become increasing concentrated – with around 75% of grocery sales in the UK now controlled by the 'big 4' supermarket chains (Tesco, Asda-Walmart, Sainsbury's and Safeway-Morrisons) – there has been a parallel growth in calls for more equitable modes of production, such as Fair Trade, and more ethical forms of consumption. Recent years have also witnessed a significant reform of the EU's Common Agricultural Policy with a shift away from direct forms of agricultural subsidy, where import tariffs and exports quotas effectively prevented the entry of new players into global food markets, towards a system of financial support for rural communities in economically 'marginal' areas of Europe.[9] Morgan et al. (2006: 116) conclude their review of the current state of the global food economy by identifying two competing meta-regulatory trends where the development of an increasingly globalised 'neo-liberal economy' has been accompanied by the emergence of a 'new moral economy' of food – a debate to which we have also contributed (Jackson et al. 2008).

Within these broader changes, specific events have occurred which have intensified the politicisation of food in contemporary Britain. During the last two decades, Britain became embroiled in a series of 'food scares' and farming crises that seriously undermined consumer confidence in the safety and quality of British food. These include the political crisis over Salmonella in eggs (which led to the resignation of Health Minister Edwina Currie) and outbreaks of Bovine Spongiform Encephalopathy (BSE or 'mad cow' disease) and its human-variant

Creutzfeldt Jakob Disease (vCJD) which led to a Europe-wide ban on the export of British beef. Then, in 2001–2, Foot and Mouth Disease (FMD) returned to the UK with devastating effects on British farming and the rural economy. The occurrence of microbiological 'food scares' such as Salmonella, *E. coli* and Listeria have continued at much higher levels than elsewhere in Europe and an outbreak of avian influenza (including the H5N1 strain which may pose a direct threat to human health) remains a constant danger (Davis 2005; Knowles *et al.* 2007). The government's response to these various crises was widely criticised (see, for example, Van Zwanenberg and Millstone 2003, Ward *et al.* 2004) and led to the break-up of the long-established Ministry of Agriculture, Fisheries and Food (considered by many to have been too close to the food and farming industries) and to the establishment of a new Department for Environment, Food and Rural Affairs (DEFRA), with an independent Food Standards Agency (Marsden *et al.* 2000).

Government policy in the wake of these crises urged a closer re-connection between producers and consumers at all points along the food supply chain 'from farm to fork'. The Curry Commission's report on the 2001 FMD crisis, for example, concluded that:

> Our central theme is reconnection. We believe the real reason why the present situation is so dysfunctional is that farming has become detached from the rest of the economy and the environment.
>
> The key objective of public policy should be to reconnect our food and farming industry: to reconnect farming with its market and the rest of the food chain; to reconnect the food chain and the countryside; and to reconnect consumers with what they eat and how it is produced (Policy Commission on the Future of Food and Farming 2002: 6).

Food manufacturers and retailers have struggled to restore consumer trust in food and there have been calls for better food labelling, more effective risk management strategies and improved means of hazard control, such as the widespread adoption of Hazard Analysis and Critical Control Points (HAACP) procedures (Busch 2000).[10]

More recently, from 2005 onwards, the global food industry has been rocked by the rapid rise in commodity prices for grain and other food staples as well as for fertilisers, pesticides and other key agricultural inputs. Driven by rising energy prices, a series of poor harvests, increasing demand from consumers in the 'emerging economies' of

China and India, and the conversion of former agricultural land to the production of bio-fuels, key agricultural commodity prices rose sharply in 2006 after a long period of relative stability. Food riots and civil disorder broke out across the world (including 'tortilla riots' in Mexico, 'pasta strikes' in Italy and 'tomato boycotts' in Argentina) and governments introduced export bans and swingeing penalties for anyone found guilty of stockpiling food. In 2008, the World Bank reported that the price of staple foods had risen by 80% in the last three years. The UN Secretary General declared that the world was facing its worst food crisis in a generation and *The Economist* reported on 'The end of cheap food' in the West (8 December 2007).

Changing families, changing food

Bringing together the two strands of our research, the early 2000s were a period of heightened public, policy and media interest in the relationship between families and food. Almost as soon as he became Prime Minister in 2007, Gordon Brown called on the Cabinet Office Strategy Unit to produce a wide-ranging report on food safety and security rapidly followed by a series of policy recommendations (Cabinet Office 2008a, 2008b). The Institute of Public Policy Research (IPPR) issued a separate report, debating the need for a national food policy (IPPR 2008). As a result of all this activity, there were encouraging signs of more joined-up thinking about farming, food and families, compared to the government's previous policy position on food which David Barling and Tim Lang (2003b) described as 'reluctant'. Policy-makers also began to acknowledge the social embedding of food practices rather than their previous emphasis on individual choice. In the government's Foresight report on *Tackling Obesities* (OST 2007), for example, it was conceded that 'policies aimed solely at individuals will be inadequate'.[11] There was, the report concluded, a need for 'wider cultural changes', with action required by 'government...industry, communities, families and society as a whole'. This was a welcome change from the previous, highly individualised, approach to 'consumer choice' that characterised earlier government reports on public health including the 2004 White Paper, *Choosing Health* (DoH 2004), which argued that 'The opportunities are now opening up rapidly for everyone to make their own individual informed healthy choices'. More worryingly, however, the individualisation of food choice now seems to have percolated into popular opinion, with members of the Food Standards Agency's new Citizens' Forums placing overwhelming responsibility for healthy eating on the individual (*FSA News*, October 2008).

What, then, does the research reported here add to these debates? The programme on which this book is based was divided into three research strands on pregnancy and motherhood, childhood and family life, family and community (see Figure I.1).[12] A fourth strand included both quantitative and qualitative 'time-lines', tracing changes in food and families since the early 1900s, and some international comparisons, designed to highlight the specificity of contemporary British family life and culinary culture. We also identified various cross-cutting themes (gender, ethnicity, class and place) which enabled us to integrate our findings across the individual projects and research strands.

We begin with some of the findings from the first strand on pregnancy and motherhood. Here, our evidence suggests, pregnancy and motherhood are understood as 'projects' to be managed, balancing (often conflicting) professional advice (about feeding on demand, for

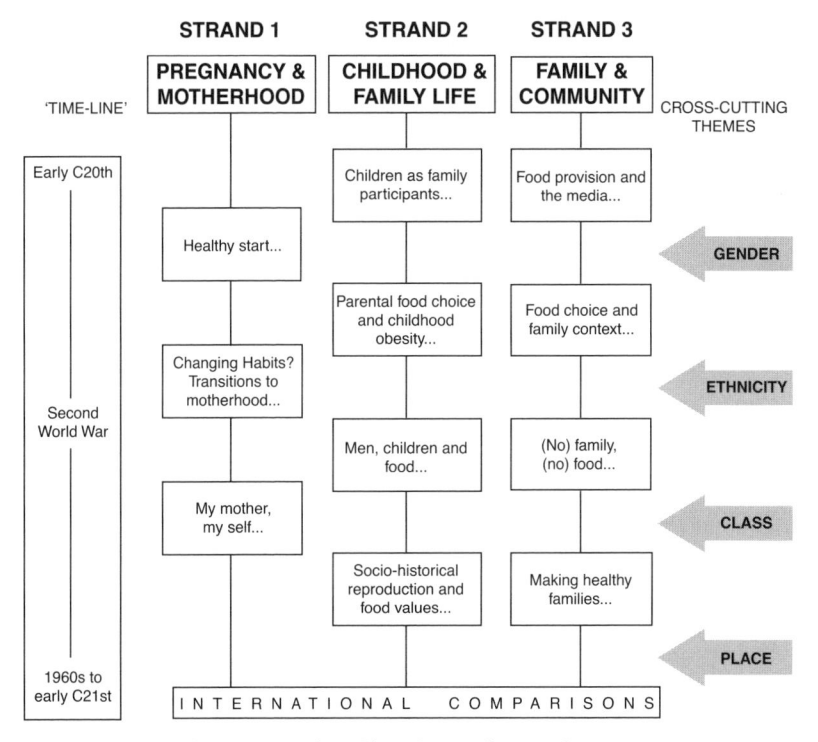

Figure I.1 The *Changing Families, Changing Food* research programme

example) with the idea of motherhood as an intuitive identity based on everyday embodied knowledge. Our research confirms earlier work suggesting that pregnancy has become increasingly medicalised over the last 40 years, through the introduction of technologies of surveillance and the promotion of 'healthy living' during pregnancy (in government initiatives such as Healthy Start whose introduction is evaluated in Chapter 1). While expectations about pregnancy have changed over recent years, these changes have had mixed results. Young mothers may feel more confident in public, for example, with greater social acceptance and public support for breastfeeding. But women face growing social pressure regarding the maintenance of an ideal body shape and size even when pregnant (a situation that has been exacerbated by the rise of so-called 'celebrity mums').

The findings from the second research strand on childhood and family life suggest that 'feeding the family' remains a highly gendered practice with women doing the majority of routine foodwork. Our research does suggest, however, that men are taking on an increasing and diverse share of domestic responsibilities with (some) men cooking more, though mostly still on special occasions, where they have professional skills or where their female partners are indisposed. We also find that children do little cooking themselves, except for making snacks and other treats. Many of the mothers in our study retained a commitment to cooking 'proper' family meals, made 'from scratch', but their commitment was often undermined by practical limitations of time and other resources, or offset by the need to balance other (family and work-related) demands, including the need to feed hungry children as soon as they got home from school. Mothers also showed great ingenuity in varying the content of the 'family meal' in order to accommodate the food preferences and tastes of different family members.

Our research confirms recent findings about changing mealtimes, away from a clear pattern of three meals a day at set times towards more frequent, informal eating events (often described as snacking and grazing). But, as with previous studies (Cheng *et al.* 2007), we found little evidence of an overall decline in the amount of time families spend eating together, particularly when eating outside the home is taken into account.[13] The making and eating of proper 'family meals', remains an important symbol of family life – a widely-shared (middle-class) aspiration though one that is not regularly achieved in practice. Recent media campaigns about the decline of the family meal therefore seem exaggerated and not supported by firm historical or sociological evidence.

Similarly with school meals, which (as noted above) have become an intense focus of recent media and policy interest, our research suggests that school lunchtimes are a space in which several discourses compete for supremacy.[14] School lunch is seen by some people as a site where civility and good manners should be taught. By others, the emphasis is on nutrition and the promotion of 'healthy eating'. For others again, the discourse of responsible consumer choice prevails or the emphasis is on efficiency, getting students to eat their food and return to the classroom as quickly as possible. If school meals are a site of discursive contestation, their common alternative, the school lunch box, can also be seen as a transitional space between home and school, family and peer group, imagination and reality. In one of our projects, children were invited to draw their dream and nightmare lunch boxes, providing tantalising insights into the psychological and social meaning of food for children and their carers (Metcalfe et al. 2008). The children in our research were often critical of the standard and cost of school meals. But they did not see them as key eating events, more as opportunities for re-fuelling or socialising before returning to class. This suggests that policies promoting healthy eating for children which position the school as a critical site for their delivery may be misguided.

The final research strand focuses on the relationships between food, family and the wider community. Our findings here are of particular relevance to current policy interventions where our research suggests that recent government initiatives may acknowledge the diversity of contemporary family life and the impact of poverty and other structural inequalities but still tend to adopt a deficit model (focusing on the paucity of cooking skills, for example, or the perceived weakness of current parenting practices). Here, our research reveals significant gaps between lay opinion (among the general public) and professional ideas about 'healthy eating' (among health managers and practitioners) where there are frequent tensions between idealised notions of the nuclear family and the diversity of family forms that are encountered in people's day-to-day experience. The image of the 'ideal' nuclear family is deeply rooted and continues to influence policy and practice. For example, our research finds health managers and practitioners making assumptions about the virtue of sitting down at the table to consume a proper 'family meal' and even thinly-veiled prejudices about what constitutes good manners and socially acceptable etiquette (learning to use 'the appropriate spoons' as one Sure Start manager put it).

Our research clearly supports those who argue that improvements in 'healthy eating' require more than an improvement in the information available to families and individuals. Research by the Food Standards Agency demonstrates the inadequacy of an information deficit model since, according to the latest Consumer Attitudes Survey (undertaken in February 2007), almost three quarters (71%) of consumers are aware of the government's 5-a-day target for eating fresh fruit and vegetables but only around a half (55%) actually met these targets on a daily basis. Our research demonstrates that children and parents were well aware of dominant narratives about 'healthy eating' but that their awareness was not always reflected in practice. Some reports (on obesity, for example) address the gaps between consciousness and practice in terms of a 'social barriers' approach, asking what social and other factors prevent 'behaviour change'. This is, in our view, too narrow an approach and we would argue for a deeper understanding of the social embedding of contemporary food practices.

The specificity of contemporary British food practices is starkly revealed by our international and historical comparisons. One could, for example, compare the (largely male) tradition of hosting and toasting in Hungary with the (more female-centred or shared) middle-class model of the British 'dinner party' (a form of entertainment largely unknown in Eastern Europe). Or one could compare the (highly normative and nationalistic) connotations of official food discourse in Japan with those in Britain. Our research on the Ukrainian community in Bradford also shows the way that food practices and meanings can shift across the generations. Where for first generation' immigrants food served as a vehicle for advancing the political project of independence, among subsequent generations food now serves as a means of facilitating active citizenship within multi-cultural Britain.

These are just brief highlights from the work that is reported in this volume. Before concluding the Introduction, however, we provide a brief summary of the chapters that follow.

Chapter outlines

In Part I, we examine the relationship between families and food at the earliest stages of the life-course, acknowledging women's crucial role in nurturing their children during pregnancy and early motherhood. Fiona Ford and Robert Fraser review a range of recent food-support programmes for pregnant women before providing an evaluation of one specific programme, the Healthy Start initiative in Sheffield. Healthy Start was designed to improve the nutrition of low-income pregnant women by providing vouchers that can be exchanged for fruit and vegetables as well as milk. The results of their before-and-after study show that pregnant and post-natal women who participated in the programme significantly increased their daily intake of iron, calcium, folate and vitamin C but mostly as a result of simply eating more. Though there were clear improvements in the women's diet, many still did not meet the recommended targets for iron and folate and, to a lesser extent, for calcium and vitamin C. Ford and Fraser conclude that for such initiatives to have a sustained impact, healthy foods need to be available, affordable and accessible and that the client group need to have an opportunity to develop their budgetary, planning and cooking skills. Claiming that mothers are increasingly held accountable for the health-related consequences associated with family feeding, Helen Stapleton and Julia Keenan examine the shifts in domestic organisation and management of family feeding practices that follow the transition to motherhood. Their chapter focuses on a group of women who were at the early stages of family formation, paying particular attention to those who are defined (or define themselves) as over-weight or obese and those living with diabetes. On becoming a mother, these women assumed responsibility for family health and the socialisation of infants, with food serving as a primary vehicle for achieving their maternal ambitions. The women prioritised the health of their children over their own well-being, even skipping meals themselves to ensure that other family members were properly fed. In the final chapter in Part I, Rebekah Fox *et al.* explore the narratives of two generations of middle-class mothers in the South-East of England, demonstrating how the experience of pregnancy has changed over the past 40 years. They document the changing advice that pregnant women have received from health professionals and members of the public regarding their own and their children's food-related activities. They conclude that pregnancy and motherhood have become increasingly medicalised, with maternal bodies and eating practices coming under increasing surveillance.

The chapters in Part II examine the changing relationship between childhood and family life. Penny Curtis *et al.* challenge the common assumption that there has been an erosion of inter-generational relations whereby parents teach their children how to cook and how to take responsibility for their health and diet. They maintain that inter-generational relations remain an important part of contemporary family life, despite the increasing diversity of household composition and family forms. Through their analysis of the narrative accounts of children and parents they demonstrate both continuities and discontinuities in ideas about family life. Their research shows how the biological ties of kinship are reworked and reinterpreted as social relationships; how traditional 'food scripts' can incorporate new types of food; and how 'generation' is discursively constructed in the process of doing family. Caroline Dryden et al. focus on the changing role of fathers in contemporary British families. While they confirm the view that mothers continue to do the majority of routine food-related work in contemporary British families, their research also reveals the wide range of domestic tasks undertaken by men and the diversity of experience within different families. Listening directly to men's voices, they conclude that their presence in the kitchen is more active and more complex than previously acknowledged and that many men consider taking responsibility for shopping, cooking and eating together as a family as defining characteristics of being a 'good dad'. Lindsay Blank et al. conclude the discussion of childhood and family life with an account of how parents handle food safety issues and other risks associated with cooking and eating. Based on interview evidence, they conclude that many parents adopt a fatalistic attitude towards food safety, trusting authorities such as the Food Standards Agency and regarding media reporting of food scares as exaggerated. While this could be regarded as trivialising the risks associated with farming and industrialised food production practices, their attitudes are rationalised in terms of the effectiveness of long-term habits and learned family behaviours which are claimed to offer them protection from food-related risks.

In Part III, we turn the spotlight on family meals, a central issue in recent media and policy debate about families and food. Peter Jackson et al. suggest that the alleged decline of 'the family meal' is a contemporary myth that is reproduced in public debate as a way of 'making sense' of the present, despite a lack of convincing historical or sociological evidence. By rereading life history evidence from the Edwardian period at the beginning of the twentieth century, they find that families of all social classes rarely ate together on a regular basis. Then, as now, meals were fitted in around the family's other domestic commitments and work routines, with family meals upheld as a common middle-class aspiration, all-too-rarely achieved in practice. The chapter concludes that the alleged decline of the family meal represents a kind of contemporary 'moral panic' – a myth that is articulated by society's moral guardians, based on a partial and exaggerated interpretation of the available evidence. Joseph Burridge and Margo Barker also examine historical evidence of the changing role of food in family life through an analysis of changing representations of food in two popular women's magazines since the 1940s (*Woman's Own* and *Woman and Home*). The chapter shows how, in both editorial content and advertisements, women are portrayed as responsible not only for the purchasing and preparation of food but also for managing the emotional response of family members. Aiming to create happiness, unity and love and to avoid complaint and disappointment, women (as wives and mothers) bear an emotional burden that has not been adequately acknowledged in previous accounts of feeding the family. We turn next to a telling international comparison where Takeda Hiroko demonstrates the diversity of governing strategies within advanced liberal democracies, by focusing on the governance of family meals in the UK and Japan. She argues that food retailers play a more prominent role in regulating the UK food system while in Japan the government exercises a stronger normative role. In both countries, however, she finds that the food regulatory system assumes a particular type of subjectivity where consumers are expected to take individual responsibility for their food choices and to acquire the relevant knowledge on which to base their decisions. In both countries, she argues, not all individuals are able to take equal advantage of this enterprising, consumer-orientated system of food regulation.

In the final section, we trace the relationship between families and food out into the wider community. The first chapter continues the theme of the previous section, demonstrating how the organisation of family meals and domestic space within the household reflects the routines and rhythms of the wider society. Megan Blake *et al.* examine the social practices associated with family meals in the UK and Hungary. The authors argue that certain meals take on special meaning because of the way they are differentially situated within other family practices. So, for example, breakfast may be given added meaning because it is constituted as a 'family practice' while lunch may be foregone by some adults for whom it is a solitary activity, devoid of any wider, social connotations. For others, a cooked lunch retains its social significance as a valued part of a culturally-approved national tradition. The authors distinguish between 'objective time' (measured sequentially) and 'experiential time' (measured in relative terms as past, present and future). The distinction helps us understand the way that normative ideas such as 'the family meal' may be undermined in practice by the demands of people's working lives and other commitments. Trish Green *et al.* take a critical look at recent government rhetoric about 'making healthy families', including the worrying gaps that exist between the views of health professionals and practitioners and those to whom they provide advice. The authors suggest that current debates about 'healthy eating' have often been dominated by prejudice, myth and unproblematised assumptions, grounded in unexamined notions about what constitutes appropriate and inappropriate forms of parenting. They challenge the emphasis on individual responsibility in government health advice and urge policy makers to employ local knowledge before making recommendations about 'healthy eating'. They demonstrate the precarious funding of many current food initiatives, despite its high priority in government rhetoric and they show that poor local services and amenities frequently undermine the 'healthy choices' that government is currently urging families to make. Finally, in a chapter which draws on evidence from four different projects in the *Changing Families* programme, Oscar Forero *et al.* examine the food ideologies that characterise a variety of non-domestic settings, including the institutional provision of food in schools, homeless shelters and voluntary associations. The chapter takes a Foucauldian approach to argue that the provision of food in these specific settings can be interpreted as part of a wider governmentality agenda. In this comparative context, institutional dining halls emerge as a contested space with multiple social actors drawing on multiple discourses of nutrition, efficiency, choice and civility. The chapter concludes that, to be effective, government policy must take better account of the multiple ideologies that are at play in the promotion of 'healthy eating' including the views of clients themselves. The volume ends with a brief Conclusion, drawing together the various strands of the book and suggesting some possible ways forward.

Acknowledgements

Thanks to Allison James, Paula Nicolson and Graham Smith for their helpful comments on an early version of this Introduction (prepared for the *Changing Families, Changing Food* conference in October 2008) and to Anne Murcott for her detailed and constructive comments on a later draft. Anne Murcott, David Morgan and Libby Bishop played a valuable role as our 'critical friends' throughout the research programme. Thanks also to Mathew Wisbey, Jackie Pickering and Daphne Lai for their outstanding administrative support and to the Leverhulme Trust who funded our research.

Part I
Pregnancy and Motherhood

1
Off to a Healthy Start: Food Support Benefits of Low-Income Women in Pregnancy

Fiona Ford and Robert Fraser

Background

The health status and financial condition of mothers and their babies came into focus after the release of the *Independent Inquiry into Inequalities in Health* (Acheson 1998). It recommended that 'a high priority should be given to policies aimed at improving health and reducing health inequalities in women of childbearing age, expectant mothers and young children' including elimination of food poverty and the prevention and reduction of obesity, by increasing benefits in cash or in kind to them. The Public Health White Paper, *Choosing Health: Making Healthier Choice Easier* (DoH 2004), continued the policy commitment to address health inequalities, giving high priority to tackling smoking, and supporting maternal and child nutrition in low-income groups through the Healthy Start (HS) scheme.

A pregnant woman becomes eligible for HS if she is at least ten weeks pregnant, and either she or her family receives Income Support, income-based Jobseeker's Allowance, Child Tax Credit (but not Working Tax Credit) with a family income below £15,575 or she is a pregnant teenager under 18, regardless of her financial circumstances. Once accepted in the scheme, pregnant women and children aged between one and four receive one voucher per week worth £3.00, babies under one year old receive two vouchers, worth a total of £6.00. Vouchers can be used in a wide range of registered shops and pharmacies (DoH 2002a; DoH 2002b). Before commenting further on the introduction of HS, we provide an overview of the research evidence linking nutritional status, pregnancy outcome and deprivation in the UK and maternal and child food support schemes in developed countries.

Nutritional status and deprivation

Evidence suggests variations in nutrient intakes of women of childbearing age in the UK by socio-economic status (Mouratidou *et al.* 2006a). Rogers *et al.* (1998) demonstrated that only three out of the 20 nutrients examined in the diets of nearly 11,000 pregnant women were unaffected by financial constraints. Dietary inadequacies have been identified in the diets of low-income post-natal women whether or not they were breastfeeding, in the UK and elsewhere (Doran 1997; Schofield *et al.* 1989). Low-income mothers are at nutritional risk and more likely to have a poor pregnancy outcome such as a low birth weight baby (i.e. birth weight less than 2500 g) which is closely associated with illness and death in infancy and an increased risk of coronary heart disease, diabetes and hypertension in later life.

Apart from being undernourished, low-income women are more likely to have a low level of education, smoke, live in poor housing and have stressful lives. Intertwined with the effects of low income are stress and anxiety from many sources including increased physical work, isolation, and lack of social support, illness, close birth intervals and ambivalence about pregnancy outcomes (Dallison and Lobstein 1995). Women who are overweight or obese before they conceive have an increased risk of complications during pregnancy and birth. Women from disadvantaged groups have a poorer diet and are more likely either to be obese or to show low weight gain during pregnancy and are also less likely to take folic acid or other supplements before, during or after pregnancy (Bolling *et al.* 2007; Heslehurst *et al.* 2007; Bull *et al.* 2003; Morin 1988).

Mothers usually occupy a central position in making dietary decisions for the whole family and play a key role in ensuring that their children establish healthy eating patterns. The pre-school age is a crucial time for establishing dietary patterns and food intake. In the UK, as elsewhere, obesity is becoming more common among children, young people and adults. Almost two-thirds of adults and a third of children are either overweight or obese, and work by the Government's Foresight programme suggests that, without clear action, these figures will rise to almost nine in ten adults and two-thirds of children by 2050 (GOS 2007).

The root causes of nutritional vulnerability are complex and diverse with inter-related risk factors such as poverty, deprivation, low educational attainment, and language barriers. The reliance in much contemporary analysis of food patterns and nutritional indices on indicators of socio-economic status are likely to mask both complexities of social differentiation (i.e. gender, ethnicity, religion, age, area and community, how long individuals have been living in deprivation) and what characterises their living conditions (Dowler 2008).

The Acheson Inquiry (1998) reported that the poorest 10% of household spend 29% of their income on food compared to 18% in the richest. While a typical basket of goods purchased in local shops can cost 24% more than from a large supermarket, this difference can rise to 60% if the supermarket economy lines are compared. It also costs them more to shop because the physical inaccessibility of large retail food outlets necessitates expenditure on transport or the higher prices in small local shops. People in low socio-economic groups spend more on foods richer in energy and high in fat and sugar, which are cheaper per unit of energy than food rich in protective nutrients, such as fruit and vegetables.

Hunger is 'the inability to acquire or consume an adequate quality or sufficient quantity of food in socially acceptable ways, or the uncertainty that one will be able to do so' (Radimer *et al.* 1992). This operational definition is derived from a study of low-income women in upstate New York as part of a nutrition surveillance project to develop more precise indicators of hunger experienced by women and children. Hunger was described as not only being without food but being unable to acquire it through normal channels. It was experienced as a 'managed process' in which the women adopted a range of coping mechanisms in their attempt to keep hunger at bay. Hunger provoked anxiety and uncertainty about where the next meal was coming from. In other words, the central issue for these women was one of food security.

A more empowering definition is that provided by the Ontario Public Health Association (Ontario Public Health Association 1995), which states that food security is when people 'can get enough food to eat that is safe, that they like to eat and that helps them to be healthy. They must be able to get this food in ways that make them feel good about themselves and their families'. Achieving food security should be a central goal of public policy and should engage questions not only of critical welfare policy and social security reform, but of basic human rights, community health, food policy, agricultural reform, community development and local control of food supply.

Food support schemes

The twentieth century saw the introduction of social policies with nutritional objectives but there was widespread debate about whether malnutrition and poor dietary quality were attributes of poverty or a reflection of ignorance. Hence the long-standing debate continued about whether it was more effective to offer food supplements or seek to teach poor pregnant and post-natal women how to manage better. Free school meals, were initially introduced for those who were, in the words of the 1908 Act, 'unable by reason of lack of food to take full advantage of the Education provided for them'. The school milk service was developed in the 1930s partly because a depressed farming industry needed a steady market for milk. Some would argue that food subsidies, rationing and food support benefits such as the Welfare Food Scheme (WFS) and the establishment of the Ministry of Food in 1939 at the start of the Second World War were introduced with a view to curbing inflationary wage demands as well as for nutritional purposes.

The National Birthday Trust Fund

The National Birthday Trust Fund (NBTF) was started in 1928, by a group of affluent women who were concerned by the high death rate of mothers in pregnancy and childbirth in the context of high rates of unemployment and poverty. Poor health was linked to poor nutrition as part of the 1930s health movement, and mothers were identified as the most undernourished Britons.

Some of the earliest evidence that special feeding of expectant mothers might lessen infant mortality was obtained in the Rhondda Valley after the miners' strike in 1926 (Williams 1977) when, in response to food supplements, infant and maternal mortality rates fell. This was in contrast to the situation after the strike of 1921, when there wasn't any food supplementation and mortality rates rose. This was attributed by the NBTF to their distribution of marmite, ovaltine and dried milk to vulnerable mothers.

In March 1939, the Joint Council of Midwifery (1939) circulated a report on the feeding of expectant mothers and babies in the north-east of England. The women were again given marmite, ovaltine, and liquid and dried cow's milk, distributed by the Medical Officers of Health to 'necessitous cases' at antenatal clinics for a period of ten weeks before and three weeks after birth. Maternal and infant mortality rates were reduced and again this was attributed to the supplementary foods provided by the NBTF.

The assumption that NBTF food supplements reduced maternal mortality appears to have been less of an evaluation of the research, than a statement of support for a programme of relief that reached many impoverished women. Many in the scientific and medical establishment of the day criticised the nutrition research, saying it was unscientific and inconclusive. This is because of the difficulty in disassociating the effect of food support from enhanced maternity care given to the same women. Yet many social reformers have credited the NBTF's food supplementation with smoothing the way for the World War II Ministry of Food and the initiation of the WFS to ensure adequate rations for pregnant and breastfeeding women.

The People's League of Health

The objective of the People's League of Health (PLOH), instituted in 1917, was 'to raise the standard of health of the British nation' (Nethersole 1922). In 1935, they instigated a research study to assess whether supplements of vitamins and minerals to the diets of pregnant women would benefit the course of pregnancy and labour, and the health of the newborn child. They undertook a pilot study of the dietary intakes of 1000 pregnant women over one week to assess which constituents to include in the nutrient supplement to be tested in the trial. Results showed that the women were not deficient in protein but only 70% of them were having enough calcium and only 2% appearing to have an adequate iron intake.

Following the pilot study the main nutrient supplementation trial was undertaken in 1938 and 1939 with 5000 pregnant women in ten London hospitals. The study group were given pills containing iron, calcium, iodine, manganese, copper, vitamin B, containing all factors of the B complex known at that time, vitamin C, halibut liver oil (which contained vitamin A and vitamin D) and essential fatty acids. The control group was given similar tablets without the addition of any of the above nutrients.

The PLOH trial found that women who had received nutrition supplements during pregnancy were less likely to have developed 'toxaemia' (raised blood pressure in late pregnancy) and to have delivered too early. It is considered one of the largest and best controlled trials of a dietary intervention in pregnancy. Although the trial was not a randomised controlled trial, the characteristics of the women in the study and control groups were similar as care was taken to ensure unbiased allocation to comparison groups. The study was reported in two articles in 1942 in the *British Medical Journal* and *The Lancet*, and in a final report published in 1946 (People's League of Health 1942a, 1942b, 1946). Despite the implications of the results, the trial received a mixed reception at the time.

Toronto supplementation study

Ebbs *et al.* (1941) published the results of a feeding experiment in Toronto. They divided their patients into three groups: (1) where the diet was poor; (2) where a poor diet was supplemented by food distributed to the home; (3) where the diet was also poor but the mother was judged to be able to afford to buy adequate food but had not done so and was therefore given dietary advice. It was found that the number of babies born prematurely and the stillbirth rate were significantly reduced in the group given food support and the group given dietary advice, when compared to the group given neither food support nor dietary advice. This study has been criticised because of small numbers of participants and some doubts about whether the groups were strictly comparable, because of differing obstetric histories. However, this study was one of the first to recognise that food supplements and dietary advice were both effective in improving dietary intakes in vulnerable pregnant women.

Special Supplemental Nutrition Programme for Women, Infants and Children

In the USA, the long-standing Special Supplemental Nutrition Programme for Women, Infants and Children (WIC) has been running since 1972. The WIC programme is directed towards low-income pregnant and postnatal women, breastfeeding mothers and children from birth to five years. Elements of the programme include: food supplements of dairy products, infant formula, juice, eggs and cereals provided via market vouchers or home delivery, dietary advice, and referral to health services which are usually available on site (Kowaleski-Jones and Duncan 2002).

Evaluations of WIC show that it has a positive impact on birth weight and length of pregnancy, with the highest-risk populations deriving most of the benefits and the longer the benefits were received, the greater the positive effects. Other beneficial outcomes were increased gestational weight gain, improved dietary intakes, reduced maternal and childhood anaemia and increased rates of breastfeeding. Some have argued that the beneficial effects of WIC cannot be attributed to food supplementation or dietary advice alone, since antenatal medical care was also enhanced.

Expanded Food and Nutrition Education Program (EFNEP)

The EFNEP programme currently operates in nearly 800 counties throughout the 50 states in the USA. EFNEP is designed to assist low-income families in acquiring the knowledge, skills, attitudes, and changed behaviour necessary for nutritionally sound diets, and to contribute to their personal development and the improvement of the total family diet and nutritional well-being. One of EFNEP's primary audiences is the low-income family with young children. Practitioners and local peer educators deliver EFNEP as a series of lessons, often over several months. This hands-on, learn-by-doing approach allows the participants to learn how to make food choices which can improve the nutritional quality of the meals they serve their families. They gain new skills in food production, preparation, storage, safety and sanitation, and they learn to better manage their food budgets and related resources from federal, state, and local food assistance agencies and organisations. They also may learn about related topics such as physical activity and health.

The Canadian Montreal Diet Dispensary

The Canadian Montreal Diet Dispensary (MDD) programme has been running since 1963 and delivers food supplements of milk and eggs, dietary advice, and inter-agency referral for other health needs, antenatal care and social support. Evaluations of the scheme have shown that the rate of low birth weight was reduced from 10% in pregnant participants to 5.6%, which is similar to the rates prevalent in non-disadvantaged areas (Heaman *et al.* 2001).

Food supplements v food advice

In 1936, Boyd Orr (Boyd Orr 1936) showed that diets became inadequate when food expenditure fell below a certain level per week. Yet others including the British Medical Association (BMA) disagreed and argued that *'given wisdom, a nutritious diet could be constructed by those on low-incomes'* (BMA 1933, 1939). The BMA view prevailed, despite the fact that their proposed diets were thought to be unpalatable and neglected all that was known about UK food habits. It was the BMA's concept of a theoretical minimal diet, and not Boyd Orr's idea of a practical level that reflected actual food habits, that became the basis for the budget on which post-war national assistance and later supplementary benefits were based.

The BMA view was taken further in the 1940s by some who believed that *'the supervision of diet should be one of the primary functions of all working in maternity and child welfare clinics'*. These clinics are attended by many women who could be instructed in the art of buying and cooking food. A food advice bureau could be established in the waiting hall of the clinic, including a gas-stove of the type found in most working-class homes. *'Thus food can be prepared in front of the women who can take notes, ask questions, collect Ministry of Food recipes, and taste the food until it is their turn to be examined'* (Nixon 1944). The bureau's success depended on *'having the right type of demonstrator who must be practical, sympathetic, and aware of the difficulties that beset so many women in the cramped space of their homes. Her function is to advise the women; what to buy, how to buy, and what to do with the food when bought. She should buy the food in the neighbourhood of the clinic, in the district where the mothers live'*. Such a bureau was first started in the out-patient department of The Soho Hospital for Women, London, at the end of 1941 and in two further London hospitals the following year. It was hoped that these maternal food advice bureaux could be rolled out nationwide but unfortunately that was not the case and a food and vitamin supplement scheme i.e. the Welfare Food Scheme (WFS) was introduced.

Welfare Food Scheme

The WFS scheme was introduced in 1940 (Welfare Food Regulations 1996) as a war-time measure to help ensure an adequate diet was provided for pregnant and breastfeeding mothers and young children under rationing conditions. Winston Churchill said of the scheme: *'there is no finer investment for any country than putting milk into babies'*. Foods supplements initially included were liquid and dried cow's milk, concentrated orange juice and cod liver oil. These were provided free or at reduced cost depending on the recipient. In the 1940s dried eggs were added for children under five years. Cod liver oil and orange juice were removed from the list of Welfare Foods in 1975 and vitamin drops and tablets containing vitamins A, C and D substituted.

The WFS began as a universal programme for all children under five years, pregnant and lactating women, regardless of family income; however the criteria for entitlement changed over time. In 1968, beneficiaries of the WFS were called 'families in special circumstances' and were described as for those for whom 'requirements exceeded resources' (Welfare Foods Order 1968). In 1971, when Social Security legislation was passed, new categories of beneficiaries developed to include those on Supplementary Benefit (SB) and Family Income Supplements (FIS). There was a discretionary inclusion of low-income families. Free and subsidised provisions for each group varied over time but WFS was free for all those on SB and FIS by the 1980s. The number of beneficiaries in Great Britain in 1999 was approximately 55,000 pregnant women and 808,000 young children – some 23% of those aged 0–4 years. Its provision in the UK cost £167 million in 1999/2000 (WFS review).

In 1999 the UK government's Committee on Medical Aspects of Food and Nutrition Policy (COMA) decided to review the WFS and the COMA Panel on Maternal and Child Nutrition was asked to undertake a scientific review of the WFS with a remit to:

- Review current dietary recommendations and available evidence on the nutritional status of women from conception to birth and/or the end of breastfeeding, and of children from birth to five years of age,
- Identify from national data, population groups particularly vulnerable to adverse nutritional outcomes,
- Evaluate the contribution of the current scheme to prevention of these vulnerabilities, and
- Identify further information needs and highlight improvements likely to be cost-neutral.

In October 2002, the DoH launched a public consultation on proposals to reform and replace the WFS with Healthy Start (DoH 2002a). The WFS was a volume-based food supplement for low-income pregnant women and infants and tokens could be exchanged for the equivalent of 1 pint of milk per day during pregnancy and lactation and liquid and formula cow's milk for children up to the age of five. Vitamin supplements previously available to WFS recipients were withdrawn in the early 1990s because of fears about the high content of vitamin A. The HS scheme was designed to offer more flexibility and choice because it provided monetary vouchers that could be exchanged for fresh fruit and vegetables as well as liquid and infant formula cow's milk and vouchers for free vitamin supplements containing vitamins D and C and folic acid. Another major change was to transfer the application process from the benefits system under WFS to midwives and other health professionals under the HS scheme. The role of midwives and other health professionals would now include advising women and families about HS and encouraging anyone who might be eligible to apply for the scheme, make sure they knew where to get an application form and how to fill it in. HS was also designed to ensure that pregnant women and families participating in the scheme had the opportunity to access good quality information and advice about health and lifestyle, including diet in pregnancy, breastfeeding, stopping smoking, and the roles of milk, fresh fruit, vegetables and vitamins in the diet.

Breastfeeding and non-breastfeeding mothers were set to benefit equally from the scheme.

Therefore, for the first time since the Second World War, the UK had a scheme that should enable dietary food advice as well as food and vitamin supplements to be given to low-income pregnant women, new mothers and their children.

Sheffield Healthy Start 'before and after study'

Having reviewed a range of food support programmes in different places, at different times, we now turn to evaluate the current Healthy Start programme in Sheffield.

Design and conduct of the study

The HS project in Sheffield is a 'before-and-after' study investigating nutrition practices in pregnant and post-natal women and their infants before and after the introduction of the new HS scheme. Dietary intakes and eating patterns in WFS and HS women were assessed at 20 weeks of pregnancy and in a different cohort at four weeks post-natally, to evaluate the short-term effect of the new HS benefit on these behaviours.

Sheffield, the fourth largest city in England, is a city of stark contrasts. Since the decline of the steel industry in the 1970s, Sheffield's 530,000 population have continued to face considerable economic difficulty, with rising unemployment causing a widening division between the richest and poorest areas. Sheffield has a minority ethnic population of 40,000. Deprivation is one of the most powerful determinants of health and almost all health indicators are adversely affected by poverty. Deprivation indicators bring together a range of social and material deprivation factors to produce an overall summary score. Sheffield's score is 26.1, which ranks as the 25th most deprived out of 354 local authorities in England. Within Sheffield, 13 electoral wards are among the 10% most deprived wards in the UK (Gordon 2001).

Methods

A 'before and after' study design was used to compare the nutritional behaviour of pregnant and post-natal women who were either beneficiaries of or eligible for WFS (Phase 1) with pregnant and post-partum women who were either beneficiaries of or eligible for HS (Phase 2). Data for WFS pregnant and post-natal women were collected between November 2005 and November 2006 (i.e. before the introduction of

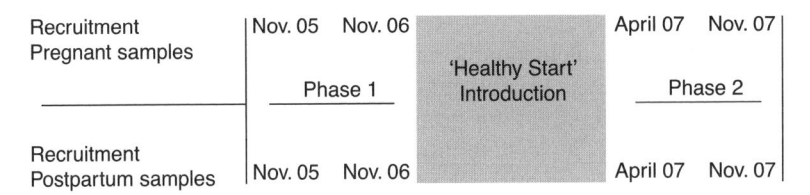

Recruitment Pregnant samples	Nov. 05 Nov. 06		April 07 Nov. 07
	Phase 1	'Healthy Start' Introduction	Phase 2
Recruitment Postpartum samples	Nov. 05 Nov. 06		April 07 Nov. 07

Figure 1.1 Recruitment timeline

HS) and for HS women between April 2007 and November 2007 (i.e. after the introduction of HS) (see Figure 1.1).

Settings and study participants

Pregnant women were recruited and interviewed in the antenatal clinic of the Jessop Wing of the Royal Hallamshire Hospital in Sheffield. Postnatal women were initially approached on the inpatient wards and then interviewed at home. The identification of potential pregnant and post-natal participants was via the Patient Administration System (PAS) of the hospital. The PAS was interrogated monthly to generate lists of pregnant and post-natal women, which were then filtered to reflect some of the eligibility criteria for the study i.e. maternal ethnicity, maternal age, and subject's postcodes. Postcodes were used to identify subjects living in deprived electoral wards of Sheffield using the Index of Multiple Deprivation (see Noble *et al.* 2008). Thereafter, women fulfilling those criteria were approached, given information and an explanatory information leaflet and invited to participate in the study. Participants were recruited at the antenatal clinic of the Jessop Wing at 20 weeks of pregnancy. Eligibility criteria included: white-British, English speaking, living in Sheffield, free of any nutrition-related pre-existing medical condition such as diabetes or coeliac disease and a recipient of, or eligible for, food support benefit.

Midwifery staff on the post-natal wards approached potentially eligible mothers for the study, to see if they were willing to be introduced to the study. Following a study overview and provision of an explanatory information leaflet by one of the research team, potential participants were asked for their permission to be telephoned by a researcher at four weeks post-natally to determine if they were still willing to participate. The eligibility criteria for post-natal women were similar to the pregnant group in addition to having a live, healthy baby.

Face-to-face, interviewer-administered, closed-question questionnaire interviews were conducted to obtain socio-demographic and anthropometrical data such as age, height and weight, maternal education level, maternal occupation, partner's occupation, household pets and receipt of benefits. Behavioural data collected included smoking habits, peri-conceptional, pre-natal and post-natal vitamin and mineral supplement usage, cooking skills and shopping habits of the household.

Dietary intakes were determined using a validated, interviewer-administered, semi-quantified food frequency questionnaire (FFQ), adapted from the FFQ used by Rogers *et al.* (1998). The FFQ asks questions about the weekly frequency of consumption of 43 foods and uses standard portion sizes. Mean nutrient intakes were calculated from foods and did not include any provided from supplements. Q-Builder was used to analyse daily intakes of energy, nutrients and food items obtained from the FFQ. The software has been described in detail elsewhere (see Mouratidou *et al.* 2006b).

Results from the Sheffield 'before and after' study

One hundred and seventy-six WFS subjects (90 pregnant and 86 post-natal) and 160 HS subjects (96 pregnant and 64 post-natal) were recruited. The results suggested that pregnant and post-natal HS women had significantly higher dietary intakes of energy, iron, calcium, folate and vitamin C compared with the WFS women (Ford *et al.* 2008). In addition, HS women ate significantly more portions of fruit and vegetables per day and were more likely to achieve the five-a-day target for fruit and vegetables. It should be noted, however, that in both pregnant and post-natal WFS and HS women, a significant proportion of participants did not meet the recommended intake for iron and folate and to a lesser extent for calcium and vitamin C. The observed differences between HS and WFS women remained significant after controlling for potential confounding effects of known factors, i.e. education and age. It appears that these differences are because the HS women were simply eating more. HS pregnant women consumed an average of 611 calories per day more than WFS women and HS post-natal women had an average of 394 more calories than WFS women. The source of these increased energy intakes was primarily increased milk consumption, but they also ate more chocolate bars, cakes and buns, puddings, cheese, sausages and burgers, and crisps.

The incidence of neural tube defects such as spina bifida can be reduced if women increase their folate intake before conception and during the first three months of pregnancy. It is now recommended that in this period folic acid supplements are taken (400 mcg per day) and dietary intake is increased to 300 mcg per day. About half of all pregnancies in the UK are unplanned which limits the usefulness of peri-conceptional supplements in reducing the risk of neural tube defects. Results from the present study showed that about 50% of both WFS and HS women planned their pregnancies but far fewer women took peri-conceptional folic acid supplements. None of the pregnant or post-natal HS women had been supplied with HS supplements which contain 400 mcg of folic acid.

Evaluating the impact of Healthy Start

The HS scheme is an agent for nutritional intervention aimed at supporting low-income mothers and families. One of the biggest challenges when trying to improve the diets of women, children and families is how to help them change their behaviour (rather than just their knowledge and attitudes).

A systematic review of food support interventions for childbearing women in the developed world emphasised the need to develop robust study designs to measure effectiveness and cost-effectiveness of food support programmes, such as HS (D'Souza *et al.* 2006).

Designing supplemental food packages which optimise the potential benefit for long-term health poses a variety of challenges. Problems of malnutrition for energy and essential nutrients must be addressed in the context of the current high prevalence of overweight and obesity in the UK. Health professionals advising women in their care about food support schemes should have sufficient nutritional skills to advise them competently about the foods to include to improve nutrient intakes and also in compensation the foods that should be excluded, to reduce the risk of excess energy intakes (NICE 2008).

Concern has been raised recently that obesity is a by-product of food support programmes such as WIC that enable participants to consume more food than they otherwise would. A meta-analysis of food support programmes in the USA showed that non-elderly adult women, who account for 28% of the caseload, are the only group of food support recipients for whom multiple studies show a link between food support receipt and an elevated BMI and obesity. According to these studies, food support participation over a one- or two-year period increased the probability of a woman becoming obese by two to five percentage points and may lead to a 0.5-point increase in BMI, or about 1.4 kg for a woman 165 to 170 cm tall (Ver Ploeg *et al.* 2008).

Healthy foods need to be available, affordable and accessible, and women need the opportunity to learn how to make the right choices and develop their own budgeting, planning and cooking skills. Money for food is often seen as the 'elastic item' in a tight budget – it is whatever is left over when the non-negotiable bills such as utilities have been paid. Maternity Alliance reported that 'Healthy Start vouchers will contribute to the food budget but in a very limited way, meeting little over 10% of the cost of a "modest but adequate" pregnancy diet' (McLeish 2005).

It is difficult to compare our findings with those of others because of differing dietary intake methodologies, age categories, socio-economic status and the inclusion of populations that were neither pregnant nor breastfeeding. The recent Low Income Diet and Nutrition Survey (Nelson *et al.* 2007) conducted by the Food Standards Agency failed to find either malnourishment or evidence that poor individuals are forced into unhealthy diets compared with the population as a whole. Individuals in low-income households were less likely to consume wholemeal bread and vegetables, both of which make a significant contribution to nutrient and dietary fibre intakes. Additionally, 39% of individuals from low-income groups reported that they worry about having enough food to eat before they receive money to buy more, i.e. food insecurity. Similarly, about a third reported that they cannot afford to eat balanced meals. Overall, one-fifth of adults in low-income groups reported reducing the size of, or skipping, meals. Also, 5% reported that, occasionally, they did not eat for a whole day because of insufficient money to buy food.

In cities like Sheffield a programme for action in maternal nutrition must be delivered which will engage and empower the local community to improve the diets, eating patterns and cooking skills of our vulnerable parents. This will result in sustainable change; connecting the support, enthusiasm and commitment of local people working in partnership with a wide range of local, regional and national agencies. It will still be essential to generate evidence about the effectiveness of nutrition interventions.

Sheffield has recently been successful in bidding to become a 'Healthy Town' as part of the National 'Change4Life' programme and, as a result, will receive £5 million of additional funding to spend on initiatives to reduce child obesity (www.nhs.uk/Change4Life). Change4Life is intended to mark the start of a lifestyle revolution which aims to help families eat well, move more and live longer. A major part of this project will be to improve parents' infant feeding practices and develop nutrition-screening tools and nutrition training resources that can be used by personnel with little or no nutrition training (such as peer support and family workers) and health professionals (such as midwives and health visitors). The tools and resources must be valid, reliable, and easy to administer to help practitioners work through the screening and care planning process in a systematic and logical way to help them to identify those individuals that require further specialist dietetic advice.

The findings of nutrition research are often misrepresented in the media, and the conflicting and negative nature of nutrition claims are confusing and frustrating for practitioners as well as the general public. Nutrition and diet fill a large amount of media space and time, with food-related stories guaranteed to make the headlines. Practitioners must communicate clear and consistent messages about food, health and the concept of a healthy, balanced diet to a wide range of people. In theory, this should be simple, because the underlying messages relating to public health nutrition are fairly consistent. But simply improving people's knowledge about a healthier diet is not enough. Any comprehensive attempt to improve diet and nutrition within the population must look at interventions across a range of levels, settings and groups of people. Therefore a capacity building project for maternal and infant nutrition needs to be developed including the use of community food workers who have specialist nutrition training and can undertake much of the dietary education work required to improve the nutritional status of low-income women, in particular 'cook and eat' sessions, shopping advice and how to eat more healthily on a low income. Recent guidance on maternal and child nutrition from the National Institute for Health and Clinical Excellence (NICE) recommends that 'a multidisciplinary approach (involving and supporting the families themselves and the wider community) is the most effective option'. It is important that advisers adopt a non-judgemental, informal and individual approach based on advice about food (rather than just nutrients). Three recent models that could be adapted for promoting dietary change are health trainers/ community volunteers for health, breastfeeding peer supporters and the food competencies framework (FSA 2007).

Conclusion: unanswered questions and future research

Food support benefits of the kind reported here are important because of their long-term effects on those who receive such benefits, as revealed by recent epigenetic research. Epigenetic processes are those in which the genome is subject to certain environmental influences to which it is exposed, particularly early in life, which cause modifications in the expression of genes. On occasion, these changes may even be passed on from one generation to the next. Malnourishment in the womb causes genetic changes that can still be seen when people reach middle and old age; according to new research it shows how strongly environmental influences can interact with the human genome to shape health. A study of children born during the Dutch 'Hunger Winter', a famine that struck at the end of the Second World War, has found that some still bear its lasting genetic legacy more than six decades on (Heijmans et al. 2008). The results offer some of the best evidence for the importance of epigenetics, a process by which environmental factors can change the way genes are switched on and off in the body.

A limited number of nutritional interventions targeting low-income women in the UK with dietary and health outcomes have been reported. Despite the limitations of the current study design, this is the only research with data on maternal dietary intakes and eating patterns before and after the introduction of Healthy Start. These findings are based on preliminary results and only short-term effects are reported. There are still a number of unanswered questions though and analysis of other priority outcomes such as gestational weight gain, post-natal weight retention/loss, breastfeeding rates, infant feeding practices, reasons why distribution of HS vitamins is problematic, women's practical cooking skills and nutrition training for health professionals who give dietary advice, would allow a more comprehensive picture of the effectiveness of new schemes such as Healthy Start.

Acknowledgement

The authors wish to express their appreciation for the book by A.S. Williams (1997) *Women and Childbirth in the Twentieth Century* which was a particularly valuable resource for them in relation to the UK historical scene described in this chapter.

2
(New) Family Formation and the Organisation of Food in Households: Who Does What and Why?

Helen Stapleton and Julia Keenan

Introduction

The provision and preparation of food and meals are highly gendered activities which are invested with practical and symbolic importance in our everyday social lives. This is very evident within a family context where food-related activities are traditionally understood to be the responsibility of women (Lake *et al.* 2006). As evidenced by current UK government campaigns concerned with rising levels of childhood obesity (Cavendish 2008), mothers in particular are held increasingly accountable for the health-related consequences associated with family feeding. Indeed, 'the ethical possibilities around the provision of nutritious foods are likely to be made more evident in women who, through discourses on motherhood, have been given the responsibility of providing food – and "good" food at that – to the family' (Coveney 2000: 156). Although amongst heterosexual couples and within some families there is evidence that (some) men are becoming more engaged with meal preparation, they are likely to reside in middle-class families (Warde and Hetherington 1994) and to be in relationships without children (Kremmer *et al.* 1998). Furthermore, any involvement tends to be highly selective and generally does not include responsibility for day-to-day, routine, tasks.

Drawing upon longitudinal interviews with 30 first-time expectant women/mothers and established mothers, we explore transitions from couple to parenthood/family when processes, attitudes and expectations around food and consumption practices may change. We also explore the significance of new identities (mother/father) and transmitted understandings of gender roles, and idealisations thereof, in relation to family 'foodwork', particularly the ways in which different households organise food-related practices including shopping, preparation and consumption. Although we attempted to recruit women from a variety of family settings, in the event the majority indicated they were married to, or cohabiting with, male partners and were sharing the same residence. A small number of participants continued to live in the family home, with or without their partners and some lived within extended/inter-generational family settings. Within these family groupings mothers and daughters generally supported each other in meeting the food-related needs for the whole family.

In addition to normal weight women, participant cohorts included women managing a variety of diabetic states (including Type I, Type II and gestational) and women who were medically, or self, defined as overweight or obese.[1] We recruited such women because we wished to explore personal and family feeding/body management practices in the context of possible limits or controls imposed by pre-existing health and/or weight-related concerns. We also wished to investigate whether, and in what ways, concerns about health and body shape/size might influence women's decision-making processes within the family food/eating environment. Finally, we wished to examine the possible effects of partner influence as previous research has demonstrated that women reported to eat more unhealthy foods and tend to put on weight when they move in with a male partner whilst his diet tends to become healthier; a female partner's influence also has a long-term positive health impact (Lake 2006).

We began interviews by asking participants to describe their memories of food and eating in their families of origin and to draw comparisons with their current circumstances. Whilst it is generally accepted that interpretation and meaning are co-constructed and ongoing processes involving researcher and researched, interviewers are nonetheless 'deeply and unavoidably implicated in creating meanings that ostensibly reside within respondents. [...] Meaning [...] is actively and communicatively assembled in the interview encounter' (Holstein and Gubrium 1997: 114). Memory is integral to storytelling and the co-construction of dialogue is facilitated by shared understandings between interviewer and interviewee. Recalling past experiences, especially those which refer to the emotional context of events and/or relationships, is complex, not least because:

> What we, or at any rate what I, refer to confidently as memory – meaning a moment, a scene, a fact that has been subjected to a fixative and thereby rescued from oblivion – is really a form of story-

telling that goes on continually in the mind and often changes with the telling. Too many conflicting emotional interests are involved for life ever to be wholly acceptable, and possibly it is the work of the storyteller to rearrange things so that they conform to this end. In any case, in talking about the past we lie with every breath we draw (Maxwell 1980: 27).

A potential drawback with respect to our study is that although we did not recruit men, we nonetheless offer proxy accounts of their views, attitudes and behaviours as recounted by their female partners. Although we have no reason to believe these accounts are inflated or fabricated, we cannot guarantee they are representative of these particular men's memories, or their current practices.

Through an analysis of women's narratives, this chapter engages with both the considered and the more taken-for-granted aspects of influences on the division of household labour. We consider a range of factors which potentially influence the division of labour within contemporary domestic settings including inter-generational (dis)continuities with respect to food-related events, household employment patterns and financial management, culinary skills and experience, the significance attached to catering for individual food preferences/requirements, and responsibility for the healthy development of dependent, 'vulnerable' bodies. We will also explore how some domestic roles and divisions come to be constructed as 'natural', 'proper' or 'fair', and how these constructions may help to explain shifts in identities during the transition to parenthood and the process of family formation.

A brief overview of the salient literature underpinning the development of theoretical concerns in this area follows. Within this context we examine continuities and discontinuities in family food and consumption-related practices and at the division of household labour, particularly with respect to men and women's changing roles within domestic spheres.

Family structures and (changing) gender roles

Singular definitions of 'family' have been problematised in recent decades, primarily reflecting socio-demographic changes resulting from increased rates of separation, divorce, co-habitation and the birth of children outside marriage, single households including lone, and same-sex family units, re-constituted families, and childbearing occurring at a more advanced age.[2] New understandings of 'family' recognise the contributions made by alternative family groupings, including step-families (Smart *et al.* 2001), gay and lesbian families (Weeks *et al.* 2001), and lone-parent families including lone mothers (Silva 1996), lone teenage mothers (Allen *et al.* 1998; Stapleton 2006), lone black and ethnic minority mothers (Duncan and Edwards 1999), and lone fathers (Simpson *et al.* 1995). As the macro elements of family structures have changed, so have the microstructures with increasing emphasis placed on children's psychological well-being in contrast to an earlier focus on their physical and material needs (Wade 2005). These changes are characteristic of an ever more 'intensive' parenting style, especially amongst middle-class families (Hattery 2000; Furedi 2001; Perrier 2007) and perhaps go some way towards explaining why, in catering for their babies' food needs, mothers' efforts extend so far beyond mere 'provision'.

Families, and family life, are historically, socially and culturally complex phenomena (Laslett 1965 [2000]; Christensen 2004) and changing notions of family and kinship (Silva and Smart 1999; Smart *et al.* 2001) suggest that attempts to portray the individuals constituting family groupings as pre-determined, or as representative, are untenable. That said, gender norms with respect to the division of household labour remain firmly entrenched, despite more than three decades of persistent challenge by feminists to tackle men's lack of participation in the domestic sphere (Everingham *et al.* 2007), particularly in relation to food and related work (Charles and Kerr 1988; DeVault 1991; Beagan *et al.* 2008) and more so with the food offered to babies/infants (Murphy *et al.* 1999; Murphy 1998). Whilst men's relative contribution to household tasks has reportedly almost doubled over the same period (Bianchi *et al.* 2000), their role is primarily that of helper: 'chipping in' to perform 'provisional, discretionary and secondary' tasks when requested, rather than making the first move and/or insisting on a more equitable distribution of the workload (Sanchez and Thomson 1997). This reiterates the message of one feminist commentator who asserts that advancements in gender equity have not so much plateaued, but are moving in a retrograde direction (Summers 2003).

Women not only undertake the majority of traditional household work, they are also more likely to take the lead in new initiatives such as recycling (Oates and McDonald 2006). Their over-involvement in all aspects of domestic labour is regardless of their espoused ideology, time availability, or earning power (Bianchi 2000; Coltrane 2000; Shelton and John 1996). Furthermore, they appear to accept the unequal division of labour rather than regarding this as unfair (Mederer 1993; Beagan *et al.* 2008), even when they themselves report having done substantially more than their male partners/spouses (Baxter 2000). Indeed, it has been argued that normative female identity, including investment in intimate relationships, is so strongly linked to the performance of domestic labour, that admitting to an asymmetrical division may be 'tantamount to admitting that one's relationship as a whole is unfair or unsatisfactory' (Baxter 2000: 627).

As research efforts have shifted from studies of 'the' family as a social institution under a capitalist/patriarchal organising system, to a focus on the interiority of family life and the personal relationships of individual family members (Williams 2004), the diversity of family structures, and their unique and individually constructed arrangements for self-management, have emerged. The significance of 'emotion work' within a family context, and the impact of this on the division of household labour, exemplifies this orientation (Erickson 2005). Although there appears to be general agreement that family patterns and practices have changed, the *rate* and *extent* of change have been contested with some sources (Silva and Smart 1999) claiming that household-related change is often framed in 'alarmist' terms and is frequently exaggerated for political expediency.

Mothers and mothering

Feminist theorists have long argued that the organisation of the household mirrors the articulation of, and the tensions between, production and reproduction. The combined forces of capitalism and industrialisation have created particular difficulties for women as they attempt to balance the demands of intimate relationships and caring responsibilities with those generated by their domestic, and sometimes community, environments, and the workplace. The 'time crunch' associated with the transition to parenthood has been identified as a significant factor in shifting couples towards a more gendered division of household labour although pre-parental attitudes influence the actual distribution of tasks (Sanchez and Thomson, 1997).

However, women continue to be significantly more disadvantaged than men, and for longer periods, in their efforts to combine motherhood with employment (Hochschild 1989; Spain and Bianchi 1996). Internalised pressures to demonstrate proficiency across the spectrum of female experience is thought to contribute to mothers who aspire to be: 'supermum, superwife, supereverything' (Choi *et al.* 2005: 167). Traditional gender divisions have been challenged by those who argue that relationships which are open to negotiation, and which uphold the principles of reciprocity and egalitarianism, are more mutually satisfying and rewarding than those based on obligation and duty (Williams 2004); such relationships are more common in middle-class populations (Presser 1994).

Patriarchal societies have long emphasised the exclusiveness of the mother-infant bond and the importance of biological connectedness: the woman who bears the child is best placed to raise it (Hattery 2000). The 'pregnancy police' (Meredith 2005) increasingly ensure that mothers' responsibilities for infant welfare starts early and is enacted through legal processes[3] and health policies.[4] The role of the father (if one is identified) has tended to be defined by the exigencies of financial provision and vague notions of male 'protection'. Mainstream theories have tended to promulgate a belief in maternity as a biological imperative, situating women who voluntarily choose childlessness within discourses of deviance (Gillespie 2000). More recent analyses (Scrimgeour 2006), however, suggest that more extensive employment and relationship opportunities have significantly influenced women's decisions regarding the benefits of combining a professional and maternity career; this work has reduced the tendency to frame childless women negatively.

Although many of the practices associated with motherhood have changed, psychoanalytic theorists nonetheless tend to promulgate images of 'ideal' (middle-class) mothers whose (unconditional) love for, and attachment to, their children is perceived as essential to their healthy development (see critique by Chodorow 1999). Hence, the reification of an idealised ('classed') representation of motherhood as a happy and fulfilling enterprise (Benn 1998). Essentialist interpretations of motherhood have also been critically analysed, and repeatedly demolished by decades of feminist scholarship (de Beauvoir 1953; Friedan 1974; Oakley 1985; Phoenix *et al.* 1991; Lawler 2000) which further supports the thesis that mothers, and their capacity for mothering, are made, not born.

In the following section we draw on our data to illustrate key theoretical points. By way of enlivening the text and illustrating theoretical points, we have included verbatim, but anonymised, quotations derived from interview transcripts. The 'identifier' following each quotation indicates whether participants were pregnant at the time of recruitment to the longitudinal cohort [C1] or were already mothers of young children [C2]. Recruitment was also on the basis overweight/obese [O], diabetic [D], or 'normal' weight [N] status. The final figure indicates a first [1], second [2] or third [3] interview. Where text has been removed for the purpose of condensing a quotation, this is indicated [...]; additional text which has been inserted into the quotation to clarify meaning is similarly bracketed. Text in italics inserted within quotations indicates the voice of the interviewer.

Transmitted patterns? continuities and changes in food and related work

Socialisation processes expose individuals to a variety of food-related influences, including those which take place within the family setting. The division of domestic labour in participants' families of origin was generally reported along traditional lines: *women tend to do the serving and kind of wait on the men:*

> ...as my Dad were at work, my Mum were just a housewife, she just looked after the house, that were her job, so yeah, she, that's what she did. I suppose it were only fair really, weren't it, you know? [*laughs*] C1-D1/Jessica

With the exception of a very small number of families, the justification for the distribution of tasks was almost entirely, and rather matter-of-factly, described in pragmatic terms: fathers were the (usually sole) wage earners and were hence privy to certain entitlements, including discharge from routine household chores. Mothers were generally at home all day and were therefore expected to maintain the house, and its occupants. If fathers did participate in domestic work, it was generally at weekends and in the role of assistant, undertaking menial tasks with instructions from their wives:

> I can remember my Dad doing things like peeling vegetables for Sunday lunch because he was obviously off work. But the main cooking was done by my Mum. C1-N1/Amely

> My dad opted for the simpler things like putting a chicken in the oven [...] he'd help out and he'd like take things in and out of the oven and lay tables... C1-D1/Amanda

Unlike the way in which they described their mothers, most participants did not assume an active role in directing their husbands/partners engagement in foodwork but tended to busy themselves with other tasks around the home, returning to the kitchen only when the meal was finished. The (untidy) state of the kitchen, and men's attempts in cleaning up afterwards, were roundly condemned:

> He [husband] does try, bless him, but I'd rather, I just say to him, 'Leave it, I'll do it'. Because you know, he'll wash the pots and you'll find little bits on the plates and stuff, and so I'm like well leave them, I'll do it [...] it's really hard with pregnancy because you can't keep to that standard. C1-D1/Alisha

Men's (lower) cleaning standards were particularly frustrating in late pregnancy and the early post-natal period when women were often feeling tired and unwell and thus less able to cope with a double workload.

A small number of participants described their fathers performing the majority of day-to-day cooking; this break with traditional patterns of labour division was articulated primarily in middle-class families where mothers were engaged in paid employment. In a minority of families, fathers cooked because they were deemed to be more skilled, and/or because mothers voiced their dislike of this task. One father was described as cooking *the ordinary bog-standard every day meals* whilst *mum would cook if it was a proper meal*. The presentation of 'proper' meals, which are enjoyed by the whole family (Makelakel 1996), is invested with significant symbolic value, at least insofar as this concerns the reproduction and maintenance of female identity (Bugge and Almås 2006). In our study family meals signified healthfulness and family cohesion and, as such, were valued events. Even when couples did not report sitting down to eat together as a customary practice, participants generally voiced such aspirations for the future as modelling affirmative eating behaviours to children was widely regarded as integral to the project of parenting. Eating together around a dining table, and transmitting the importance of both routine and 'special' family meals such as Sunday lunch, was identified as an important feature of parenthood:

> ...we're umming and aahing whether to have a conservatory with a table in. Erm, because also when the baby's born we need somewhere to put the high chair [...] when there's a baby we need somewhere. [...] 'Cause I want to sit round the table to eat when the baby's here. C1-O1/Ellen

When reflecting on differences between their family of origin and that of their current situation, participants often made distinctions between home-made foods – which mothers normally made *from scratch* – with those which were purchased.

> ...his mum weren't a baker, she never baked buns or cakes and her own pastry or anything. She bought a lot of her things. C1-D1/Amanda

Home-produced foods were generally more highly regarded than shop-bought varieties; home-made pastry, made exclusively by mothers, was especially revered. Producing such food was very labour-intensive, however, and hence participants who reported this to be a regular feature of domestic life, generally lived in households in which mothers were not engaged in paid employment outside the home. Within their families of origin – most of which were described as nuclear – the vast majority of participants identified their mother as primarily responsible for day-to-day cooking; Betty was alone in declaring that she and her siblings *started to cook, but out of pure necessity* [laughs], *not wanting to eat any more of that food* [i.e. cooked by their mother]. Only very occasionally then, did participants make reference to mothers who were uninterested in food and meal preparation. Those who did cite this as a feature of family life often described their own attitudes in a similar vein; a high degree of inter-generational coherence with respect to disliking foodwork was revealed in the narratives of some mother-daughter dyads:

> I suppose I take, take after my Mum. [...] I'm not that bothered about food. It's just something to satisfy your hunger and you have to eat.
> *Do you think your Mum enjoyed cooking or do you think it was...?*
> No [*laughs*]. No, I think she just did it 'cause obviously she had to but er, I don't, I don't think she's ever really enjoyed it [...] no I think she just did it because she had to [*laughs*]. C1-D1/Helen

Both generations of women in Helen's family might thus be described as contradicting traditional understandings of the female role and responsibilities, particularly in relation to taken-for-granted assumptions regarding family food provision. Narratives frequently reflected the limited career opportunities available to the previous generation of women and if mothers were employed in paid work it was usually in part-time, menial jobs which were viewed by significant others as inconsequential. As Helen intimates, however, contemporary women are not necessarily burdened by 'having' to do it (cooking) but are more able to exercise their economic freedom to purchase a range of alternatives, including 'ready made' meals, eating out and domestic help.

Mothers, then, were often *stuck to the kitchen all day* although a minority of fathers were reported to assume a more prominent role, especially following retirement when they had more time *to do it [cook] for pleasure*. A number of male partners in this study were also reported to enjoy cooking, occasionally to the extent that they assumed overall responsibility for the provision of family meals. Men were noted to be particularly adept with using machinery in food production and even those who did not routinely cook were reported to derive satisfaction from their efforts, despite the (sometimes excessive) amount of time involved:

> If he's cooking pasta I won't let him do it in the evening because we wouldn't, he'd be doing it all night. [...] I was away at my mum and dad's the other day so he kind of did it then when he had the evening to himself. Took him almost two hours, and he kept saying it wouldn't take him any longer than like half an hour. But see that's his latest thing. He got a pasta kind of, you know one of those things that rolls it out? [...] he got that for Christmas. C1-D3/Julia

> We've got a bread machine [...]. That's actually his. He can use the bread machine. I was quite surprised at that.
> *And does he regularly use it or?*
> Yeah, he does use it quite often, yeah. C1-O1/Katrina

Participants born and raised in non-British cultures (our sample included Chilean, French, Pakistani and Indian), or who were living in Britain as children of first-generation immigrant families, articulated differences in the food-related roles ascribed to family members. Many of these participants also talked about food and eating in terms of culinary activities being culturally emblematic, particularly with respect to the transmission of essential, and sometimes highly specific, norms and values. Participants of Pakistani and Indian origin reported family norms which were much more rigidly gendered although changes were reported to be underway, particularly with respect to the *division* of household labour, including men's involvement in cooking:

> ...now they [Pakistani men] are expected to learn how to cook because like, er, time is changing [...] everything should be in div-

ision like household work and, erm, like in terms of earning also […] So nowadays men also know how to cook. C1-O1/Nighat

Second generation Asian fathers are thus expected to replicate the production norms of their female partners: to be both wage earners and homemakers.

Performing gender: individual roles and domestic management

Foodwork is an aspect of the maternal repertoire which is performed relationally and, as such, reflects the gender/care interface. When discussing food shopping and meal preparation in the antenatal period, participants' narratives often conveyed a strong sense of obligation and duty; this emphasis was enhanced, and there was some evidence that it was sometimes internalised, when women became mothers and acquired primary responsibility for the food-related needs of both partners and children. Only a small number of participants – notably teenagers – readily admitted that they lacked proficiency in basic culinary skills:

> I think the first thing I ever cooked for him was cheese on toast. […] And I burnt it. So I put brown sauce on it so he didn't know. And I think he knew what he'd let himself in for ever since then. C1-D1/Natalie

Narratives suggested that prior to parenthood there was more negotiation between study couples around food purchase and consumption. This was particularly so with respect to the evening meal which, although it was often eaten together, not infrequently consisted of different ingredients and required different cooking methods which reflected individual preferences and time availability. The arrival of a baby, and the desire to model 'family' eating practices, resulted in more compromise with both partners demonstrating greater flexibility and tolerance for less than 'perfect' meals.

Narratives frequently attested that the socialisation of children into 'appropriate' food and eating environments is implicit to the mothering role and attending to the nutritional needs of the family is widely regarded as an intrinsic aspect of maternal performance. The gendered division of childrearing responsibilities, which holds mothers as primarily responsible for the behaviour and welfare of children (Lee 2000), assumes they will also take an active role in monitoring body size and weight, disciplining family appetites, and remaining attuned to the need for a 'healthy balance' in the provision of family meals. Food norms in families of origin did not necessarily reflect these values, however, and hence many participants struggled with, or actively resisted, adopting these maternal responsibilities. Furthermore, some overweight women were concerned about transmitting (in)appropriate food/body image messages to children, whilst diabetic mothers were apprehensive least their 'scientific' approach to food preparation and consumption negatively influenced family attitudes and behaviours. Mothers of diabetic participants were also reported to be concerned about inadvertently highlighting (stigmatising) their child's special dietary needs by cooking different meals; balancing insulin requirements, and avoiding hypoglycaemia, however, required close scrutiny of ingredients, especially with respect to carbohydrates.

The prospect of leaving (full-time) employment and beginning maternity leave was both positively anticipated and dreaded by participants. During antenatal interviews in the final months of pregnancy, some women voiced feelings of relief: that respite from the workplace and the transition to motherhood would provide opportunities to be more creative and imaginative with food preparation, whilst others anticipated feeling guilty and blamed by partners and other family members when they opted to use this additional time for non-domestic activities. The arrival of the baby resulted in a greater or lesser degree of role switching with even women who disliked shopping and cooking assuming primary responsibility for family foodwork. This was not without difficulty and narratives described a range of adaptive responses and coping strategies. Being cast in a more domestic role was also not without concern for the integrity of some women's maternal identities:

> ...since I've been at home and I can kind of keep on top of things like what food we've got in [...] I kind of quite enjoy being prepared like that but I also get totally freaked out by how domesticated I'm getting and how it's just not me. [...] But in a way I kind of like it because then it means that it's less stress. C1-N3/Elsie

Despite the benefits of education and the experience of an independent lifestyle, many participants anticipated that the transition to motherhood would also result in household labour patterns increasingly reflecting traditional gendered stereotypes:

> I can see it definitely being, you know, mothering and then, but that's because he'll be at work and I'll be at home and I've decided that that's what I want to be like. And therefore he will let me be

like that…It's really weird because when we met we never thought of ourselves as traditional you know, and as I say I went to this grammar school where I was supposed to be completely independent and but, and yet we've just fallen into those roles just because that's what we like doing. Which I think is a bit freaky [*laughs*]. C1-N1/Emma

Regardless of the fact that Emma has elected to remain at home *mothering* whilst her husband continues full-time employment, she nonetheless appreciates the *freaky* possible consequences of role switching and lack of independent status. Couples who did not replicate gendered norms risked the disapproval of (female) family members:

[Husband's] mum thinks I should have a dinner on the table because I'm at home all day not doing anything. [Laughs] […] We took McDonalds with us to their house before we went out and she went, 'Are you having McDonalds for your tea?' And I said, we said, 'Yeah', she went, 'What, and you've been at home all day and you haven't cooked a meal?' [Laughs] I'm like, 'No, I've been busy'. C1-D2/Anne

Release from the time constraints associated with paid employment signalled Anne's availability for foodwork, despite the fact that her husband had previously undertaken this responsibility.

Some women looked on food production, and the demonstration of culinary proficiency, as an opportunity to position themselves more favourably in comparison to their mother's achievements, particularly with respect to modelling healthy food relationships to children. In the following quotation, Joanne criticises her mother for not being sufficiently *bothered* to cook; the inference is that she fails in providing adequate care for her children:

…both my grandmothers were really good cooks and they cooked absolutely everything from scratch, literally everything. And my mother just never did. And I just don't understand why because she never worked, so it's not like she didn't have time to cook. And I… [*sighs*]…there was research published yesterday, that was on the television, about junk lifestyles for children and I thought, 'Well that's how I was living as a child 30 years ago because my mother just couldn't be bothered.' (C1-O1/Joanne)

It is interesting to note that Joanne, who is educated to post-graduate level, does not question a prevailing norm: that providing healthy meals is singularly the responsibility of women (as mothers). Not all participants welcomed the food-related responsibilities which were perceived as integral to the maternal role, however, and preferences for engaging in non food-related activities were articulated:

> It's not that I would be a bad cook particularly, it's not that I don't know how to cook, it's just, I don't know, I'd rather spend my time doing something else really. C1-D1/Julia

Indeed, a number of participants anticipated these actives with little enthusiasm; they referred to cooking as a *chore* and considered eating to be a perfunctory activity which primarily served to stave off hunger:

> I can't say I get excited about it [cooking] really. It's a bit of chore. [...] it's just something I don't want to take time out of my day to do 'cause I can think of more interesting things like making jewellery or [*laughs*] something else that I'd rather be doing. C1-D1/Helen

For a few participants, the transition to motherhood and responsibility for the routine provision of family meals, impacted negatively on their previously pleasurable relationship with shopping and food provision. It was at this juncture that food-related tasks became burdensome:

> I do enjoy cooking but I think when you have to do it [cooking] every day it does become a chore. [...] It's not as fun as before. C1-D1/Amanda

Indeed, shopping for food was singled out as an activity which some participants particularly disliked and considerable numbers avoided it altogether by undertaking the *big shop* online and using local shops, farmers markets, and pre-ordered food boxes to top-up supplies. Women reported differences between their own, and their partner's, shopping patterns with partners generally shopping only for items on a list (and often failing to get everything) whilst participants described themselves as mostly knowing what was in fridges and cupboards (and hence not needing a list), as being more likely to shop spontaneously especially with respect to trying new foods, and buying treats which both enjoyed.

In the majority of households, the contribution made by male partners to the organisation of household food was often described in terms of a single meal or food item, usually prepared on a weekly basis. These 'special' food events tended to take place at weekends, regardless of male partners' employment status.

> ...he [partner] always makes a nice Sunday dinner.
> *That's one of his specialities?*
> Yeah, yeah. I like his Sunday dinner. C1-D1/Vicky

> *So do you make your own muesli?*
> He [partner] started doing that. That was his, erm, thing. He used to do it on a Sunday. C1-N1/Emma

Participants described a similar pattern of food-related roles and responsibilities in their families of origin where the reputation and culinary expertise of men (as fathers) similarly rested on their ability to produce one occasional meal. In this respect, male partners appeared to emulate, and perhaps even transmit, patterns of behaviour enacted by the previous generation.

The justification offered for maintaining traditional (gendered) divisions of labour was almost entirely accounted for in pragmatic terms: men were the wage earners and breadwinners, who needed to be adequately, and appropriately, nourished in order to work effectively. Participants, however, rarely constructed foodwork in terms of these activities being more suitable and 'natural' occupations for women. Rather, narratives suggested that domestic roles became less distinct over time, sometimes coinciding with mothers entering paid employment and children becoming more independent. It was at these intersections in family trajectories that some fathers became more involved in cooking and, indeed, a few discovered they not only enjoyed this activity but that they were also talented. A few participants reported attempting to teach their menfolk basic cooking skills in anticipation of new motherhood and greater pressures on their time:

> I'm too tired to make his tea [laughs] so...
> *Do you think it'll carry on when the baby's here that, he'll do more cooking?*
> Yeah, I've told him it will [laughs].
> *Right, and how's he taken it?*
> Well he's okay actually, yeah. I'm trying to get him to be a bit more adventurous. I was trying to teach him how to make cottage pie last week, so I think he might learn that one soon. C1-O1/Katrina

Men who enjoyed discussing food, and who contributed significantly to household cooking were very occasionally reported:

> A lot of the time when him [partner] and his dad and his brother get together they talk about food a lot and about different things they've done. C1-D3/Julia

> My brother is a very, very good cook and actually went to catering college and is now a total foodie and is sort of properly trained and works in that industry. [*laughs*] [...] in the early days (following birth) he was bringing stuff round and we were stocking up the freezer you know. He'd bring round loads of pasta sauces or curry or what have you and we'd just stick it in the freezer. [...] he's taken over baby food production, which is just fantastic. So we bought about 30 little plastic pots [...] he sends them back and they go in the freezer. [...] And again, [husband] made like big batches of home-made soup, which I've had at lunchtime and stuff. C1-N3/Hayley

As were men who were presented by their partners as being the more proficient:

> [Partner] actually enjoys it and finds it quite relaxing and takes a lot more care over it than I do. I, I think I probably, when I do cook, I probably cook more healthily than he does. Erm, but he cooks more stylishly than I do. You know, he thinks about, oh, a bit of double cream and that'll make all the difference where it would never occur to me that kind of thing. So he'll probably carry on with cooking 'cause he just is a better cook than I am. C1-N1/Elsie

Men's flair for food preparation tended to be countered, however, by their greater use of 'unhealthy' (and fattening) food items, including butter and cream. They also tended to focus on the *creative* and *stylish* aspects of food preparation and this compared with women's more *functional* approach which demanded that they first check to see *what needs eating up, what's in the fridge that's going off*. Men with culinary skills were a rare, but much appreciated, group and participants envisaged they would be an invaluable resource during the post-natal period, particularly following a difficult pregnancy and/or birth, or when new mothers were struggling to establish breastfeeding.

Food, eating and body management in the post-natal period

The arrival of a new baby put pressure on all couples, especially those in more traditional relationships where women assumed responsibility for all food-related events within the household. New mothers were often heavily reliant on their partners for help with shopping and food preparation – especially in the early post-natal period – and hence tended to eat what was presented to them rather than make requests for foods which they might have preferred, but which were unlikely to be offered. Narratives from some new mothers suggested, that they felt obliged to accommodate, rather than challenge, their partner's poor culinary skills and/or lack of nutritional knowledge:

> *You say your boyfriend's cooking a lot and he enjoys doing that for you?*
> Yeah, [but] I'd rather cook something healthy. My boyfriend rather cooks like something what's easy, but I don't like saying.
> *Yeah, because he's gone to the effort?*
> Yeah, I just think Oh, I'll eat it now but when I cook [for] him I'll like to cook healthy. But he likes a lot of pasta, so he'll like cook pasta stuff but most of the time it's just like pizza and chips and stuff. And so then I think, well, I'm supposed to be like eating healthier now but then he's cooking me pizza and chips and it's like I don't want to say anything because then it's right ungrateful. But when I cook I usually cook something like chicken stuff.
> C1-D2/Shauna

Shauna hints at a difference between men and women's approach to meal preparation which is echoed throughout our data: women were more likely to cook *something healthy* (chicken) whilst men resorted to food which was quick to prepare and which emphasised carbohydrate (pasta, pizza) and/or fat (chips). Although Shauna is appreciative of the fact that her boyfriend is attending to her needs for sustenance, like many new mothers she is nonetheless anxious about eating healthily in order to regain her figure;[5] breastfeeding mothers were also concerned about eating healthily in order to produce high-quality breastmilk, in sufficient amounts, to nourish the baby. Women managing diabetes expressed concerns about the need to eat regularly and appropriately, and with due regard to the overall caloric balance of food, matching this against insulin requirements.

The aspiration to eat healthily, and to make choices which reflect this aim, may be difficult to realise in the context of a relationship which is in transition. This is not least because embedded (and embodied) habits are not necessarily available for changing at this time and also because change is perhaps more likely to succeed when the consensus of all parties can be secured. The use of shop-bought 'ready meals', and/or home-cooked *batches* of food which had been prepared and frozen in advance of childbirth, provided male partners with an alternative culinary repertoire, at least in the immediate post-natal period. Such provision did not, however, necessarily assuage women's feelings of distress as they compared themselves with an unattainable feminine ideal:

> ...I was not able to cook for a few days [...] it was adding on my guilt, like I am not able to do anything. Like there are so many mothers in the world who can look after their baby and who can look after their house, a home also. C1-O2/Nighat

A small number of *lucky* women lived in middle-class households where male partners assumed a primary role in foodwork. In these households, female identity was not so closely bound with the successful accomplishment of domestic work.

> [Husband] cooked every single evening meal because I was still breastfeeding [...] So for a whole year, I've eaten [husband's] meals in the evening, which I think, first of all, I need to be extremely thankful for, you know, the fact that he was willing to do that because I've spoken to other new mums and, you know, they say that they feed their babies and they come down and cook the meal for their husbands [...]. C2-N/Mabel

Ongoing support from male partners was seen as essential in establishing, and maintaining, breastfeeding, particularly for mothers also managing diabetes. Breastfeeding was cited as the principal reason for men's greater involvement in food preparation in the post-natal period because during this time mothers saw themselves as needing to be *on tap* and immediately available to meet the unpredictable feeding requirements of their new infants. Breastfeeding was widely perceived to be onerous and time-consuming work which could not easily be combined with other household tasks; it was generally appreciated that maternal nutritional standards would suffer when breastfeeding women lacked adequate support:

> I don't think I actually made a cup of tea probably for the first, certainly for about the first week, first ten days. [...] it's the breastfeeding thing, everything comes back to breastfeeding [...] because I was like constantly had to be available to [son, aged 5 months] [...] the thought of going in the kitchen and getting food, getting a meal prepared, wasn't workable because there was every chance that I'd have to abandon it half way through then to feed him. [...] I just had to be on tap, literally available you know, at the drop of a hat to do anything [...] I kept thinking, what do single Mums do? I have no idea how they manage. They must just live on cup-a-soups or God knows what for the first few weeks. They really must or just you know, snack food. C1-N2/Elsie

Mabel and Elsie appreciated their good fortune in having partners who were competent and capable cooks, and who shared their food preferences. For most couples, however, adapting to a new baby entailed changes in consumption patterns with meals frequently eaten in relays and/or which were often cold (or reheated). If infants needed feeding during adult mealtimes, couples generally rotated eating to accommodate the baby's needs. Narratives from working-class participants suggested they were less likely to demonstrate egalitarian relationships in this respect; men's food needs were generally prioritised:

> We do two sittings normally when we have us food: (husband) eats his while it's warm [laughs] and I feed [son, aged 2 months] and then I have mine and [husband] carries on feeding [son]. C1-D2/Anne

Men's involvement in infant care was reported to vary considerably with some taking a very active role in most activities and others offering a highly selective input. Activities such as feeding, bathing and playing were generally relished whilst changing nappies was generally disdained:

> My husband's not very hands-on in a practical sense if you like, so he won't change his nappy and stuff. I think he feels a bit, because he's a boy and he's a man that he shouldn't. I don't know why but he just feels that way I think, or he just doesn't like dirty nappies

[...] that's what the real thing is. But you know, things like playing with him and entertaining him, he does things like that, so he does give me a bit of a break so I can do stuff that I need to do.
C1-D2/Alisha

Whilst participants generally welcomed their partner's participation in childcare, this was not necessarily because of the opportunities it provided for men to build relationships with their children, but because it released women to *do stuff* around the home. Although anecdotal reports suggested that men enjoyed their involvement with infant feeding activities, this is not to suggest that women necessarily considered them particularly competent in this domain:

So [husband's] involvement with [son, 7 months] has mainly been around bathing and putting him to bed?
Yeah, yeah.
Feeding him?
He does at the weekends. [...] He's not very good with actual food. [Son] can be awkward and I've just learned how to navigate round him, and I'm probably a little bit firmer than [husband] [...] [He] goes, 'Oh well he doesn't want it', and I say, 'Well let me try' and sort of like [*makes noise to imitate a full mouth*].
C1-O2/Theresa

I think [husband] tried to give him [son] it [food] once and said, 'He doesn't want it' and then I think he's given up.
C1-D3/Anne

Weaning, and the introduction of solid food, provided increased opportunities for men to become more involved in infant feeding. Somewhat paradoxically, however, weaning was perceived to be women's work, perhaps not least because policy directives and interventions about this transition tend to be directed at mothers, not fathers. For example, in a widely advertised 24 page weaning leaflet (DoH 2008) there is only one photo involving a male interacting with a baby (aged nine months) and this image emphasises a potential role for men in socialising children into a hetero-normative family setting. The only other male image in the leaflet depicts a General Practitioner (GP) which is interesting in view of the fact that the gender mix of GPs currently practising in the UK is now almost evenly distributed (General Medical Council 2008).

Conclusion

This chapter draws attention to a number of significant shifts in domestic organisation and management of family feeding practices following the transition to new parenthood. When discussing parenting expectations, participants' narratives frequently referred back to their family of origin and to the family practices, roles, attitudes, and patterns of behaviour to which they had been exposed, and which appeared to inform their own parenting styles. The gendered nature of domestic work was reiterated by participants, with the majority of women reporting that they were largely responsible for organising, and undertaking, the bulk of domestic tasks, especially foodwork. Becoming a family and managing the unpredictability of infant feeding demands emphasised the need for support, particularly for breastfeeding mothers. A small number of *lucky*, middle-class participants reported being in relationships with men who enjoyed cooking and were highly skilled in this area; such expertise was understood to be essential to the success of all initiation and maintenance of breastfeeding endeavours. Additional help also enabled women to make the transition to motherhood at a more gradual pace; this was especially appreciated by first-time mothers. Participants from backgrounds which featured highly demarcated gender roles sometimes reported tensions when traditional values clashed with the norms of the host country. This was very apparent in foodwork when established cultural practices were eschewed, not least because they contradicted customs assimilated through processes of enculturation.

Maintaining, or improving the health of the family was an additional concern for many participants; those managing diabetes drew on their (sometimes considerable) experience in this regard. This aspect of family life emphasised the connection between food and care and the centrality of mothers in catering to individual preferences and maintaining family cohesion. The dining table – and eating together as a 'family' – were highly regarded symbolic, and social, references in this respect. Once they became parents, couples made more of an effort to eat together at the table with one partner eating their own meal whilst the other fed the baby. Women were more likely to take the first 'shift' with infant feeding and hence they were more likely to eat cold/reheated meals. This was frequently the case for breastfeeding mothers who regularly reported missing meals altogether; those who lacked sufficient support were particularly vulnerable in this respect.

Our research thus reiterates many of the ideals associated with contemporary motherhood with participants assuming responsibility for family health and the socialisation of infants into the family; food served as a primary vehicle to achieve maternal aspirations. Once they became mothers participants generally assumed (and were expected to assume) overall responsibility for the organisation of family feeding including decisions about when, how, and what was consumed; this was the case even for the few couples where men had previously been more involved in these tasks. The few participants who were not planning to return to work in the immediate future framed their new maternal role in terms of a 'job' which served to legitimise both their decision and their status.

3
Pregnancy Police? Maternal Bodies, Surveillance and Food

Rebekah Fox, Paula Nicolson and Kristin Heffernan

> We used to call them the pregnancy police. Quite a few girls at work were pregnant the same time as me and it's unbelievable how much people think they have a right to interfere. We've all had experiences where complete strangers told us what to do, or what not to do. One of my colleagues refused to have lunch with me because I was eating tuna sandwiches and he said he couldn't bear to watch me being so irresponsible to the baby. Another time I wanted to buy a hair colour in Boots, and the pharmacist came rushing out and said 'You can't buy that' and I said I thought it was fine after the first three months. 'No, absolutely not, you know, there is a very slight risk, but any risk is a risk.' So I went to put it back on the shelf. Another colleague said that her hairdresser refused to highlight her hair, because it wasn't worth the grief she would get from the other customers. My friend was furious; she said it was her choice (Kirsty, 36).

Drawing upon accounts of recent mothers and their own mothers in south-east England this chapter examines the ways in which experiences of pregnancy and early motherhood have changed over the past 40 years. Pregnancy is a biological process but exists within social, economic, political and cultural realms and is both spatially and temporally located (Longhurst 1999: 89) with individual women in different times and places experiencing pregnancy in a variety of different ways. In this chapter we take food as a lens to explore these changes by examining advice to mothers in relation to feeding the pregnant and infant body across recent generations. While it is clear that research evidence has identified the effects of food and drink on the pregnant and post-natal body leading to burgeoning new information and advice, women themselves have been peripheral to the evidence gathering.

Feminists have argued for the ever increasing 'medicalisation' of motherhood during the twentieth/early twenty-first centuries (Oakley 1980, 1984; Conrad 1992; Barker 1998; Ussher 2006) which has constructed pregnancy as a physical 'condition' in need of medical management and control (Young 1990). At a time when pregnancy is becoming an increasingly 'public' phenomenon, with increased visibility and acceptability of the pregnant body in public life, workplaces and the media (Longhurst 2005), pregnant women are simultaneously subjected to new and expanding forms of 'insidious social control' (Deveaux 1994) in the form of 'expert' advice regarding health, diet and lifestyle.

In this chapter we consider the ways in which these various changes have affected the lives of pregnant women across two generations, drawing upon the experiences of mothers and daughters from a specific cultural group in south-east England. It is important to note here that those interviewed were all heterosexual, white and mainly middle-class, so cannot be seen to speak for the experiences of all pregnant women, but provide a snapshot of how changes in technology, media and medical 'knowledge' have influenced women's pregnancies across this time period, whilst recognising that other women, even within Britain, may have very different experiences based upon their age, race, class, sexuality or other circumstances.

Here, we briefly describe the methods used in this study before considering this inter-generational shift from two different perspectives. Firstly, we examine food 'advice' to mothers *during* pregnancy through Foucauldian notions of surveillance and governmentality, whereby previous structural or physical constraints on women's freedom are replaced by more subtle forms of 'bio-power' or self-regulation through scientific 'knowledge' and medical technologies. Secondly, we examine advice on *infant feeding* to new mothers, in the light of changing constructions of the breastfeeding discourse. Both of these mechanisms function not only as a tool of surveillance, but as a form of moral obligation and neoliberal governance over women's behaviour in accordance with culturally specific ways of 'doing' pregnancy and motherhood (Butler 1990; Longhurst 2000) to which women may or may not choose to comply to varying extents.

Methodology

This chapter is based upon research carried out in London between May 2006 and September 2007 as part of the 'My Mother, My Self' project. The aim of the project was to consider inter-generational changes in experiences of 'motherhood' between new mothers and their own mothers, through exploration of a variety of issues relating to pregnancy, diet, body image, infant feeding practices and medical advice.

The initial phase of the research involved a pilot e-mail questionnaire survey, involving both open and closed questions. The questionnaire was initially sent out to the personal contacts of all three authors and a mailing list of university departments seeking women of all ages who were mothers (or pregnant). These respondents were asked to pass the e-mail attachment on to mothers they knew (including if possible their own mother or someone from their mother's generation). It is estimated that using this 'snowballing' method the questionnaire was sent out to approximately 100 respondents. In all we received 34 responses from mothers aged between 28 and 66. The sample was not intended to be representative but to act as a basis for exploring a variety of issues relating to pregnancy and seek potential respondents for later in-depth interviews.

The second phase of the research involved one-off in-depth interviews lasting between 45 minutes and three hours with 12 recent mothers (those with a child under one year of age) and seven of their own mothers (the other mothers were either deceased, lived abroad or declined to take part in the project). The women were offered the choice of whether they wished to be interviewed together or separately with five pairs choosing a joint interview, whilst two chose to be interviewed alone. This raised interesting questions regarding the pros and cons of privacy versus sharing of memories, with many of the women reporting greatly enjoying speaking with their mothers about these topics and touching on a variety of issues that they had never discussed with them before. Talking with two individuals disrupts the standard researcher-subject dynamic and allows for information to be fed back to respondents during the process, with the interview sidetracked by mother-daughter conversations which often yielded extremely valuable information or revelations and reflection upon the generational changes that had taken place.

All interviews were held in the women's homes, providing a relaxed and informal atmosphere, with several digressing into offers of refreshments, 'off-the-record' chat or perusal of family photo albums. All interviews were digitally-recorded and transcribed verbatim and loosely based around a set of semi-structured questions designed to probe a variety of issues (personal biography, pre-natal care, diet and lifestyle, body image and inter-generational continuities and changes). None of the children's fathers were present at the interviews, although some were designated as baby-sitters in the next room, with one particularly helpful partner shouting comments through the thin partition wall – much to the annoyance of the respondent! Several of the children were present, with interviews disrupted by crying, feeding and older children's requests for entertainment or toys.

The sample was self-selected via e-mail questionnaire respondents, personal contacts and an advertisement at two local nursery schools. The younger 'my self' generation were aged between 25 and 39 whilst the older 'my mother' group were aged 53 to 70. Of the 'my self' generation one was pregnant with her first child, two had one child, five were pregnant with their second child, one had two children and one had four (all with at least one child under one year of age). Of the 'my mother' generation two had two children, four had three children and one had four, with ages ranging between 22 and 41, giving birth between 1966 and 1985. All the 'my self' generation lived together with the baby's father, eight of which were married, five of the 'my mother' generation were married and two divorced. This may reflect the fact that the 'my self' sample represented a disproportionately large number of older middle-class mothers, who had 'settled down' before planning pregnancy, although not all of the pregnancies were planned. Age at first birth varied between 19 and 36 for the 'my self' group and 18 and 31 for the 'my mother' cohort. Where some of the women had had children over a period of years (up to 16 between first and last child) marked differences were noted in the experiences of pregnancy even *within* generations.

Data from the interviews were analysed into several main themes, involving advice during pregnancy, changes to diet and lifestyle, media and body image, surveillance/self-surveillance, medical intervention and infant feeding practices. Current media sources were also examined for articles relating to pregnancy, advice, body image, maternity fashions etc, although no comparison was made with similar sources for the 'my mother' generation. It is also important to note the distortion of time upon the recall and perceptions of pregnancy, with the current embodied experience of the recent mothers being very different from the memories and reinterpretation of the past taking place amongst the 'my mother' generation, allowing for more critical distance and analysis of feelings, experiences and actions. Whilst the original brief was to examine the *changes* and *continuities* in experiences of pregnancy across the generations, the nature of the project and the way in which the questions were framed led to an emphasis upon the *differences* between mothers' and daughters' experiences, which is reflected in the focus of this chapter. We will now move on to consider some of these experiences in more detail: firstly through an examination of surveillance and control of diet/lifestyle during pregnancy and secondly through changing advice relating to infant feeding practices.

Public surveillance and control: constructing the 'foetal person'

> I mean, you know, I was talking to my aunt the other day, and she smoked through her pregnancies, and my mum was drinking and stuff. That was socially acceptable, and it wasn't really questioned. Whereas now, I feel a bit of guilt, like if someone sees me drinking a glass of wine. I hardly go out these days anyway, and it's not like I drink excessively or anything, just a glass of wine when I go out, but if someone see's that, they might think, 'oh, that's not very responsible'. I think it's changed a lot, I think there's a lot of pressure on...pregnant women to conform...and I agree, some of it's like...but some of it's just so anal, I mean, like, some of the food stuff is like, you know, really extreme (Lola, 37).

Feminists have criticised the increasing medicalisation of childbirth in the latter half of the twentieth century, arguing that this dis-empowers women and submits them to unnecessary medical control, surveillance and intervention over what is an essentially natural process (Oakley 1980, 1984; Fox & Worts 1999). Pregnancy, it seems, is now viewed as a 'normal illness' (Ussher 2006: 17) positioning women in the role of 'patient' and 'the unruly reproductive body as a legitimate object of medical and scientific surveillance, amenable to containment and control' (*ibid.*: 16). Markens *et al.* (1997: 354) argue that pregnancy and women's behaviour have always been controlled, what has changed is how and by whom. In the past many religious and cultural taboos and rituals existed surrounding the female reproductive body (Ussher 2006: 16), which has now been simply transformed into scientific 'truths' by the process of medicalisation.

This surveillance can be seen within a Foucauldian framework of neoliberal governance, whereby women internalise dominant discourses and actively engage with the medicalisation of their own pregnancies (Nicolson 1998; Armstrong 1995). Medical or technological 'wisdom' exerts increasing power in a society where it is often viewed as scientific 'fact' or 'truth', becoming internalised as a specific form of social control to which many willingly submit (Foucault 1973, 1979a). Thus, surveillance is not only imposed 'top down' by the 'nanny state' (*The Times*, 26 May 2007) or public scrutiny of everyday behaviours, but policed by pregnant women themselves engaging in reflexive practices of risk management, embedded within culturally specific ideologies of 'good' and 'bad' motherhood (Tyler 2008):

> Discipline is instilled from within and punishment if we waver from the norm, self induced. The effectiveness of this disciplinary power lies in the fact that it doesn't rely on coercion but on willingness, or desire, of individuals to submit to it, a submission that is invariably unwitting because of its taken for granted nature (Ussher 2006: 4–5).

A major shift in pregnancy discourses in recent years has been the increasing construction of the 'foetal person' (Daniels 1993; Ruddick 2007) which sees the woman herself as little more than a 'container' for the foetus during pregnancy (Young 1990; Bailey 2001). Whilst in the past concern was more with maternal health and reducing infant mortality, today it focuses on the health of the unborn child. Women who fail to follow recommended advice regarding diet, lifestyle and medical intervention are constructed as antagonistic towards their foetus, who becomes an object of collective concern, with its own public identity as the 'potential citizen' (Longhurst 1999). In the United States, women who fail to follow legally or morally sanctioned behaviour have been charged with pre-natal abuse of their children (Chavkin 1992) leading to an erosion of their autonomy and reproductive rights (Petchetsky 1987). Whilst this is not yet the case in the UK, people tend to view themselves as societal supervisors of pregnant behaviour and women are subject to constant advice regarding their everyday habits and lifestyles.

In her study of the cultural history of pregnancy in Britain over the last 250 years Hanson (2004: 6) argues that 'throughout the period pregnancy has not been a private matter, but particularly susceptible to social intervention and control'. Women have always been held accountable by their behaviour for birth outcome, with notions of maternal responsibility developing in the eighteenth century, when maternal emotions were believed to affect the foetus. The early twentieth century saw the recognition of the effects of physical conditions such as poor diet and working conditions on pregnancy, bringing about genuine developments in early pre-natal care for working-class mothers. Initially the concern was with maternal health, but as birthrates fell the mother became recognised as 'an environment for the foetus' (Ballantyne 1914) and women who refused routine check-ups or advice were accused of 'ignorance and slackness' in the health of their baby (Hanson 2004: 128). This continues today in the naturalisation of the 'necessity' of ultra-sound scans and other technological interventions (pregnancy tests, midwives appointments etc) as a 'natural' part of the pregnancy process.

Wainwright (2003) discusses public health surveillance over working-class mothers in Dundee at the end of the nineteenth century, and the ways in which new discourses of 'scientific motherhood' (Apple 1995) constructed them as irresponsible and in need of 'constant medical supervision'. Simultaneously mothers were made responsible for the outcome of their pregnancies through 'errant' behaviour (such as going out to work), but seen as incapable of proper care of their children and in need of expert advice/guidance. Health visitors did a lot to improve maternal/infant health, but also submitted them to a middle-class 'gaze', making pregnant bodies both visible and problematised and constructing working mothers as 'ignorant' and 'careless' in the health of their children.

Similar discourses exist surrounding working-class British mothers today, in particular the emergence of the figure of the 'chav mum' (Tyler 2008) who is stereotypically young, unmarried, uneducated, unemployed and engaging in a variety of unsuitable behaviours such as smoking during pregnancy. Race and class have always played a key role in shaping dominant discourses of what constitutes good motherhood, with certain groups such as young black teen mothers in the United States becoming pathologised (Pillow 2004) whilst new trends in the media glorify celebrity pregnancies.

However, even 'celebrity mums' are not free from criticism where they fail to conform to dominant ideals of 'good' motherhood. *Star* Magazine (10 March 2008) features a cover story declaring 'Pregnant Kerry drinks a bottle of wine a night' followed by a story vilifying pop/reality TV star Kerry Katona for apparently drinking, smoking and snorting cocaine during pregnancy, as well as breaking several unwritten 'celebrity pregnancy' rules, such as appearing overweight and unattractive and returning to her working-class roots by marrying taxi driver Mark Croft after the breakdown of her marriage to pop star Brian McFadden.

The media plays a big role in 'naturalising' dominant discourses of 'good' motherhood, with an increased flow of information between public and private spheres in the forms of new technologies such as internet, television, newspapers and magazines. Scientific 'knowledge' regarding pregnancy is readily available to anybody that wishes to hear it and over time certain discourses (such as the harmful effects of smoking or drinking) become naturalised and seen as 'common sense' (Markens *et al.* 1997). Such public 'knowledge' is used to construct people in their role as societal supervisors of women's behaviour and anyone who chooses to deviate from these norms opens themselves up to potential criticism of their irresponsibility towards the 'foetal person':

> I think people frown upon certain things and are certainly not slow in telling you. I found a lot of people (particularly men!!) had something to say about me having one glass of wine, which I found quite offensive and insulting. Often from people who hardly knew me and had little or no experience of pregnancy (Anna, 28).

> I think there is a general awareness of what people should do, but you do occasionally see very pregnant women outside somewhere smoking. And I just want to go up and shake them and say 'Do you realise what you are doing to that baby, smoking?' I saw only the other day, there was a children's party down at the community centre round the corner and there were a group of women outside, all smoking. One of them was very, very, you know, obviously pregnant. I thought if I was desperate for a cigarette I would be too ashamed to stand out in the main road and be seen to be smoking (Janice, 65).

Women are advised not to smoke, drink alcohol, eat blue or soft cheese, caffeine, nuts, pate, raw eggs, shellfish, undercooked meat and an ever-changing variety of other foodstuffs. Whilst the period between these two generations has seen some backlash against the medicalisation of pregnancy (with the promotion of breastfeeding and home/natural births by organisations such as the National Childbirth Trust) at the same time other technological innovations (e.g. Caesarians, scans, induced births) have increased dramatically (21.5% of babies in the UK born by Caesarian in 2006 compared with 2% in 1950) and less overt forms of medical control have exerted themselves in women's everyday lives. This often takes the form of 'advice' from family, friends, colleagues, medical professionals and even complete strangers (Longhurst 1999):

> I once went into a restaurant when I was about five months pregnant and was about to order a glass of wine with my meal, but the waiter said 'a soft drink for you madam?' and I know he was only trying to be nice, but then I felt I couldn't order one because he'd said that (Lola, 37).

Here, Foucauldian self-governance can be seen in action, with Lola restricting her own behaviour in accordance with accepted norms of 'doing' pregnancy, despite her knowledge that such 'facts' may be based upon dubious scientific authority. This governance operates not only in relation to the gaze of others, but on a more personal level, with women subjecting themselves to private guilt if they stray from such recommendations. Freedom of access to information was a factor in this, with many women believing there was almost an overavailability of information, making it difficult to decipher what the real 'risks' were. In an age of 'intensive parenting', rules are not enshrined in law but in moral obligation, with 'expert' advice turning parents into 'paranoid risk managers' (Furedi 2001). Sarah described one such incidence:

> I once ate a rare steak early on in my pregnancy with Daisy and I got myself into such a state over it and started reading up about toxoplasmosis and what it could do to your baby and made myself really upset. I went on the internet, that was the worst thing...oh my goodness...just, just, I'd never do that again. You know, it's the worst you can do, because there's just all this very extreme information (Sarah, 36).

These ideas have become so hegemonic that members of the 'my mother' generation have begun to question their own knowledge and practices during pregnancy and feel that they were not fully informed at the time:

> My doctor advised me to drink raw egg mixed into a glass of full fat milk every day as the best source of protein – Sarah [daughter] was horrified when I told her this because of course today we know all

about the dangers of salmonella. We weren't so well-informed as our daughters are today (Janice, 65).

It was the summer of 69 when I was pregnant with Lola and I remember sitting at my desk sweating away and drinking gallons of coca-cola. God knows what it was doing to the baby but we didn't know about things like that back then (Carol, 60).

However, others felt that the new 'discoveries' should be taken 'with a pinch of salt' and that their daughters were 'over-reacting a bit':

As far as eating, there were no restrictions, but recommendations about what you should eat, like dandelion tea is good for you, and all those sort of things. It was always stuff that was good for you, never anything that was bad for you. Erm...and to be perfectly honest, with Karen, with a pregnancy where you're so anaemic, half-raw liver is probably worth thinking about. And I did eat it, and I'm sure it helped, certainly towards the end of it...but there definitely wasn't a list of things that you're not supposed to eat (Sylvia, 64).

I did smoke in fact. Not with Dan, I think I'd stopped smoking then. But I wouldn't have been a heavy smoker. I'd only smoke a few a nights when I sat down, only about three or four cigarettes at night but that was all. And it didn't seem to do them any harm that I can see (Hazel, 64).

Mothers were also cautious about giving advice to their daughters, aware that it may be seen as 'out-of-date' or 'non-scientific'. Whereas in earlier times friends and family were often the main source of information regarding pregnancy, this seems to have given way in many cases to the reign of the 'expert':

R: *Do you give advice to Karen? And does she listen to your advice?*
S: [Laughing] Ohhhh that's really tricky...Did I give Karen...? I must have done I can't not have done. Did she listen to me? I think I was aware from fairly early on, that my information was likely to be 30 years out of date, erm...so, I think it was with caution that it was really given or accepted (Sylvia, 64).

The extent to which women followed or rejected advice depended upon a variety of factors including age, education, social class and the number of previous pregnancies, with women often much more relaxed about following the 'rules' during their second pregnancy and trusting in their own 'embodied knowledge', including management of nausea and food cravings:

> Yeah, I mean I don't eat soft cheeses, when I got to my dad's on the farm, he has unpasteurised milk, I don't drink that. I'm not sure about shellfish and stuff like that, I have eaten prawns, but...and people have gone 'Oh God' and stuff...but other shellfish, I wouldn't eat other shellfish. Err... you know, cooking your eggs properly, that kind of thing. So I follow it vaguely, but I'm probably not as careful as, you know. I didn't drink at all for the first 12 weeks, then, since then I've had the odd glass of wine. I'm definitely more relaxed this time than I was last time. Last time I was really like...one glass of wine a week, that's it. Now I'm like, if I fancy it, I'll have it. When you're more advanced it's not really an issue. Early on it's more of an issue, you know with alcohol...so I'll be really careful the first few weeks, then have a nice glass of wine every so often (Susie, 37).

> R: Do you think apart from not eating certain things, do you think you changed how you ate when you were pregnant? Do you think you ate more healthy things...or?

> K: Quite the opposite for me really, 'cause I felt so ill, I found myself eating chocolate biscuits. I would have had bran flakes for breakfast, get a healthy start, but it wasn't an option, 'cause I just felt so nauseous. I ate very unhealthy foods, chocolate, and biscuits, so no, my diet became worse. I did drink glasses of milk, and smoothies, but no, I wasn't eating my greens! I felt too queasy (Kirsty, 36).

In their study of the production of 'authoritative knowledge' in American pre-natal care Markens *et al.* (1997) argue that women often balance adjustments in their diets to provide acceptable solutions for both themselves and their unborn child, for example giving up coffee, but continuing to eat chocolate which also contains caffeine. The women in this study also revealed themselves as 'active consumers' of advice, picking and choosing which bits to follow and actively seeking out the most up-to-date evidence via internet sites, books and magazines. This also highlights a new space in which the politics of pregnancy is played out in the twenty-first century, through the virtual community of internet chat rooms and health sites, which are used to replace or supplement more traditional forms of pregnancy advice from mothers, grandmothers or medical professionals. Such disembodied spaces construct their own ways of 'doing' pregnancy which are in turn re-embodied in the actions and dilemmas of pregnant women in everyday life.

Personal evaluations of available advice deny simple readings of pregnant women as 'docile bodies' (Foucault 1979b; Deveaux 1994) within a surveillance society and reveal the ways in which such knowledge can also be used to resist and empower (at least to certain sections of the population who have the education or resources to do so). Whilst the majority of the mothers within this survey constructed images of themselves as 'good' mothers through justification of choices and actions, similarly these popular discourses disempower other mothers who do not conform to them and are constructed as 'bad' or irresponsible in the public eye, because of their age, race, class, weight, diet, clothing or lifestyle. This is something that needs to be studied further in future research on the subject, taking a wider sample of women from a variety of different social and cultural backgrounds.

Infant feeding practices

It is not only during pregnancy that women are subject to advice and judgement regarding food, but also in changing discourses surrounding infant feeding practices. In today's society breastfeeding is vigorously promoted as an indicator of 'good' and 'natural' motherhood, with unsuccessful attempts and recourse to formula milk regarded in certain circles as almost something of a failure as a mother. Numerous studies promote the benefits of breast milk which are believed to include protection from infections and allergies, reduced risk of various illnesses in later life and improved emotional and intellectual development (www.nhs.co.uk, 2008) and indicate that bottle-feeding may predispose children to obesity and related diseases in later life (Bergmann *et al.* 2003). However, discourses surrounding appropriate infant feeding practices have changed over time and are shaped by a range of physical, cultural and economic circumstances.

During the early twentieth century until its peak in the early 1970s there was a rapid growth in formula feeding, led by paediatricians and formula producers under the dominant discourse of 'scientific motherhood' which led many mothers to question the quantity and quality of their breast milk (NCT 1999; Carter 1995). Backlash against the medicalisation of pregnancy in the 1980s and 1990s led to increasing rates of breastfeeding; however this did not necessarily increase its acceptability in public space where it is still seen as a private and feminine activity (Pain *et al.* 2001). In their study of infant feeding practices in Newcastle, Pain *et al.* (2001) argue that breastfeeding in public is still seen as making something of a statement and is particularly unacceptable due to the traditional masculine working-class culture of the region, where unusually high levels of bottle-feeding persist. Indeed Britain still has one of the lowest breastfeeding initiation rates in Europe (66%) with large variations according to socio-economic status (Earle 2002). Nor is breastfeeding, or even expressing milk via a breast pump, seen as very acceptable within workplace environments (Boswell-Penc & Boyer 2007), providing a public-private dichotomy for mothers returning to work and wishing to live by the dominant ideologies of 'good' motherhood.

Within our study we found that breastfeeding had become both more vigorously promoted and more acceptable over this period, with women from the 'my mother' generation reporting that they found difficulties, if they were not actively dissuaded from breastfeeding at the time:

> At the time breastfeeding wasn't really the done thing amongst my social circle, I felt like a bit of a freak and I wouldn't have dared to do it in public so I was pretty much tied to the house for most of the time. When I was in the hospital the midwives weren't very supportive and kept saying why don't you give her a bottle dear so you can get some sleep (Cath, 60).

> Although it was the 70s, erm...no it was not accepted at all and you really had to find a corner and tuck yourself away. There weren't rooms provided anywhere so you really had quite a juggle trying to work out where you would be when the baby was likely to need a feed. So for example if you were going shopping, you would have to somehow work it so you could get there and back in time to feed the baby again. There wasn't anywhere, there was absolutely nowhere apart from public toilets and that's not a very nice place to do it is it? I can remember my friend fed her baby; she was much more laid back and didn't care about conventions, and what other people thought at all. She fed the baby in a restaurant, in a little corner and the fuss that caused...I mean it wasn't even a restaurant, it was a fish and chip café in Cumbria (Janice, 65).

The 'my self' generation by contrast were strongly encouraged to breastfeed and were often quite comfortable about doing it in a variety of locations. However, it was still seen as a potentially embarrassing situation requiring careful thought as to when and where it was done and who was present. Whilst many of the women happily breastfed in front of me during the interview, doing it in very public situations or even in front of male family members or visitors was still seen as a problem:

> I'm happy to breastfeed most places because it's a natural thing and people shouldn't be allowed to make women feel uncomfortable about doing it. No-one's ever said anything to me but I've seen some people looking. The only place I wouldn't do it is on the tube, because it wouldn't feel right and I don't really like doing it in front of my dad! He makes a real effort to stay in the room to show he's not embarrassed, but I know he is and we'd both really rather he left! (Sophie, 24).

> I felt it was expected of me to breastfeed. It's not something I felt great about doing, but it was expected. I did breastfeed for six months. Not the whole, by the end of six months I was just doing one feed a day, and the bottles, but...I am gonna breastfeed this time, but I'm not really looking forward to it. It's more that I don't like breastfeeding in public, I don't know what it is, I just don't like it. It's fine if you go round to your friend's house and they're all feeding and stuff, but...like in a cafe or something. I just don't feel comfortable about it (Susie, 37).

Whilst better public facilities are now available (and indeed mandatory) and public health discourses legitimate feeding in all manner of situations, many women still feel uncomfortable about doing it and it is difficult to remove the embedded conception of breasts as a male sexual object. Other physical or social barriers function to restrict women's use of public space during pregnancy and early motherhood, including difficulties of movement with a young baby, inaccessibility of public transport etc. and breastfeeding is still largely place-specific and related to class and cultural identities:

> For me personally I suppose I'd consider me and my family to be quite middle-class and to be linked in that network quite closely, and breastfeeding, everybody seems to breastfeed...but if you say my husband, his family is a very working-class family, his mum breastfed his sister actually, which was really quite unusual I think.

His sister for example, I don't think…her sort of network is far more bottle-fed, and certainly the doctor friend of the family we've got, they're based in Newcastle, and he's described it as a dying art up there, people just don't do it. So I think it's really regional and related to class. That sounds really awful, I'm saying it's related to class and it shouldn't be, but it seems to be (Sarah, 36).

Whilst all but one of the 'my self' group had tried breastfeeding, several had given it up within a short time period due to lack of success or support. However, within certain spaces and social networks particular moral geographies of motherhood develop (Holloway 1999) and breastfeeding becomes seen as the norm. Many of the women mentioned the strong pressure from midwives or other mothers to breastfeed, particularly within certain groups and the simultaneous lack of support for doing this:

I wouldn't say they encourage you to breastfeed; it's much stronger than that – you're made to feel like the devil if you don't want to! (Sophie, 24).

When you go in to the maternity bit at the hospital they're massive boards up about breastfeeding everywhere you look, there's leaflets on the table and I thought God it is all over the place, everywhere you look there's something, you'd feel really bad if you didn't want to do it (Emma, 27).

The worst thing is the bloody middle-class breastfeeding mums. I went to a baby group after Caroline was born and they were all like blah blah blah breastfeeding this and breastfeeding that and looked at me like I was a piece of crap because I wasn't doing it. I think they're just jealous cos they have to stay in and not drink for another six months and I'm out having fun! (Hayley, 26).

Where women were unsuccessful in their breastfeeding attempts, this led to feelings of failure surrounding the competence of their maternal bodies:

I always knew that I wanted to breastfeed and then when Esme was born I wasn't producing enough milk to feed her and she wasn't gaining weight fast enough, so the doctor was really rude and told me I'd have to use a bottle or she would be taken into hospital. It was just the most awful thing in the world, so much wanting to give her what was best and not being able to. I was really upset and felt like a complete failure. I could feel people looking at me when I was out and thinking why has that baby got a bottle, why isn't she breastfeeding? (Anna, 32).

They were really pushy about breastfeeding at the hospital and I was exhausted and said 'I think I'm just going to try a bottle for now'. But they were really disapproving and gave me a cold bottle and obviously he wouldn't drink from it, so I was nearly in tears and said 'please could you heat it up for me' and they said 'no, why don't you just try breastfeeding again?' (Katie, 27).

Thus infant feeding provides yet another form of surveillance over the maternal body. In the early twenty-first century women are encouraged to breastfeed and given greater freedom to do so within public space (both overtly and in the form of baby changing facilities). However many women are uncomfortable in exerting this freedom and dominant ideologies of 'successful' motherhood are now used to denigrate those who do not wish to breastfeed or are unable to for personal or practical reasons. The largely older middle-class sample of mothers interviewed in this project may also have very different experiences from those of other social groups (for example teenage mothers) where different ideologies and 'moral geographies' prevail. Once again this is used to create 'ideals' of 'good' and 'bad' motherhood which serve to accentuate social distinctions and put pressure upon women who do not conform.

Conclusion

In this chapter we have examined the changing perceptions of pregnancy and motherhood over the past 40 years, arguing that this has become experienced more publicly across this time period, yet is still subject to a number of ever-changing rules and social surveillance regarding appropriate behaviour, diet and lifestyle. Drawing upon the experiences of mothers and daughters in south-east England, we argue that values and attitudes relating to pregnancy are not only transmitted generationally and related to specific local, cultural and class identities, but also greatly influenced by dominant temporal discourses of 'good' motherhood, with public surveillance of pregnancy asserting increasing influence in today's information-dominated society. Whilst today's mothers experience increased freedoms to work or dress attractively during pregnancy, or breastfeed in public in comparison with their own mothers, they also experience new pressures in the form of surveillance regarding feeding and eating practices.

The medicalisation of pregnancy and its associated 'knowledge' and visibility (via scans etc.) of the foetus (Petchetsky 1987) have served to construct the notion of 'foetal rights', which although not yet on a legal level as in the United States, nevertheless functions as a powerful form of self-governance over pregnant women's autonomy and behaviour. Pregnant women are bombarded by an ever-changing number of 'forbidden' foods and new scientific 'evidence' regarding the dangers of eating, drinking, smoking, colouring their hair or engaging in numerous other everyday practices during pregnancy. Similarly, aggressive government health campaigns have promoted the 'Breast is Best' message, providing something of a backlash against promotion of formula feeding by medical and industrial interests earlier in the twentieth century. Thus today's mothers experience increased support and acceptability of breastfeeding in the public sphere, however modern infant feeding discourses are also used to denigrate those who are unable or do not wish to comply, leading to added pressures upon recent mothers in an age of 'food fascism' (*The Times*, 26 May 2007).

This is not to argue that women are merely passive recipients of advice, but see themselves as active consumers, using a variety of sources to make decisions about their feeding practices and place themselves within various ideologies of 'good motherhood' that are both time- and space-specific. Whilst women of both generations mentioned various forms of medical and public surveillance over the pregnant/post-natal body, they also found various ways in which to challenge and resist dominant discourses, denying simple Foucauldian readings of them as 'docile bodies' (Deveaux 1994).

The fact that the women interviewed were predominantly white and middle-class means that this is a group who are largely empowered within British society in general and other groups may have different ideals and norms of motherhood, which may be less easy to justify within dominant 'scientific' or 'popular' constructions of 'appropriate' maternal behaviour. However, this may also be the group who are most concerned to be seen to behave 'correctly' and judge themselves on the ideals of 'paranoid parenting' (Furedi 2001). It would be interesting to conduct further research with women from wider ethnic and social groups to compare the influence of new scientific, media and breastfeeding discourses upon their experiences and perceptions of pregnancy and motherhood across recent generations.

Whilst recognising the limitations of this study, the findings show that there has been a significant shift (both tangible and in the perceptions of mothers and daughters) in the way in which pregnancy/early motherhood is experienced in British society. Food provides a useful lens through which to examine these wider changes in medicine, technology, gender relations, career opportunities for women, media focus and the rise of the 'celebrity mum', which have all served to push pregnancy to the forefront of public attention in the early twenty-first century. This focus upon feeding and eating practices reflects wider shifts from more overt forms of gender inequality towards neoliberal forms of governance which seek to control populations through self-regulation of accepted behaviours and bodily norms embedded within twenty-first century health discourses.

Part II
Childhood and Family Life

4
'She's got a really good attitude to healthy food...Nannan's drilled it into her': Inter-generational Relations within Families

Penny Curtis, Allison James and Katie Ellis

Over recent years, the UK tabloid press has been vociferous in highlighting a wide range of social issues, from an alleged decline in cooking skills among young people to the enthusiastic reporting of anti-social behaviour orders – all of which have, to a greater or lesser extent, been associated with the erosion of inter-generational relations. In July 2008, for example, *The Daily Mail* ran a headline, which asserted: *Pushover parents to blame for generation of children who 'lack discipline and moral boundaries'* (30 July 2008). It would seem from this that inter-generational relations are in crisis – a crisis characterised by adults' failure to teach and to control children appropriately and by children's lack of responsibility and failure to discriminate between right and wrong.

However, in spite of such banner headlines, inter-generational relationships and 'exchanges of support' (Mitchell 2007: 98) have been shown to remain an important part of contemporary family life (Morgan 1999; Silva and Smart 1999; Smart 2007) and recent work suggests that, though household composition has become increasingly diverse, three-quarters of the UK population acknowledge their participation in a three or more generational family (Dench *et al.* 1999). This would seem to counter the suggestion that inter-generational relations have lost their role in the everyday lives of families.

It is against this background that this chapter sets out to examine, in detail, the ways in which inter-generational relations transpire in families – what they represent and what they accomplish – using food as a lens through which to examine these social processes. While drawing on contemporaneous narratives of family life, we are nonetheless also able to explore the temporality of these inter-generational relations. Through the accounts of children and parents, we demonstrate the continuities and discontinuities of ideas of 'family' that are integral to the inter-generational relations through which 'the family' is continually affirmed.

Family relationships

This chapter takes as its theoretical starting point an understanding of family as socially constructed. Following Morgan (1996), rather than a concern for how family is structured or what purpose family serves, we focus upon the ongoing, dynamic process through which family is created. Morgan's analysis highlights the significance of family 'practices'; those activities and relationships by which and through which, individual family members 'do' family and experience family life. Yet as Finch (2007: 66) has pointed out, this emphasis on social actors creatively constituting family as a facet of social life 'means that an individual's understanding of "my family" is subject to change over time' and during a person's life-course (Hockey and James 2003). For example, although a child, once grown, becomes a parent to their own children they, nonetheless, also continue to be a 'child' in relation to their own mother and father. In addition, the significance of particular kin and non-kin relations can shift over time for any individual; changing sentiments that may be a product of personal conflicts or the outcome of busy lives.

Family is therefore fluid rather than fixed and in late modernity is, increasingly, unlikely to be synonymous with household (Finch 2007: 68) and one of the consequences of a focus on what families 'do' has been a realisation – or at least a reaffirmation – of the importance of kin (Smart 2007). Doing family can be achieved through the interactions that take place between individuals beyond the immediate household and, for migrant families for example, may well extend across national boundaries (Fog Olwig 2003). This is because family is accomplished, not through people's occupancy of kinship roles *per se,* but through the activities and relationships that characterise 'linked lives' (Bengtson *et al*. 2002): the life of each individual family member is embedded within a web of inter-linked relationships which intermesh across and between generations such that lives can 'become interwoven and embedded at a material, emotional and metaphorical level' (Smart 2007: 45).

Family and generation

If Smart's (2007: 44) contention, that 'vertical kinship matters' is correct, how then is family to be understood in generational terms since, following the work of Qvortrup (1994), generation, like other categorical structural indices such as social class and gender, 'distinguishes and separates' children from adults through 'relations of division, difference and inequality between categories' (Alanen 2001)? From this perspective, childhood is both a structural and structuring phenomenon (Qvortrup 1994; Alanen 2001) which variably enables and constrains the individual child's experience of childhood and, thus – through this emphasis on separateness – might seem to threaten the connections and connnectivities through which 'family' is practiced. This underscores, as Alanen (2001) points out, the need to problematise and understand how these different generational positions – child, parent and grandparent – are constituted, and how relations between subject positions are enacted and reproduced on a day-to-day basis. To this end, Alanen emphasises the importance of children's practices, as well as those of adults, to understanding how individuals 'do' generation, highlighting the:

> Complex set of social processes through which people become (constructed as) 'children' while other people become (constructed as) 'adults'. 'Construction' involves agency (of children and adults); it is best understood as a practical and even material process, and needs to be studied as a practice or a set of practices. It is through such practices that the two generational categories of children and adults are recurrently produced and therefore they stand in relations of connection and interaction, of interdependence: neither of them can exist without the other, what each of them is (a child, and adults) is dependent on its relation to the other, and change in one is tied to change in the other (Alanen 2001: 20–21).

In this chapter, we therefore see as key, a focus upon family practices as enacted by and through generational relations since children, parents and grandparents are relational categories embedded within a generational frame. Thus, as we will show, generation is discursively constructed, in the process of doing family, through the narratives of children and their parents as they discuss their food-related practices, for as Caplan (1997: 25) has noted, as social beings we 'use food to express significant relationships' and often, indeed, to display who belongs or does not belong to 'our' family (Morgan 1996; Finch 2007).

Methods

The data that this discussion draws upon derives from semi-structured interviews with children, aged between 11 and 12 years, and separate interviews with parents. Children were recruited from year seven form groups in four schools in the North Midlands and South Yorkshire (UK). Three of the schools were located in urban areas: an inner city school in an area of significant social deprivation; a multi-ethnic inner city school and; a school located in an affluent, suburban area. The fourth school was located in a rural area with a wide geographical catchment. Consent was obtained from 108 children and their parents to participate in the first phase of data collection (54 girls and 54 boys) in which interviews were carried out in small friendship groups, usually consisting of two children, during the school day. Children described themselves as having a range of ethnic identities. However, the majority described themselves as 'white British'.

A second phase of data collection was also undertaken. A sub-sample of children was selected to represent a diversity of (overlapping) family forms: single parent families; families with only one child; families with two or more children; and families following a restricted diet due to health, religious or social reasons. Thirty children agreed to take part in a second interview (18 girls and 12 boys) which was carried out in the family home of each child. One parent from each family also participated.[1]

Grandparents, parents and children

Recent work, focusing upon specific family contexts,[2] indicates that grandparents continue to play a significant role in their grandchildren's lives. However, much of this work has been concerned with what grandparents 'do', rather than how generational relations are negotiated and understood within everyday family life and, in particular, how children participate in and make sense of this process.

One of the factors which may influence what grandparents 'do' within families is the nature and frequency of contact that takes place across generations. A diversity of patterns of contact between generations was evident in the families of the children who participated in this study. One child, Sofia, for example, lived in an extended family unit which spread across two properties which the family planned to connect together. In this three generational unit Sofia shared her living space with 11 other people: her sister; two brothers; the wife of her eldest brother; an aunt and uncle and their two children and a grandmother and Sofia's own parents.

More usually, however, inter-generational contact was maintained between households. Melissa, for example, described seeing her grandmother *nearly every day*. And contact with the grandparental generation was generally welcomed and spoken of fondly by children. Peter, whose parents were divorced, described his family as being 'really well-connected':

> I'm really lucky actually 'cause like my Mum lived in [*Another Town*]. And she couldn't take it like living on her own so she moved here. And I've got my Grandma, my Grandpa. My Uncle and my, erm, my Uncle's wife and my cousin. And then in [*Different Town*] I've got, er, my cousin and my, erm, my like my, erm, aunts and stuff. And they're all like. And, erm, my Dad's Mum lives in [*Big City*] so it's like my Dad's mum'll, ring up and say, do you want them to come round for the weekend it's like, oh, yeah, it's fine.

Not all children, of course, live within such close proximity. A few reported that they had to travel a considerable distance in order to visit grandparents ('to my country', Ahmed) and some therefore saw their grandparents only rarely.

However, everyday contact is neither necessary nor sufficient (King and Elder 1995; Brannen *et al.* 2000) for children to feel that they are embedded within such three generational family networks. For many children, because contact with their grandparents was occasional, it was seen as a special experience that occurred at family events or weekends and, at such times, food was seen by children to play a key role in maintaining these generational relationships. Regular eating routines, for example, helped to maintain contact between children and their grandparents in reconstituted families where parents were separated or divorced. For example, Kerry and her sister go out on a regular basis with her grandparents; *every Friday I go out for tea like to have a roast dinner. And maybe my Dad or my Mum and Stefan [Mum's boyfriend].* Food can also be the catalyst that brings the extended family together: *if grandparents are here then we do generally all eat together. As a family* (Harry's mother).

Even when grandparents were no longer able to be active participants in family eating practices, children were able to locate their relationship with their grandparents through food-related memories. Sam's grandfather was suffering from dementia and being cared for in a residential home: *he can't remember anything, he can only remember the past. Not like, say he had say, er, 'Shreddies' for breakfast, like two, one or two hours like he'll probably have forgotten what he had.* Yet Sam's grandfather remains an important focus for his own memories around food.

He recalled birthday celebrations with his grandfather fondly; memories which have become part of Sam's own biographical account:

> He used to set out this massive snack table with all these like sandwiches and birthday cake [for Sam's birthday]. We're all gonna die one day so you might as well eat it now [*laughs*].

Memories, as Smart (2007: 3) notes 'are part of a sense of self' and as such have particular importance to how individuals relate to one another at the level of personal life. And, since parents were also once children, with grandparents of their own, these memories may become important to the ways in which the 'doing' of family takes place in the present, as Carrie's mother recalls. In contrast to her own mother's cooking in the 60s, when industrial convenience food first became popular, Carrie's mum likes to cook meals from scratch for her own children using raw ingredients:

> My Nan and Granddad they used to have allotments. And my Nan was a bit of a, you know, she'd shove a lettuce in between her rose bushes and that sort of thing and, and I'm, and I do the same. And at an early age I used to like sitting in my Granddad's shed with his tomatoes and sort of messing around with the stuff in there. I suppose...as a family we've always gone like foraging like berries and bilberries. And I've just took that that bit further. And I suppose my Mum sort of dabbled in little bits now and again I remember, you know, occasions when she might have had a go. But it was always too much messy.

Food continuities and the family

If generationality is negotiated, within families, through interpersonal interactions between differently positioned actors within a generational frame then, as we will demonstrate, individuals' experiences of family life are also 'linked' (Bengtson *et al.* 2002) through the construction of shared narratives *about* family life. Indeed, it is these which help to embed generational family relationships at the emotional and the metaphorical levels (Smart 2007).

Nick, for example, described his grandmother as cooking *the same thing as my Mum does really it's like, just, they'll try something like new like a crazy idea or something but it's mostly roast dinner*, and Abdul said that his mother *got plenty of ideas off her Mum*. The continuity in food practices across the generations is thus remarked upon by children in their accounts and these position parents – and particularly mothers – as important mediators of inter-generationality.[3] Thus scripted into family narratives about what 'our' family is and what our family does are important food-related understandings which mediate between past and present generations. James's mother, for example, describes herself as still cooking 'traditional' food, similar to that cooked by her own mother: ...*my Mum's meat and potato pies and shepherd's pies.*

Indeed, the very notion of 'traditional' food, which is often closely allied to that of 'home cooking' in family narratives, works to locate the family in inter-generational terms through emphasising temporality. So, James's mother described the family in which she grew up as a 'meat and two veg sort of family':

> I was brought up with eating a lot of vegetables, and a lot of fruit and a lot of home-made cakes. And I still do all the baking. We eat a lot of home-baked cakes. And we're basically still a meat and two veg and, fish and vegetables and salads which is what I ate when I was little. I think I cook exactly the same things as what my mum does.

This allusion to the home cooking of traditional foods can be understood as what Gross (2005) refers to as a meaning-constituted tradition. Meals that were *freshly cooked* (Emma's mother) and which *were always cooked from scratch* (Edith's mother) reflect and convey a notion of domestic moral order across the generations, helping to construct a 'sense of coherence' in family life that is enduring (Moisio *et al.* 2004: 379). Such inter-generational family scripts also serve to display to individuals that the relationships between generations are also family relationships (Finch 2007: 67) and, moreover have significance for the day-to-day experience of family life. As Beth's father noted *I think we've all got our mothers sitting on our shoulder.*

Such traditions stem, in part, from the ways in which cooking is learned in families and although few of the present-day children admitted to doing much cooking at home, or to being taught how to cook directly by their mothers, in the following narrative can be glimpsed ways in which the implicit knowledge about family food can be imparted:

> Luke: Well, it's just, er, I, I used to watch my Mum.
> Oliver: Yeah, that's the same here, kinda just.

> Carrie: I know how to do like basic cooking so.
> Interviewer: *Who taught you to do that do you think?*
> Carrie: Just watching my Mum.
> Interviewer: *Yeah. Just learning how to do it.*
> Carrie: Mm.
> Interviewer: *and then trying it yourself? Yeah?*
> Carrie: And you, you have cooking lessons at school as well.
> Interviewer: *Yeah.*
> Carrie: But that, that dun't really help much because it just tells you how to make chocolate cakes and that dun't really help you.

Here an important contrast is drawn between cooking food that is meant for the family and is part of the family tradition and school cookery lessons – *it just tells you how to make chocolate cake* – which are dismissed as not really part of the cooking that is about family food.

In some families, however, such family scripts about traditional food and home-cooking can best be described as aspirational since pressures on mothers' time may make this a difficult ideal to achieve. Nonetheless, that they represent a moral backdrop for contemporary eating practices serves to reinforce the continuities through which 'the family' is reproduced. Peter's mother recalled that when she was a child *we used to be meat and two veg everyday*, and she feels the need to apologise for her neglect in not following this tradition: *I know it sounds awful but some days, if I've been working, it's just like a quick pizza put in the oven*. A distinction between the cooking practices of his mother and grandmother is also made by Peter:

> Here we have like pasta bake and stuff and like lasagne and sometimes hotpot. But that's not home-made and stuff. But over there at grandma's, 'cause she doesn't work, she'll have a ready, she'll make like lasagne and stir fry and stuff like that.

However, although grandmother's cooking constitutes a benchmark for food practices across the generations, family food scripts may be reflected upon and modified in light of the complexities of contemporary family life and changing consumerist values. In this sense, family food practices also act as markers for different familial and historical generations. Indeed, 'putting in a pizza', as a number of parents noted, is emblematic of changes in eating cultures which have taken place over the adult life-course. Likewise, the availability of 'ready meals' has increased as have opportunities for eating out, food practices which mark out generational distinctions as Martin's mother highlighted through comparison with her own childhood experience: as a child, the only exception to a diet of 'proper cooked dinner' had been the family's Friday night visit to the chip shop.

Similarly, generational distinctions are highlighted by the accommodation within family scripts of 'new' foods such as jacket potatoes (which Britney's mother could not recall eating during her own childhood), tinned tuna and pasta.

> Other people might have been having it years but as a teenager, all of a sudden, my mum brought home. We had tuna salads on French bread that is what we used to have. On a Saturday for tea. So that were quite new, revolutionary for us (Kirsty's mother).

Thus, family scripts are often sufficiently robust to encompass new types of foods and the incorporation of convenience meals into family eating practices, without challenging the meanings conveyed by and through those scripts. Moreover, despite the difficulties that the contemporary family experiences in realising the ideal of 'home cooking', it remains 'a metonym for a model of household activities that marks intergenerational care-giving' (Moisio *et al.* 2004: 379). Similarly, as we have shown elsewhere (James *et al.* forthcoming) the symbolic importance of 'eating together' has lost none of its potency, across the generations, just because it is only infrequently achieved:

> We always used to sit down as a family. You know, mealtimes you sit round the table. I wouldn't have any of this sitting in front of the television or up in their bedrooms it just, I suppose 'cause I did that when I was a kid, we were allowed occasionally to sit in front of the telly, but it's nice 'cause it's a time to catch up and everything isn't it and see what everybody is up to. And as they got older and now they're into their teens it's like a battleground and they're trying to [*laughs*]…ordering them to the table (Carrie's mum).

Discontinuities of food and family

While food practices may be fundamental to the process of 'doing' family, as Morgan (1996: 158) has pointed out, food-related activities and relationships may also demonstrate difference and divisions between family members. In a small number of families, discourses concerning family food practices served principally to emphasise generational difference and to suggest a new – and improved – moral order within the contemporary family. Emma's mother recalled that, as a child, she had hated vegetables which she felt compelled to eat after her sister had been punished for leaving food: *I didn't like my meals at all...to be truthful, I've never liked vegetables very much at all. Smelly vegetables, if it's got a smell...* In such families, compulsion and lack of choice is highlighted in relation to the food practices of parents' childhoods and then contrasted, by parents, with the greater liberalism and opportunity for choice the current generation of children have in relation to food practices. This serves to remind us that different familial generations are located differently in historical time so that the biographical choices that people make have to be understood in relation to that (Harris 1987), and to their positioning in the life-course (Brannen 2004). As Beth's mother recalls:

> we just used to sit and be plated up whatever you got and you ate whatever you got...And you had to finish everything on your plate, didn't you, whereas I don't think it's quite as much like that now.

Similarly, James' mum recalls:

> When I was little your tea was your tea and there wasn't an alternative whereas nowadays it's, there are alternatives. Because it's quite often that other people are having a other, other meals. At the same time. Whereas when you were little my Mum just made the tea and that was that. That's the end of it [*laughs*] you either had to eat it or go hungry and it was not, there wasn't an alternative to it [*laughs*].

However, despite changes in eating practices from those of her own childhood, James' mother acknowledges the powerful tug of tradition in relation to food practices with her own children:

> I suppose I'm still guilty sometimes of saying, Oh, you know, eat! You haven't finished it. You're not having anything else. But you know, I don't think it's as much now. They have some aspect of saying what they want for their tea whereas we used to just be plated up what we'd got and that were it.

Thus, while family scripts can, as Moisio *et al.* (2004) have suggested, serve to construct and communicate a 'sense of coherence' in family life, the construction of a notion of domestic moral order across the generations does not necessarily imply continuity – as Carrie's mother suggests when she compares her own cooking to that of her mother and grandmother:

> I suppose I was brought up more on quick, instant, junk food, you know, the sixties and all that...but I actually preferred proper food 'cause I used to go to my Nan's a lot and she did proper food. So now the kids are like [*pause*] I do the proper food but they'd rather eat the junk food. So I don't know.

Indeed, for some parents and children, such family scripts about the food-related moral order are a means of negotiating new understandings of family which contrast with past practices and which accommodate the realities of contemporary family life. Thus, when Beth visits her grandparents, her grandma cooks vegetarian food for Beth who, like her parents, is committed to vegetarianism and although her grandparents do not often visit, when they do, they have to accommodate the family's eating practices and eat the vegetarian food with which they are presented. Beth's mother notes that Beth's grandfather does complain, but she is determined not to cook meat for him. This, she acknowledges may be the reason why *they don't come very often*.

In the narratives of children and their parents, family food scripts reflect elements of the typology suggested by Byng-Hall (1995).[4] Thus, for example, the ongoing idealisation of 'traditional' food, home cooking and eating together, described earlier, is a script that is replicated in successive generations. In other families, such as Beth's, scripts may be corrective. Here traditional family stories are experienced as discomforting and there is dissonance between how things were and how they are now: parental control of food preparation and eating is challenged and new stories are required to recognise and enable children's influences on food and eating. Families may also develop food-related scripts in which myths are improvised, where new stories are given prominence as part of the re-writing of the life-course and the development of vegetarianism in Beth's family may also be seen in this way.

However, we suggest that this typology may not be sufficiently nuanced. Rather, family food-related scripts may provide an anchorage in the shifting generational sands of family life which, through continuity, refinement and revision, link a child to practices and relationships in the past (Smart 2007; Hoskins 1998). Grandparents provide, as Brannen *et al.* (2000: 136) have noted, 'a sense of symbolic importance to children – giving them a sense of continuity and belongingness'. However, even when apparently discontinuous, such food practices nonetheless constitute linkages with earlier practices and relationships through the very difference which they represent. Beth's nuclear family's vegetarianism is such a strong contrast to the meat-and-two veg eating practices of her grandparents that it may serve, through the difference it represents, to remind Beth of her relatedness to them. Family scripts, we suggest, thus form a backdrop to children's experiences of family life but are not necessarily determinant of them.

Negotiating generational order within the family

If, as we have suggested above, inter-generational family food scripts contextualise children's experiences of, and interactions with, generational practices, this raises questions about the extent to which children are active in negotiating the potency of family scripts as they are replicated, corrected or improvised in day-to-day family life, and how children understand their own subject position/s within the family generational frame. In order to explore these questions, we consider children's narratives about their interactions with grandparents and with parents' and children's reactions and contributions to generational family food practices.

In some families, children can be highly receptive to the 'teachings' of adults. Edith's mother, for example, suggests that Edith's grandmother has been an important source of influence for her daughter:

> Edith's mum: She's got a really good attitude to healthy food... Nannan's drilled it into her. [...] She's been really, really good. She does listen. *(And what sort of things will your mum say to her do you think?)* She'd just tell her straight what's in there. And like how bad it is for her, how, you know, like McDonald's, how rubbish they are and
> Edith: Yeah, when I sleep at hers she makes me watch all them programmes like 'You Are What You Eat' and things like that. And like when that, that guy were doing that thing where you had to eat McDonald's how many weeks. And things like that.
> Edith's mum: so it has been drilled into her.

But, family life and generational relationships are never entirely consensual nor wholly conflictual. Children do not necessarily accept such messages passively but may negotiate across the generational order to manage their relationships with adults, as Kerry highlights:

> Kerry: My Gran. Erm, she'd be like, 'Well, you've got to drink milk' and I'm like well I don't really like milk. And she said, 'Well you'll have brittle you'll have brittle bones.' Erm, and I said, well, like. And she said [*laughs*] erm, 'Well, I take these tablets. Which gives you calcium.' And, erm, [*pause*] and I said, 'Well, haven't they' er, she said, 'Well, one day you'll have to take them if you don't start drinking milk.' And I said, 'Well, they've got gelatine in them.' Some, sometimes. And then she said, erm, 'Well,' then she said, 'Well, it's either that or like would you like to have snapped bones' or something and I said, 'Well, I'd rather take the tablets' but you know. So. But, er, I said, I was trying to resolve the like not drinking milk and I just said, you know that like Nesquick powder? I said, 'Well, I drink that so [*laughs*] if you want to get me that you can do.' And she said, erm, 'Well, I've got some of that at my house so you, so you can have some tonight' and I'm like well I don't really want it but you know [*laughs*].
> *Interviewer: So you were hoping she wouldn't buy it?*
> Kerry: Yeah.
> *Interviewer: So do you have to drink that then now?*
> Kerry: Well, er, hopefully she'll forget if you know what I mean. So. Fingers crossed.

Although recognising the good intentions of her grandmother, Kerry was able to skilfully subvert these intentions without upsetting generational relations.

However, particularly when their parents were not present, children were often able to influence their grandparents' food practices since grandparents, according to children, were highly receptive to their food tastes and were willing to accommodate their preferences. Peter, for example, describes his grandma in this way: *If I go to my grandma's she'll usually make something that we like but if she can't make, she likes she'll try and make another meal.* Similarly, Susie, who had stayed with her grandparents for three weeks during a school summer holiday, noted that her grandmother was happy to cook whatever she would eat: Susie could eat *anything I wanted...she like told me to like write it down and the stuff that I liked and she just like made it for me.* Although her grandmother did cook 'traditional' foods such as *shepherd's pie and hot pot*, Susie was also allowed foods that were not allowed at home such as Coco Pops[5] – though her grandma *won't let me have too many unhealthy things*. Such independent inter-generational negotiations between grandchildren and grandparents do not pass unnoticed by the parental generation. Susie's mother knows that her grandmother may be less strict about what she provides, suggesting that Susie probably eats: *you know, fatty puddings and treats really, 'cause I suppose she gets a bit spoilt.*

Grandparents' provision of treat foods, as a meaning-imbued generational practice, was reflected in the narratives of a number of children. Bret, for example, recalled that when his dentist grandfather went to bed at the end of the night he and his Nannan would stay up and: *she'll just feed me owt. Right, once he's gone to bed, me and my Nannan stay up and watch a film or something and my Nannan just lets me have chocolates and stuff.* Similarly, Amanda suggested that when she stays at her gran's house *we do have quite a lot of unhealthy things…We don't like loads and loads and loads, but we eat like a bit more than we should. Like we like, if I go to my Gran's then we usually have pizza and then I have a pudding, like a chocolate mousse, and then a chocolate bar but then I finish.*

And when children learn to cook with their grandmothers it is often treat foods that are made, *like some buns or sommat like that* (Rose).

> Interviewer: *And where do you think she's learned to cook? Is that from you do you think?*
> Vanessa's mum: *Probably not [laughs]. Er, her grandma I'd say. Her, her grandma bakes constantly. She bakes all the time and she, and she's been teaching 'em to bake and, and they can do it more or less without looking at a recipe now, buns and biscuits and things like that so.*

The provision of treats by grandparents and their 'spoiling' of children are complained of by parents and yet relished by grandparents; these practices are highly suggestive of the ways in which power is negotiated inter-generationally. Being by-passed in the inter-generational interactions that take place directly between children and grandparents, interactions that as we have seen often challenge the moral food order of the nuclear family, parents try to re-frame or re-script them as 'spoiling' as a way of softening their impact. 'Spoiling' has been commented upon previously in the academic literature with, for example, both Hill (1989) and Brannan *et al.* (2000) alluding to grandparents' 'indulgence' of their grandchildren through the giving of sweets, money and presents and 'letting them get away with things' (Brannen *et al.* 2000: 138) or 'letting children do as they please' (Hill 1989: 201). However, while 'spoiling' is generally framed within parental discourses as a problematic practice, such practice is nonetheless constitutive of the active and ongoing negotiation of generationally-specific relations and a means through which different subject positions are enacted and reproduced within a family generational frame. As children's narratives clearly illustrate, interactions with parents and grandparents are imbued with generational distinctions and these distinctions are also reflected in other forms of social interaction within the family. Thus, for example, Harry recognises the need to 'tone down' his behaviour and be less boisterous in the presence of his grandparents:

Interviewer: Do things change when your grandparents come and stay?
Harry: Sort of. We have, I have to like be a lot calmer. A lot less like nuisances. Mm. Less, a lot less loud but [*pause*] normally just the same thing.

Such sensitivity to generational differences is also illustrated by Sofia, whose grandmother *never lets us fight*. However, when the grandmother is not present, child-parent relations may be reconfigured: when Sofia's grandmother *goes out with my Mum and that and me and my brother start on each other messing round and being, erm, me and my brother. Well, two brothers against my sister and my Dad and my other brother.*

Conclusion

The 'doing' of family life is characterised by the fluid interplay between biological and social relatedness, as biological kinship ties between children, parents and grandparents are continually reworked and reinterpreted as social relationships within the local context of the family (Carson 2000). Generational identities are, as we have illustrated, established through the denotation and articulation of similarities and differences: both these processes of identification manifest through family narratives such as food-related scripts. Children's own narratives evidence continuity in food practices, within some families, which help to construct a coherent notion of family life and a sense, for the child, of what it is like to be in 'our' family. Food scripts can therefore symbolise continuity with the past and act as moral referents against which current practices are compared.

However, as Jenkins (1996: 52) has noted, similarity and difference are the dynamic principles of identity which 'reflect each other across a shared boundary'. And, as we have shown, food-related scripts may also convey difference, such that changing food practices act as markers for different familial and historical generations. Thus, food scripts can incorporate new types of food and new forms of practice which contrast with, rather than signify continuity between, generations. Nevertheless, such differences – through their very construction and articulation – are also constitutive of inter-generational relations and of generational identities. Similarly, the notion of grandparents' spoiling of children models grandparent-child relations in direct contradistinction to parent-child relations; 'spoiling' serves as explicit contrast to the moral responsibility exercised by parents for children's eating practices and therein helps to constitute the family generational frame and mark out distinct generational identities.

In sum, therefore, we have argued in this chapter that generation is discursively constructed, in the process of doing family, through the food-related narratives and practices of children and adults. Generational identities are negotiated, on an everyday and ongoing basis, between differently positioned actors within a family, generational frame such that children come to negotiate and understand their subject position/s as children *vis-à-vis* adults *and*, significantly, as children *vis-à-vis* adults at different stages of the life-course.

5
Fathers, Food and Family Life

Alan Metcalfe, Caroline Dryden, Maxine Johnson, Jenny Owen and Geraldine Shipton

Introduction

In this chapter, we consider the ways in which fathers of school-aged children in three contrasting localities in England describe their 'food practices' within the family. The chapter draws on in-depth interviews with 29 fathers so we are not attempting to map large-scale trends in household divisions of labour here; other studies have done just that, as we note below. Instead, our aim is to explore the meanings attached by fathers to their involvement in shopping, preparing and consuming food in the household. Research on family food practices has rarely reflected men's voices directly, and the study we carried out is one contribution to addressing that gap. What part do food practices play in fathers' daily lives, and in the ways in which they see themselves, their own family histories and their relationships with partners (current or former) and children?

Background: food, family and fatherhood in recent research

Feminist research in the latter part of the 20th Century produced systematic evidence of entrenched gendered inequalities in household divisions of labour. Analyses from a range of feminist and allied perspectives reframed domestic labour as hard work, requiring physical, managerial and emotional skills, rather than something that women were just 'naturally' good at (Friedan 1965; Gavron 1966; Oakley 1974; Bernard 1982; Ussher 1991; Delphy and Leonard 1992; Duncombe and Marsden 1993, 1995; Dryden 1999). Specifically with regard to food practices, Murcott (2000) reviewing the field following her groundbreaking 1980s study, found that, in the household, women still continued to do more food-related tasks than men. So, for example, women tended to do most of the cooking (Charles and Kerr 1988; Murcott 1983) whilst also carrying out a great deal of the 'invisible labour' in food provisioning (DeVault 1991).

Murcott's review came at the end of a century in which a vigorous feminist critique of gender-based power relations in western societies might have been expected to challenge such patterns. It is the case that feminist critiques have become embedded in societal discourses in many respects (Segal 1990). In the public realm it is now widely expected that women gain qualifications and work in a wide range of careers and occupations. Likewise, in the private realm there is some evidence that women's expectations have risen, as regards what they expect of their partner in the home as well as their own career aspirations (Beck 1992). These raised expectations can become an issue once children are born: examination of the career and employment trajectories of men and women, once they become parents, demonstrates that an egalitarian division of labour becomes very hard to sustain (Joshi 2002). Nevertheless, alongside a general discourse of increased equality, there has also been the emergence of the notion of the 'involved father'. Politically, pressure groups such as 'Fathers Direct' have shared the debating table with Government Ministers to discuss child and family policy. Changes in Government policy and the law have also reflected an increased acknowledgment of fatherhood, for example through the shift away from the concept of custody to an emphasis on the importance of the child's contact with both parents, and through the recognition of a child's right to information about her or his biological father.

This shift in the politics and ideologies of fathering has been accompanied by a mushrooming body of academic studies. There is now a wide range of theoretical and empirical research on modes and styles of fathering from psychology (Lamb 1987; Marsiglio *et al.* 2000), policy studies (Equal Opportunities Commission 2006) and sociology (Brannen and Nilsen 2006; Lupton and Barclay 1997; Dermott 2008), for example. Within each, a central argument has developed that the distant and authoritarian father associated (rightly or wrongly) with previous generations is being replaced by the 'involved father', who changes nappies and takes children to and from school (Lamb 1987; Marsiglio *et al.* 2000). Brannen and Nilsen suggest that this denotes a shift from 'fatherhood to fathering' (2006), in which the former referred to the main breadwinner whose paid work exempted him from childcare, while the latter term speaks to the practical and relational aspects of parenting, it is involved and 'hands on'. For some, this shift may also be seen as part of a trend towards more democratic family forms in a broader sense (Giddens 2000).

What can a focus on food practices tell us about contemporary fatherhood in this context? As part of the wider *Changing Food, Changing Families* programme, we were interested in examining fathers' own ideas and perceptions about fatherhood, through their accounts of involvement in food-related activities. In taking this approach, we acknowledge that to date there has been a distinct lack of research based on men's own accounts of their involvement in 'foodwork'. This gap was noted by Murcott in the 1980s, when she called for more studies involving men, in order to provide a balance to the growing number of studies that explored food themes from the perspectives of women. Therefore Murcott's work remains an essential point of reference. She proposed four inter-related points about household food practices, supported by many (though not all) other researchers in this field. First of all, food is significant because it is symbolic of and integral to the practice of family life: for example, a 'proper meal' has commonly been seen as a key indicator of 'a proper family'. Second, along with the majority of other routine domestic tasks, women undertake the majority of cooking and meal preparation activities (Charles 1995; Charles and Kerr 1988; Harnack *et al.* 1998; Kemmer 1999; Lake 2006; Cheng *et al.* 2007; Warde and Hetherington 1994). Third, women are more likely than men to take overall responsibility for food acquisition and preparation, and to take account of others' wishes in their planning about food. In this connection, some researchers have emphasised women's lack of authority; others have emphasised the ways in which foodwork contributes to the construction of identity (Bugge and Almås 2006; DeVault 1991; Murcott 1983). Finally, for many of these writers, women's food-related roles have been seen as central to their subordination and oppression, both within the household and in patriarchal society generally (Charles and Kerr 1988; DeVault 1991).

Few took heed of Murcott's call for research on men's perspectives, and by the time of her review in 2000 she was still making the same point (Murcott 2000). Amongst the early studies, only DeVault interviewed men, and only three men out of the 30 households in her study. The clear implication was that men contributed little, if anything, to household food practices. Men in the 'stereotypically "masculine" environs' (Julier and Lindenfield 2005) of the public or commercial kitchen have been the focus of rather more studies especially as they focus on the ways in which men seek to construct particular masculinities (Deutsch 2005; Hollows 2003b; Mechling 2005; Roos and Wandel 2005; Wilk and Hintlian 2005). Against this background it is unsurprising that men's appearances in the domestic kitchen have often been framed as an anomaly in need of explanation. Explanations have usually focused on women's increased participation in education and employment, suggesting that this has led both to increased negotiating power and status for women, and to their absence from the home at the times when family meals are prepared (England and Farkas 1986; Harnack *et al.* 1998; Kemmer 1999; McIntosh and Zey 1989; Warde and Hetherington 1994). Here, men have often been portrayed as recalcitrant figures 'forced' into an essentially feminine domestic space. At best, they are represented as rational figures, reacting to changes beyond their control; at worst, they are deemed to be lazy and emasculated, with their power and their identities under threat.

The qualitative research discussed here takes seriously Murcott's call for men's voices to be included in research about families and food practices. In particular, we seek to examine men's understandings of food and food tasks in relation to their identities as fathers and as partners. In the next section we outline our research, and the locations, samples and methods we chose. Following this, we focus on three key moments in household food practices: shopping, cooking and eating. We explore men's accounts of their involvement in these, and examine the ways in which such food practices play a part in the negotiation of responsibilities, identities and relationships within the home. We argue that the impact of women's participation in employment and education does play a continuing part in understanding men's presence in the kitchen, but that this presence is more active and more complex than has previously been suggested. We also argue that many of the fathers in our study integrated food practices into the ways in which they positioned themselves as good fathers, good partners and family men. However, this does not mean that men and women are on an equal footing when it comes to the domestic kitchen. We argue that women's identities are still rooted in practices of feeding the family more deeply and more consistently than those of men, even when men do take on an active role.

About the study

The *Men, Children and Food* study included research with 29 households, and with children in 4 primary schools, in a total of 3 study localities. Our aims were to explore the perceptions of fathers and of children, in relation to their experience of food practices both at home and (in the case of children) at school. This chapter focuses solely on fathers' perceptions, drawing on in-depth interviews with 29 men (for an account of our research with children see Metcalfe et al. 2008). We recruited fathers through contacts with a primary school in each locality, and in a minority of cases through other local networks (e.g. through a local mosque and flyers placed in libraries). These fathers had at least one child aged between 5 and 11 at primary school.

We aimed for maximum diversity in our recruitment, by choosing 3 localities that reflected differences in terms of social class, employment and education patterns and ethnicity. The first locality, Christopher St., was an ethnically, religiously and socio-economically diverse inner city area of a large northern city. The second, Vale, was a disadvantaged former coal-mining village in Yorkshire, with an almost entirely white British population. The third area included two neighbouring villages in rural Lancashire – Netherhope and Upperhope – with relatively well-off populations; again, this was a predominantly white area. We interviewed 10 fathers from Christopher St., 8 from Vale and 11 from Netherhope/Upperhope.

Fathers ranged in age from their early 30s to the early 60s. For some, their only or eldest child was 5, for others their youngest was 11. Table 5.1 provides an overview of household compositions and other demographic details. The majority of the interviewees in Christopher St. and in Vale worked in manual occupations and/or were receiving benefits; only 4 out of 18 had degree level qualifications. In all but one household in these 2 areas there were 2 adults and all couples were heterosexual. 8 of the 18 were re-married or in second or third relationships. 5 of the fathers were not the biological father to at least one child in the household, and 6 had a child living elsewhere to whom they were the biological father. In contrast, the fathers of the rural Lancashire cohort were generally in more highly-paid jobs, in management or professional settings, and almost all had degree level qualifications. All of the participants here were white, and the overwhelming majority were British. They were almost all older fathers, having had their first child in their mid-to-late 30s or early 40s, often after having been married for several years already and many had developed careers before having children. In contrast with the patterns of reconfigured families in Vale and Christopher St., 8 of the 11 Lancashire households were based on first marriages, with children solely from and resident within that partnership.

We conducted in-depth semi-structured interviews with the 29 fathers, most of whom were interviewed twice. Each interview lasted on average about one and a half hours. The focus of the interviews was food, fatherhood and the family. In the first interview we asked fathers about particular food practices, such as shopping, preparing and cooking food, mealtimes and cleaning up afterwards. The second interview was a more reflective exercise, focusing not only on fatherhood, but also on childhood, including memories and feelings about food. We undertook a thematic analysis of our data (see Mason 2002; Smith 2003), aiming to build a contextualised understanding of fathers' roles in relation to food practices in the home and to use this contextualised understanding to make generalisations through grounding our analyses in the 'situated particulars' of everyday life.

Shopping, cooking and eating: three 'moments' in fathers' accounts of family food practices

Below, we explore the ways in which the fathers in our study described shopping, cooking and eating practices in their households. In line with the limited available research, we find that men do indeed continue to carry out less foodwork than their women partners, and that they acknowledge this, with reference to reasons that range from the constraints of working patterns to conformity with family and cultural norms. However, we also find that there are very few fathers who opt out of foodwork altogether, and that some play a substantial part in one or more of the three 'moments' discussed here. Overall, we suggest that food practices represent a vital aspect of the negotiation of family life, including the ways in which men now position themselves as active and 'involved' fathers.

For ease of reference, Table 5.1 provides an overview of the fathers in the sample, the key features of their households and the ways in which they described their inputs to shopping, cooking and eating within the family. We then reflect in more depth on each of these 'moments', in relation to some specific examples.

One: Shopping

As Table 5.1 shows, shopping was a task that 27 of the 29 fathers interviewed claimed to carry out, either alone or with their partner. On the face of it, despite a high reported involvement in shopping, many of the stories told by men support DeVault's (1991) argument that women do a lot of invisible work in relation to food. For example, all except four of the fathers who shopped for food either went to the shops with their partner, or shopped using a list she had prepared. In that sense, overall responsibility – and the work of planning and thinking ahead – usually resided largely with the woman.

Nevertheless, there was strong evidence in our data that suggested most men take an active interest in the shopping process and the complexities involved and demonstrate a high level of knowledge of food outlets, types of food, prices etc. For example, almost all the fathers demonstrated in-depth familiarity with the range of alternatives for food shopping. As they described these options the influence of locality and class clearly shaped their discussions of the different types of shops visited and how they were evaluated. In Vale, with no supermarket, local shops were generally perceived as selling poor quality and expensive food and the expressed preference was to travel by bus or car to supermarkets. In Christopher St., by contrast, local shops were plentiful, and among them were numerous specialist shops that some of the men said they frequented. For instance, there were butchers selling halal meats, and well-regarded grocers and organic shops. In Netherhope, there was one village shop next to the school and several of the men spoke about deliberately using this shop when dropping off or picking up children from school, as a means of supporting it. Yet, of course, its range was limited and so they did the majority of shopping in the surrounding towns.

Some fathers described collecting small items like milk or bread on the way home from work, to supplement the main shopping trip; sometimes this was at the request of their partner, sometimes it was because they were responsible for cooking that evening and wanted to ensure they had the right food available. In these accounts, fathers' references to planning for one meal at a time contrasted with what their partners were described as doing: women were more likely to plan for a week or more, as this example from Leon illustrates:

> Quite often my wife will do a kind of, or we'll all go and do quite a big shop and my wife tends to decide more what we're having then, although sometimes if we've been pushed for time I might go and get stuff and get stuff say for tonight and tomorrow night or…you know.

Some men explicitly described themselves as learning from their partners about food shopping, or as being influenced in their shopping

Table 5.1 Household composition and demographics

					C St 10	Vale 8	Hope 11	All 29
Estimated age at birth of first child	<19				1			1
	19–25				4	5	2	11
	25–35				5	2	4	11
	35+				0	1	5	6
Current Age	<39				8	5	1	14
	40–49				2	2	4	8
	50+				0	1	6	7
Family-Household Formation	Traditional				4	3	8	15
	Reconstituted				4	2	2	8
	Other (single parent, extended)				4	1	0	5
Ethnicity	White British				4	7	10	21
	British Asian				3	0	0	3
	Black African				2	0	0	2
	Other				1	1	1	3
Employment Status of both partners	Male f/t				3	4	8	15
	Female f/t				0	3	5	8
	Male p/t				4	2	1	7
	Female p/t				2	1	3	6
	Male not working				3	2	2	7
	Female Not Working				7	4	3	14
Highest Educational Qualification of Man	None				2	1	0	3
	High School				0	5	1	6
	Further Education				3	2	3	8
	Degree +				4	0	7	11
	Unknown				1	0	0	1
His shopping practices	Takes responsibility for most shopping				2	0	2	4
	Shops according to partner's list				1	2	1	4
	Shares shopping duties and responsibilities				2	2	2	6
	Goes with partner to help (she makes list)				2	3	4	9
	Does supplementary shopping				3	1	0	4
	Does not go shopping				0	0	2	2
His food preparation practices	Does majority of food preparation/catering for family				2	1	3	6
	Shares food preparation				2	2	1	5
	Cooks occasionally				2	3	5	10
	Rarely if ever prepares food for others				4	2	2	8
His description of main evening meal	Family usually eats evening meal together				8	2	6	16
	Family occasionally eats evening meal together (e.g. weekends)				1	2	3	6
	Working partner usually eats alone				0	3	2	5
	Individualised eating				1	1	1	3
	Couple and children eat separately				1	0	1	2

Notes:
1. In the shopping, food preparation and eating categories we have categorised households according to the stories told, these are hence condensed and miss out much of the nuances of real life. They are merely constructed and presented here as a rough guide to the range and frequency of practices and the stories told about them. Occasionally two stories were told, these were usually that the family eating together at weekends and the full-time working partner usually ate alone.
2. The 'Traditional family' referred to households in which both adults had no other children within the household, and/or had one or more children belonging to other partners who lived elsewhere. Reconstituted family referred to the variety of situations in which one or both partners were recognised 'step-parents' to one or more children within the household, and/or had one or more children who lived elsewhere. Such categories of course are wholly reliant on certain stories being told and therefore these numbers merely give an indication of how families were narrated to the researcher and not the validity of their claims. The 'other' household formations referred to single parents (1), and to extended families living together (3). Regarding extended families this was not just a case of grandparents living with a 'nuclear family', but to two brothers and their families, their two parents and a further brother who all lived together, across two houses situated next to one another, and to one instance in which the man had two families, though we only gained access to one of these.
3. Age of birth of first child is estimated because the question was not asked directly, it is based on age (if known) and age of eldest child.

	Age of first child (estimate)	<39	40–49	50+	Traditional	Reconstituted	Single Parent	Other (extended)	White British	British Asian	Black African	Other	Male f/t	Female f/t	Male p/t	Female p/t	Male not working	Female Not Working	No of cars in household	None	High School	Further Education	Degree +	Unknown	Takes responsibility for most shopping	Shops according to partner's list	Shares shopping duties and responsibilities	Goes with partner to help (she makes list)	Does supplementary shopping	Does not go shopping	Does majority of food preparation/catering for family	Shares food preparation	Cooks occasionally	Rarely if ever prepares food for others	Family usually eats together	Family occasionally eats together (e.g. weekends)	Working partner usually eats alone	Individualised eating	Couple and children eat separately
Abdi	<25	X			X						X						X	X	0	X				X										X					
Ben	35	X			X				X						X			X	1	X							X								X				
Carl	15	X				X			X						X			X	0				X						X						X				
Danny	23	X				X			X						X			X	0				X		X						X				X				
Dave	31	X			X				X				X			X			X	0			X					X		X					X				X	
Ibrahim	28	X						X		X					X			X	1			X					X					X			X				
Khalid	28	X						X		X							X		1			X						X	X						X				
Lomana	35		X				X				X			X				X	1				X		X									X	X				
Mukhtar	25	X						X						X			X		1				X			X								X	X				
Shazad	21	X			X					X				X				X	1	X			X					X	X				X		X				
C St.			X					X		X					X			X	1			X					X	X				X	X	X	X	X		X	
Adam	20	X						X	X							X		X	X	0	X								X					X					X
Total		**8**	**2**	**0**	**4**	**2**	**1**	**3**	**4**	**3**	**2**	**1**	**3**	**0**	**4**	**2**	**3**	**7**		**2**	**0**	**3**	**4**	**1**	**2**	**1**	**2**	**2**	**3**	**0**	**2**	**2**	**2**	**4**	**8**	**1**	**0**	**1**	**1**

Name	Age of first child (estimate)	<39	40–49	50+	Traditional	Reconstituted	Single Parent	Other (extended)	White British	British Asian	Black African	Other	Male f/t	Female f/t	Male p/t	Female p/t	Male not working	Female Not Working	No of cars in household	None	High School	Further Education	Degree +	Unknown	Takes responsibility for most shopping	Shops according to partner's list	Shares shopping duties and responsibilities	Goes with partner to help (she makes list)	Does supplementary shopping	Does not go shopping	Does majority of food preparation/catering for family	Shares food preparation	Cooks occasionally	Rarely if ever prepares food for others	Family usually eats together	Family occasionally eats together (e.g. weekends)	Working partner usually eats alone	Individualised eating	Couple and children eat separately
Darren	24	x				x			x			x	x					x	1		x							x									x		x
Gary	22	x				x			x				x					x	0		x																x		
John	35	x			x				x								x		1		x												x					x	
Jonathan	27					x			x					x		x			1		x	x					x		x						x				
Peter	25			x					x					x		x			0			x					x								x				
Richard	40		x			x			x				x						1			x											x	x					
Warren	20	x							x				x					x	2																				
(Totals)		5	2	1	3	4		1	7			1	4	3	2	1	2	4		1	5	2	0	0	0	2	2	3	1	0	1	2	3	2	2	2	3	1	0
Vale									x				x	x					2			x	x			x		x				x			x				
Bill	21	x			x				x				x	x					2				x										x		x				
Edward	40		x		x				x				x	x					2				x										x		x				
Leon	34		x		x				x				x	x					1				x												x				
Mal	38		x	x	x				x				x	x		x	x		2				x		x	x				x	x			x	x		x		

102

	Mark	Michael	Nicholas	Oliver	Robert	Ruud	Tony	Hope	
Age of first child (estimate)	26	33	37	42	22		40	27	
<39	X								1
40–49							X		4
50+		X	X	X	X	X			6
Traditional	X	X		X			X	X	8
Reconstituted			X		X				2
Single Parent									0
Other (extended)									0
White British	X	X	X	X	X		X		10
British Asian									
Black African									
Other						X			1
Male f/t	X	X	X	X		X	X	X	8
Female f/t				X	X	X			5
Male p/t									1
Female p/t							X		3
Male not working					X				2
Female Not Working	X	X	X						3
No of cars in household	2	2	1	2	2	2	1		
None									0
High School			X						1
Further Education	X			X					3
Degree +		X		X		X	X		7
Unknown									0
Takes responsibility for most shopping				X					2
Shops according to partner's list									1
Shares shopping duties and responsibilities				X					2
Goes with partner to help (she makes list)	X		X				X		4
Does supplementary shopping									0
Does not go shopping	X	X							2
Does majority of food preparation/catering for family			X	X					3
Shares food preparation	X								1
Cooks occasionally	X	X							5
Rarely if ever prepares food for others	X					X			2
Family usually eats together				X	X	X	X		6
Family occasionally eats together (e.g. weekends)	X	X							3
Working partner usually eats alone	X								2
Individualised eating		X							1
Couple and children eat separately	X								1

patterns. John, a former miner now claims disability benefits and his wife does two part-time jobs. He said:

> I've actually picked up Susan's shopping and Susan's preferences, watching and looking what she does.

And again:

> Susan is the one that knows what she's doing with the fresh so she usually does the fresh produce, I usually go along as the mule, follow through. But if it's stuff that…stuff required from day to day, bread, milk, cheese stuff like that, I'll go and get it from Netto's and sort of things and put odds and sods out to try and vary the meals – to within my limitations of cooking.

Our study highlighted considerable disparities in economic circumstances of families with some struggling just to survive whilst every penny clearly counted. For example, Carl, an unemployed father and step-father of six took the main responsibility for shopping and catering in his family. He recounted how he would shop at the cheapest supermarket:

> If we haven't got money, if we've got like £4–£5 and still got two days to last before benefits are paid then I'll go down and I'll get it worked out and then I'll bring it back and I'll cook it, I'll cook tea and then I know that's going to be, they're going to have that much left and I know that they've got summat to eat as well.

In more affluent households too, the cost of food featured in explaining shopping choices. So, for example, for Ruud, a management consultant married to a surgeon (Katrijn), the high-quality Booths supermarket was a local option he wanted to use for limited purposes only:

Ruud	Actually I try to buy meat only at Booths…
Katrijn	They have quality…
Alan	*Booths you say is your corner shop but you don't go there as a big shop?*
Ruud	No, no
Katrijn	Try to avoid that.
Alan	*So why don't you go there for the big shop?*
Ruud	Well because it's too expensive.

Most of the fathers made reference to supermarkets as an important source of family food supplies, and a comparison between the three localities suggests that supermarket access was an important factor in who did the shopping and when. With the dominance of large supermarkets, the car has become integral to contemporary weekly food shopping; this appeared to have different effects in different localities. In both inner-city Christopher St. and the former mining village of Vale, men were much more likely to go shopping with their partners. In the middle-class rural Hope villages however, the 'main shop' was more likely to be done by the woman alone. This appeared to be largely because in Vale and Christopher St. households were more likely to have only one or no car. Men often had to do the shopping themselves or go with their partner because, either they had the car for work or the woman was unable to carry the shopping alone if there was no car:

Adam   She goes to Netto's to do her weekly shopping but when she comes to do, just to get normal bits and bobs like 'tatas, milk, few biscuits, but to fill freezer up we've got to travel a bit and go to Barnsley to like Farm Foods or Iceland or summat like that when she fills freezer up...
Alan   So how often do you go to, well you say you go to Netto once a week, or your girlfriend goes to Netto once a week and do you usually go with her?
Adam   Mmm, to help her out because shopping bags are a bit heavy for her aren't they?

Overall, shopping was rarely described by fathers as a source of conflict between couples and their accounts suggested a strong emphasis on negotiation and a high level of knowledge of shopping-related issues. While only the small number of 'househusbands' in the sample took the main responsibility for food shopping, almost all the remaining fathers took an active part in some respect, ranging from shared responsibility to a support role.

Two: Cooking

For some men, 'cooking' meant cooking from scratch with fresh ingredients; for others, it meant assembling ready-prepared ingredients for something like a pizza or a pasta dish. Our emphasis here is on 'cooking' as the act of preparing a meal for oneself and/or for other family members, rather than on the differences within this spectrum. Most notably, only a minority of fathers saw themselves as taking the main responsibility for cooking or sharing the cooking. There were parallels therefore, in some respects, between fathers' accounts of preparing meals and those summarised above with respect to shopping. Most fathers took a support role, either on a regular or an occasional basis and some appeared to have no involvement in cooking at all (see Table 5.1).

Overall, our analysis of fathers' cooking accounts suggests that they can be grouped into three main categories: first, sous-chefs and occasional cooks; second, everyday cooks who share responsibility or do most of the cooking; and third, non-cooks. The accounts from fathers within each group suggest that levels of employment and of education within the household play a part in who cooks, when and why, but that the inter-relationship between these factors and household negotiations is complex.

Sous-chefs and occasional cooks

Overall, ten fathers described themselves in terms of 'helping', as being occasional or intermittent cooks and sometimes – as with shopping – in terms of learning from watching or working with a partner. So, for example, one father used the 'sous-chef' term himself, to describe his role in peeling, chopping and doing the bits and pieces for his partner, who managed the overall process of preparing and cooking a meal:

> Well I'm not a very good cook. I think they'd all agree with that. So yeah she will come home and she will cook but I will assist her as much as I can with chopping and stuff like that...I'll be the sous-chef, yeah. That tends to be my role (Edward, late 40s, married to Zoe, Netherhope, he is a salesman, she a part-time administrator, two children 10 and 7).

For some, the occasional or support role was expressed, not through the process of assisting, but through cooking a particular dish for the family, or cooking at a barbecue or other special event in the ways often associated with men's cooking in past studies:

> Well this Saturday I cooked steak, I cook a steak I do, so we'll have steak, chips, onion rings, all the trimmings, I'll do that (Darren, lorry driver, married to Michelle, housewife, former mining village Vale, late 30s, three kids 11, 8 & 2).

> I don't cook much, but when I do cook, I do it so they remember it (Danny marginally employed married to Gaynor: housewife, inner city Christopher St., early 30s & early 40s, eight children under 15).

Might do a barbecue, a barbecue would be different you see because you could chat around the cooking kit, whereas out here in the kitchen you wouldn't really...Er, yes, for some reason it does seem to be a man's thing And it gives me an opportunity, you see, to have a beer while I'm cooking so, because you've got to keep cool you see (Oliver, management consultant married to Francesca, occupational psychologist, rural village Netherhope, early 50s & early 40s, two children 10 and 7).

Fathers' awareness of taking an occasional and/or support role did not diminish their sense of making an important contribution to foodwork. Darren was keen to point this out, implicitly distancing himself from certain forms of 'traditional' male role: 'I'm not one of these husbands that sits down and expects my meals'.

The barbecue, for instance, makes an interesting parallel with the Sunday Dinner. Murcott describes how the Sunday Dinner draws the family together (Murcott 1982); similarly, the barbecue is a means by which the whole family (nuclear, reconfigured and/or extended) can be drawn together, often with friends in addition, through the social act of making and eating a meal. As Oliver says, barbecue cooking provides an opportunity to 'chat around the cooking kit', and 'to have a beer while...cooking', a familiar masculine marker of sociality.

It is also interesting to note that some of the men implied that cooking *in the kitchen* was never going to be easy because it was not 'their domain':

Alan   *Ok. So how often do you cook then?*
Bill   Me? Probably not enough. I think, well what will happen tonight, Steph will come in, we'll decide what we're having and because I'm around both of us will prepare – like I'll prepare the salad or for a chicken you know
Alan   *So you're the sort of supplementary chef?*
Bill   Probably. Probably. We have this debate, me and Steph, often and I kind of find it fascinating, that's her, she's really small, a lot smaller than me but she's big in the kitchen, because it's her dominion.
Alan   *Ok, she stands...*
Bill   Though she'll say she's really into equality – which she is – it's very strange. We have this debate often, 'how is it that this is yours, the kitchen, when you say you don't want that style' do you know what I mean? It's very interesting. And

she'll be watching over me while I'm cooking (Bill, Community Worker, married to Steph, Administrator, rural village Netherhope, mid 40s and late 20s, 1 child 11; Bill also has two children from a previous marriage)

Sous-chefs and occasional cooks may offer familiar staples that they can rely on, or may undertake an experiment, trying new recipes. These two approaches are discussed by Michael, and his wife Penny volunteers a contrasting view of her own cooking:

Michael   I will tend to experiment a bit more. I will cook with whatever's in the fridge…But that's only sometimes, a lot of the time it will be a recipe either from a recipe book or a recipe that you've done so often that you think you can remember – usually get it wrong.

Penny   I've become completely boring (Michael, stockbroker married to Penny, housewife, rural Netherhope, both late 40s, four children under 12).

Most importantly, these fathers saw what they did as making a positive contribution; their foodwork is as symbolic as the Sunday Dinner. They are capable of doing more than this in the kitchen; however, the initiative remains largely with the wife or partner to call on them to do this, and work routines often make that difficult. Michael again:

Michael   Penny cooks all the time but I wouldn't come back… after work and actually cook a proper meal, I might cook something but I wouldn't actually go and concentrate on cooking a nice proper meal, it's more it's fuel at that point in the week…just at the moment I'm working quite hard so it's quite likely that Penny might cook, she might cook me an omelette or I will have whatever the children have had, so that if they've had spaghetti Bolognese I'll have spaghetti Bolognese, that sort of thing.

The important point here is that Michael's work limits what he can do at the best of times, and at the moment with particular pressures at work his wife, Penny, is more likely to cook for him or he will have whatever the children have had earlier.

Sharing the cooking or doing most of it

11 of the 29 fathers either shared the cooking (5) or took the main responsibility for it (6). Previous work, such as studies by England and Farkas (1986) and Warde and Hetherington (1994), concluded that men are much more likely to cook when the woman is absent, usually because of paid employment. We similarly found that fathers were more likely to cook regularly, and to share responsibility for cooking and food preparation, if women worked full-time. Correspondingly, fathers were less likely to cook if their partners were not in paid employment – regardless of their own employment status. Overall, a higher level of household education was also associated with greater involvement in cooking among fathers (see Table 5.1), findings that parallel earlier studies (Harnack *et al.* 1998).

However, fathers' accounts underlined the diversity of experience across households, in terms of the ways in which employment patterns and other factors were drawn into the day-to-day negotiations of family life. For example, for some of the men, cooking was presented as necessitated by partners' absence through paid employment outside of normal working hours:

> Well, Susan has been doing the evenings, maybe about a year and a half, maybe two years...it's been, shall we say, necessity that I've done it, and necessity of just trying and experimenting (John married to Susan, he claims disability, she has two part-time jobs, Vale, mid-40s, three children 11, 8 & 4).

John is at home because of a disability, and Susan has had to take a second part-time job in the evenings to bring in enough money. Out of necessity, John has taken over the role of cooking for the children; this is not something he did before marriage. He cooks for the children so that they can eat (and he can eat with them or eats surplus food just after they have finished) then they can go on to other activities, such as judo. In this context, employment and outside activities take precedence over a family meal.

Robert, like John, is at home in the day time, as he is retired; his partner works full-time. He, too, usually cooks the evening meal, explaining this in terms of preferences about food quality:

> It will be half past five when she gets in, well if she started cooking then after she'd been out all day, this is when you end up with

a burger and one chip isn't it? (Robert, retired political party activist married to Pamela, civil servant, Netherhope, 59 and 44, one son 11).

A slightly different story is told by Ben, who has gone part-time at work in order to share responsibility for looking after his two daughters. This means that he and his partner share the cooking as well as other food tasks, and whoever is not at work is the one who cooks:

Ben So Monday, Tuesday I'm not at work so I cook tea and my partner's at home on Thursday, Friday, so it's just the Wednesday and we just sort of alternate who cooks then...And then at the weekend we just sort of, we haven't got a rota or anything so at the weekend I don't know, it just sort of works out (Ben, works for council in urban regeneration, lives with Alice, an art therapist, in Christopher St., both 40ish, two children 6 and 3).

In a fourth example, ill health appears to be a major reason for a woman's absence from the kitchen:

Gary Joanne does most of it [the cooking]. I do a bit but Joanne
Joanne Well I prepare the food out and I'll put it in pans and that he will do most of it, do you know what I mean...and Gary like sees to it because my legs get that heavy you see so I have to sit down (Gary married to Joanne, mid-30s, he is a factory worker, she does not work, three kids aged 15, 12 and 8).

As the discussion with this couple progresses, it becomes clear that Joanne does little or no cooking because of illness and that Gary appears to take major responsibility for catering for the children. However, this is not through cooking but preparing sandwiches:

Gary Well before, years ago, we used to have...when the kids would stop in and have a proper meal we used to have a set meal [...] but now it's just, with us getting older they're coming in, go straight out, see you later – that's it – gone. And then sort of like it's just cooking what everybody decides to have [...] because I mean the youngest one prefers

sandwiches to cooking so I presume like it's a lot easier for him and quicker, you know what I mean.
Alan So do you think maybe he likes it because you like it?
Gary No I think he prefers sandwiches anyway. I mean most times he'll come in and ask for a sandwich or he might be upstairs playing and he'll come down and say 'can I have a sandwich' and then you give him a sandwich and [inaudible] so he prefers sandwiches to actual cooking. So I think with him, by the time it's actually done he's fed up of waiting. I mean and then he doesn't eat a right lot of it, he's not a very good eater either, whereas sandwiches he'll eat them and eat them all but a dinner he'll leave more than what he'll eat.

For fathers who are 'everyday cooks', therefore, the woman's absence from the kitchen at the times when meals were needed often appeared to influence what happens, whether this was because of paid employment or for other reasons such as illness. However, the men we interviewed very rarely presented their involvement in foodwork as something they were 'press-ganged' into. Rather, involvement in cooking was presented much more in terms of the responsibilities that come with parenting or as a positive contribution they could make to family life.

The final point to make about this group of 'everyday cooks' is that their involvement in cooking was still described as something that they could opt into (or out of) more readily than their partners could. Men described themselves as happy to allow others to take up the reins, while the women who did least cooking were often described as making a deliberate effort to cook family meals at the weekend, as Warren noted:

My wife actually [made the evening meal] yesterday [Sunday]. I usually make it when I'm off but she wanted to make it yesterday so she did it...she fancied making a sausage casserole so who am I to stop her? (Warren, lorry driver married to Natasha, housing officer, Vale, mid-30s, three children 14, 11 & 6).

Similarly, Mal is a househusband and Paula works full-time; she usually cooks the Sunday lunch, and also insists they sit at the dining table rather than at the breakfast bar:

Mal Well we had a chicken casserole yesterday evening, which my wife made which is most unusual.

Alan So how come she made it yesterday then?
Mal It's just. Because I didn't volunteer to do it. If I'd have said don't worry I'll make it on Sunday I would have made it. But she'd got it into her head that she was going to do it and that was it (Mal, househusband married to Paula, marketing executive, Netherhope, early 50s, two children 14 and 10).

Volunteering implies a notion of being able to opt in rather than opt out, and Mal's comment that 'she'd got it into her head that she was going to do it and that was it', implies determination on her part, not just a failure to step forward on his. Overall, the accounts of the 'everyday cooks' in our sample suggested that the need to place oneself at the heart of the family through cooking is felt less keenly by men than by their partners.

Non-cooks

While 11 of the 29 fathers in our study claimed at least to share the cooking, nine did very little, other than occasionally helping. Some had moved from the original home setting to another where a woman had cooked for them; some had lived away from home only for a specific period, such as attending university. Mukhtar, for instance, said that he had not cooked since 1986 when he was a student in Tripoli. Jonathan had moved on from one cook to another when he had left home and shared a house with friends, before marrying Stacey. The last time he cooked was when his wife was in hospital giving birth to their second child, ten months before our interviews. Jonathan was employed part-time as he had become the main carer for the children; even though Stacey returned home from full-time work at 4.30 each day, she cooked the family meal. Jonathon had attempted this task but failed:

> I like the idea of being a good cook, I do, but it's the actual getting to it that puts me off. I don't know, having loads of things on the go at once, I'd totally get lost with that...I did have a go once and we did do a few meals and then I think I burnt something...It's not a burning ambition of mine but I think it would be good to say that you could do it, you know what I mean (Jonathan, Rehabilitation Assistant married to Stacey, 35, Administrator, Vale, two children 8 and 1).

A contrasting picture came from brothers Ibrahim and Khalid who lived in two houses next to one another in Christopher St. Like many

British-Asian families in the area, the extended family shared space and resources across the two households. Though neither cooked, Ibrahim claimed he was able to cook, unlike his brother, whom he claimed 'had never even boiled a kettle'. His brother disputed this, saying he'd probably made himself a pot noodle. They had no need, their wives would cook, and if they were unavailable then their sister-in-laws were next door, and failing that, their parents lived with them. Indeed, their father, who had lived on his own in Pakistan for some years, was declared to be a good cook and would still make breakfast for the children at weekends. Overall, however, these 'non-cooks' were clearly in the minority.

Three: Eating

Eating together as a family in the evening was the usual practice of 16 families and another 6 ate together on occasion, often at the weekend but 5 families tended to arrange mealtimes in such a way that the working partner ate alone. In 3 families there was individualised eating and in 2 the couple and the children ate separately. Vale had the fewest number of families who were usually able to eat together (2) compared to Hope (6) and Christopher St. (8). Previous research has found family meals to be a resonant symbol of family life, and fathers' accounts often confirmed the importance of 'proper meals', eating together and viewing the main meal as the family meal – a valuable touchstone in terms of a recognisable family and family life. These three aspects were something that many men were pleased to indicate they achieved in their family lives, or something they sought to do but for various reasons found it difficult to achieve. These points can be seen in extracts from three interviews. First, Leon emphasises a view of the importance of eating together as a family:

> Leon   I think we've always made a point of it [eating together] right from when they were young.
> *Alan   So why is that?*
> Leon   Well I think it's just a social thing and often you find out what's gone on or whatever (Leon, electrician married to Rosa, teacher, mid-40s, Upperhope, two children 11 & 8).

Leon explains that he and Rosa have always placed a value on this from when the children were young. It is a 'social thing', a time and a place when you can get to know what is going on in the children's and one another's lives. The next two stories are more complicated.

114 *Fathers, Food and Family Life*

Oliver   [Yesterday] I was in London, struggling to get out of London because someone jumped in front of a train, so all I had was a banana yesterday…Today would probably be representative of what you're doing here because I'm actually at home (Oliver management consultant married to Francesca, occupational psychologist, Netherhope, early 50s & early 40s, two children 10 and 7).

Warren   We don't always eat at the [kitchen] table actually, sometimes kids will eat at t' table and me and my wife will come in here [living room]. But not for Sunday dinner (Warren, lorry driver married to Natasha, housing officer, mid-30s, Vale, three children, 13, 11 & 6).

Oliver quickly dismisses the question of what he'd eaten yesterday as not worthy of discussion: it was not a typical day, in part because he was working away and in part because of the situation with the trains. Moreover, it is because he is home today that this would be better to discuss; today would involve the family eating together, and something more than a banana. Indeed, it is interesting how he clearly tells this story because of what he thinks the research is about. The family meal is symbolic of how he sees the research and how he wants to narrate himself within this research: as a family man.

Warren's story is slightly different; intriguingly he simultaneously undermines the normative but then quickly restores it again, indicating initially that they tended to eat as a family in the kitchen but then, it seems, in trying to reveal some of the contingencies of day-to-day living, he says that the children will eat there when he and Natasha eat a different meal in the living room. But, he quickly re-secures the sense of a proper family by commenting on how this may be done for ordinary weekday meals but it is not done for Sunday Dinner, when they all eat together.

The two stories also indicate a further issue regarding eating together. While some days, in particular Sundays, are more structured, when a proper meal will be eaten where the family-household sat together; other days, Fridays and Saturdays, are days when rules are relaxed and routines broken, or rather a different temporality comes to the fore. On these days families are more likely to have take-aways or eat 'child-friendly food' such as pizza and for many who ordinarily insist on eating at the dining table with no TV on, eat it in front of the television on sofas and on the floor. We came to know this as 'The Dr

Who Meal' as the story of eating while watching this programme on a Saturday night was so commonly told. This was a treat for the children, but in some households it was also one of the few times at which the whole family would eat together.

Eating together was for many a luxury or came second to simply ensuring that the children were fed. A number of households, Warren's included, where both adults worked late, would recruit wider kin to feed the children: Warren's children went to Natasha's parents. Others relied on schools to ensure that the children ate at least one decent, hot meal a day; food eaten at home was in some of these households seen as supplementary to what was provided by the state, the quality of which could not be guaranteed.

Practices and meanings: food and the negotiation of family life

To sum up, this chapter has taken seriously the absence of men in studies of food within the domestic arena (cf. Murcott, 2000) and to redress the balance has focused on three moments of family food practices (Morgan 1996) – shopping, meal preparation and eating, and explored the range of experiences and accounts of them given by men. We looked at these three moments because they are key points when families come together and involve tasks that have often been examined in terms of roles undertaken. By doing this we have identified the different meanings the fathers attributed to these moments, their perceptions of their place within them and through this their identities as fathers, as partners, as men.

On the one hand, our study seems to support the general contentions about the gendered division of labour made by various writers over the previous decades (Murcott 1983; Charles and Kerr 1988; DeVault 1991; Warde and Hetherington 1994; Harnack *et al.* 1998; Lake 2006). Thus with regard to shopping, men's stories confirm that in the majority of households it is women who do the planning and make lists (if lists are made), they are the ones who plan meals in the longer term, who do what DeVault termed 'provisioning' (1991). With regard to food preparation, while about one-third of our interviewees spoke of, at least, sharing, and a significant number of these taking on the majority of responsibility, overall traditional patterns remained. However, in spite of this apparent reiteration of traditional gender roles, and the gendered division of domestic labour, we would claim two points.

First of all, while we too find gendered patterning, it is not so clear cut as is often reported by the earlier studies. In contrast to the distinct set of gendered roles found by these earlier studies we have revealed a diverse range and a more blurred and interwoven set of experiences and accounts. Thus, while it remains true that women still take the major responsibility for provisioning through shopping and planning, men get involved in this at a range of levels in diverse ways. For example, if they have not led on responsibility then they accompany partners to drive and carry bags, they negotiate purchases whilst shopping, they will shop to a list, undertake supplementary shopping and take responsibility for provisioning in the short term, for that evening or the next day or two. Similarly, with food preparation, it is not just the occasional man, at least, sharing, even taking on the responsibility for this task, it is over a third of men who reported that they did so; though not always relishing the task or feeling confident in their capacities. Added to the diversity we also found a blurring of the responsibility for the task itself. On the one hand, food may have been ostensibly cooked by one person, but preparation and ideas regarding what to cook may have been done by their partner, or outsourced to supermarkets' pre-prepared ingredients and meals. Indeed, this dispersal of responsibility was very common as schools were often expected to provide reasonable meals (and occasionally the main meal of the day), while wider families were often drawn on to feed children at various times, such as weekends or when the partners were absent because of work; indeed they were called on to look after the children while parents went shopping, or to accompany them shopping while one parent would do the childcare. In short, while gendered patterning was apparent it was only very clear at a certain level. Dig a little deeper and the apparent clarity of such roles is blurred by the performance of ongoing everyday practices (Schatzki 1996; Warde 2005; Shove and Pantzar 2005).

Secondly, by talking with men about feeding the family, we discovered not simply what they do and do not do, but revealed the meaningfulness of the tasks for these men. As we have witnessed, a significant minority of men interviewed took on responsibility for shopping and food preparation, often linked to how they sought to share responsibilities, willingly, albeit hesitatingly, taken on when circumstances dictated. For these men, food practices were central to their fathering and their partnering. Yet, the majority of men, not as fundamentally involved in or identifying with such practices, also drew on foodwork as a means of demonstrating their commitment to and place within their family-household (and broader 'extended' family kinship networks). Thus, their help, occasional cooking and barbecuing, while much maligned in literatures as of little value, appears to have symbolic value to these men as they seek to redraw themselves as fathers and partners. Indeed, the identities of some men as fathers and partners, and their place in the family, is often denoted by their absence. For instance, children's 'needs' took precedence, so in order that children eat well and in a reasonable time, men are often marginalised to the periphery of the family meal; it was not uncommon for them to eat alone after returning from work (though the same was true of women who were the primary earner). Moreover, in contrast to Murcott's paper 'It's a Pleasure to Cook for Him' (1983), we found that many men spoke of not having the food they would prefer because their partner did not like it and would not make it; many also spoke of having had eating habits, even tastes changed by their partners' preferences: one of the most common stories being reduced meat eating, or eating white meat or vegetarian food instead. Meat was saved for special occasions and eating out. Thus, while a significant number of men were taking on greater responsibility, for those who were not, and for even those who were marginal, food remained symbolic and meaningful. The three moments then reveal how men construct and weave together identities, as fathers, as partners and as family men in the three different spaces of shops, kitchen and at the table.

6
'I don't go in for all that scaremongering': Parental Attitudes to Food Safety Risk

Lindsay Blank, Paul Bissell, Elizabeth Goyder and Heather Clark

Introduction

Food risks have a special standing in people's risk appraisals (Knox 2000) due to the central role which food plays in family life. Concern about food risks has steadily increased in the last few decades (Payson 1994). A survey conducted by the international market research company Ipsos-Reid (Tucker *et al.* 2006) found that the majority of respondents in 19 countries felt their food is less safe that it was ten years ago. In recent years consumers have become generally uncertain about the safety and quality of their food and their perceptions often differ substantially from that of experts (Verbeke *et al.* 2007). There is evidence to suggest that consumers expect all food to be intrinsically safe and would never knowingly purchase or consume unsafe food, and this is particularly evident in terms of protecting and nurturing the family. Nevertheless, although under normal conditions the majority of consumers are not worried about food safety, or at least accept the inherent low level risk, the occurrence of a food safety incident may result in consumer concern and anxiety (Verbeke *et al.* 2007).

Policy on food safety has also become more structured in recent years. For example the UK Food Standards Agency (FSA), established as a direct result of the Bovine Spongiform Encephalopathy (BSE) crisis, has a remit to 'make sure food is safe to eat, including funding research on chemical, microbiological and radiological safety, as well as food hygiene and allergy' (FSA 2008). Internationally, reforms in the Codex Alimentarius Commission and its World Health Organisation expert advisory committee demonstrate an increasing prevalence of food safety concerns on the international stage (Millstone and van Zwanenberg 2002).

Food scares and the inherent risk associated with food preparation and consumption are wide and varied. These are generally characterised as those related to technology (e.g. genetic modification, intensive farming methods and food irradiation) and those associated with lifestyle and food consumption (e.g. diet and nutritional quality, food hygiene and eating practices). Research into risk perception and technological hazards has focused on technology acceptance, whereas research into lifestyle hazards has focused on behaviour change and in general people have been shown to be more worried about technological food hazards than lifestyle ones (Miles 2004). This is attributed to the fact that people believe they have more knowledge and more personal control over lifestyle hazards than technological hazards; that is, the food habits which impact directly on family life. Furthermore, some lifestyle hazards are judged to pose less of a risk than technological hazards as they can be managed by decisions made within the home (Frewer *et al.* 1994). In summary, when changes to lifestyle are made, moderation and balance in terms of nutrition and health versus food enjoyment is the key; with the 'odd slip' or exception considered to be acceptable. But with technological advances the prominent view, mediated by a lack of trust, information and understanding surrounding any new technology, is that even a small amount could be damaging – and is therefore to be avoided at all costs and not tolerated or permitted within the family environment.

There is evidence that people conceptualise technological and lifestyle food-related hazards in different ways. Concern about technological risk has been shown to be associated with a lack of information from the government (or other trusted sources), potentially implying a need to increase transparency regarding risk management practices associated with technological food hazards, as well as developing effective communication practices about technological risks. Lifestyle hazards were associated with the need for improved communication in a crisis (Miles 2004). Participant concern about lifestyle hazards was also associated with changing information about healthy food and conflicting information about food safety, suggesting that communication might also address how information is derived as well as presenting the facts independent of scientific context (Miles 2004). Therefore people in general appear to be more accepting of lifestyle risks and more worried about technological food hazards regardless of the true level of risk involved.

The media also tend to focus their food risk attention on technical hazards, most notably possible problems with the food supply as well as controversies related to health and nutrition (Tucker *et al.* 2006) although in the current age of the 'obesity epidemic' this balance is changing and lifestyle issues associated with food risk (e.g. fat, sugar, salt consumption) have, in recent years, been receiving more attention. Intense media coverage can escalate into food scares particularly when food or processes are asserted to contain new or unexpected health risks (Whelan and Stare 1992; Craven and Johnson 1999). As a result, food safety coverage in the media tends to be temporal and to cluster around any crisis situation which is occurring at a particular time (Eyck 2000) with a focus on what should be done to protect the family during the crisis. There is less focus around ongoing concerns such as pesticide use or genetic modification.

In order to try to understand how people engage with the discourses around risk and food safety, our aim was to explore how they understand, interpret and use this information in their everyday lives, and how this relates to the food choices they make for their families. Our interviews represent people's accounts of their experiences, and how they choose to interpret these in terms of their decisions on what to believe and what to reject in their attempts to manage food risks and keep their families 'safe'. These data are taken from a larger project looking at the importance of food in these families and the reasons for their food choices. Our project looked at the food choices parents make for their families and the reasons and motivations behind the accounts they give. One of these reasons – the effect of perceived risks around food – is discussed in this chapter.

This chapter explores how parents perceive and make sense of the risks associated with food and eating by presenting the findings of a qualitative study of people's opinions surrounding food consumption, risk and safety. It is argued that people often take a fatalistic approach or trivialise the risks associated with food. A trust in authorities and rejection of media scaremongering combine with the use of learned and trusted family methods of cooking and shopping come together to justify these behaviours.

This study was conducted in a semi-rural population based outside Sheffield (a large, post-industrial city in the north of England). The interviewees discussed topics related to the food they chose for their families and this included how they perceived and acted upon the risks associated with food provision and consumption, and how they reasoned their decisions of what to believe and what to reject in relation to food risk and safety. Analysis of these interviews revealed that our sample talked primarily of the risks associated with farming and industrial practices. These accounts demonstrate what we have termed fatalistic approaches where people do not act on food risk due to a belief that events are pre-determined and cannot be controlled. There were also examples of ways of trivialising risk, whereby the potential risks around food are played down as a way of dealing with them and maintaining normal family life. Food scares were said to be exaggerated by the media, and were seen as transitional in the way they affected shopping and eating habits. An overwhelming trust in authority allowed individuals to justify their limited concern over food safety and this was assisted by a belief that maintaining long-term habits and learned family behaviours provided some protection from risk.

Method

Our study consisted of 30 semi-structured interviews conducted with parents of children aged 11 to 13 attending a semi-rural school and living in an affluent area of rural South Yorkshire. The parents were aged between 35 and 55 and were categorised as social class I or II by the occupation of the head of the family. Recruitment, interviewing and analysis was undertaken by the first author, with substantial support from the other authors. A qualitative approach was considered most appropriate as the aim was to obtain detailed insights into families' behaviours in relation to food. This also allowed responses to be questioned and clarified as required. However, it must be acknowledged that the accounts provided by these parents do not necessarily represent a 'true' version of social reality but are interpretative and may be influenced by parents' concerns in wanting to provide a socially acceptable account. Sampling was purposive and all those who expressed an interest in taking part were interviewed. This resulted in significantly more women than men being interviewed (29 women and four men including co-interviewees where present). It is impossible to tell whether this was due to the subject matter, as it is still the case that more women than men take responsibility for feeding the family, irrespective of employment status. Our sample may therefore over-represent women's views.

Ethical approval for the study was obtained from the Ethics Committee at the University of Sheffield. Participant families were recruited via a letter inviting them to take part in the study. The school assisted in distributing the letter to two school year groups in order to target every parent who had a child between 11 and 13. The age group was selected to complement that of other projects in the 'Changing Families, Changing Food' programme and also represented the transition between junior and senior schools where parental influence on food choice is altered. Each participant returned a reply slip to indicate their interest in the project, and each read and signed an information consent form at the time of interview. One hundred and fifty letters were sent out and all of the 30 parents who responded positively were interviewed.

Interviews were conducted between March and April 2007 during which time food scares directly related to bird flu in poultry (including a suspected outbreak at the premises of a large UK poultry products company), and salmonella contamination of chocolate (again located at the premises of a specific UK producer), were current and the obesity 'epidemic' was continuing to receive substantial media coverage. In relation to the data used here, participants were asked what risks they were aware of to do with food, and then asked how this affected their food choices and ways of shopping and selecting food. Prompting by the interviewer was avoided wherever possible. The interview guide was developed in consultation with the existing literature and was also refined as the interviews progressed.

Qualitative methods of data collection were used and interviews were individual (although the spouse was also present in three cases) and lasted between 30 and 90 minutes. The interviews were tape recorded (with consent) and transcribed verbatim. N. Vivo software was used to assist with the organising and coding of the data. Codes were developed initially at the design stage of the study, and were added to and amended during the processes of data collection and analysis. Initial 'Root' codes (e.g. food risk, healthy eating, shopping habits) were used as well as more specific coding (e.g. scaremongering, control) were used to develop a framework for the thematic analysis.

Lifestyle versus technological risks

Several overarching themes were apparent and common to each interviewee. Firstly, when asked about their perceptions of the risks associated with food and eating, in each case the interviewees spoke primarily of technological risks; of the risk associated with changing farming or industrial practices rather than lifestyle risks e.g. those associated with diet (such as obesity). Of the 30 interviews we conducted only two interviewees mentioned obesity and eating the 'wrong foods' in direct association with the concept of risk in relation to food consumption. Many of the interviewees did speak at length about their views of the obesity epidemic in other parts of the interview, but this was mentioned very rarely in relation to the risks associated with food. The technological risks discussed by the interviewees may be defined in terms of risks which, it was believed, could not be easily managed or controlled by the actions of the individual. This quote typifies the responses as it demonstrates how JC feels that she has control over the type of food she chooses to eat, but feels less sure of her ability to ensure that the food she is eating is 'safe':

> JC: well, because it's down to me what I eat in terms of I mean do I have chocolate or do I have an apple, but I can't know whether something is safe when I'm eating it, that's not always under my control.

These accounts contain differential views about the different types of risk associated with food and eating. Whereas technological risks are considered to have the potential to affect the whole population and are perceived as hard to avoid or control, lifestyle risks (such as the risk of obesity) are seen more in terms of individual choice within the family, as something which can and therefore should be controlled. Generally, there was very little overall concern about food risk in this population; in other sections of the interview, concerns about food safety and risk management were not discussed, and the issue of risk was not bought up by any of the interviewees until initiated by the interviewer.

Food scares and transitional risk

Secondly, and again common to most of the accounts, is that the main association with the term 'risk' when associated with food was in reference to 'food scares'. The term food scares is collectively attributed to a number of outbreaks of food and farming 'crises' in the UK beginning with salmonella in eggs in the early 1980s and going on to include BSE, swine fever, foot and mouth (Cooter and Fulton 2001) and most recently avian flu. Our interviewees most often mentioned BSE ('mad cow' disease), salmonella and bird flu. Perhaps as a result of this, accounts tended to mention a particular type of food or an individual food item which would be singled out, treated more carefully and often excluded from the family diet. In most cases these examples were meat or other animal-derived products, that is, the same type of foods which have been the focus of recent food scares in the UK. For example:

> WS: ...and I always cook my meat properly, beef and that, and chicken, I always make sure I cook well.

In justifying their differential response to specific foodstuffs in terms of the level of perceived risk and therefore the degree of behaviour modification deemed to be appropriate, people relate directly to food scares and, as a result, deemed products which had not received high profile media attention as intrinsically safer than those which had. This is summed up by this quote:

> KT: …well it's not like we've had a scare on carrots is it?

The interviewees also spoke at length of the transitional nature of perceived food risk. This they linked closely to media representations of food scares so that there was a perception that the particular risks around any one foodstuff were transitional. Therefore, individuals would choose to modify their purchasing behaviour for a short time, but when the media frenzy died down they would go back to their 'normal' shopping habits.

> SB: They all do don't they for a short time and I think you sort of think oh heck, but then it's like with the beef stuff, we never stopped buying beef for long, we were probably more careful which kind of beef we bought you know I was like, well just check where you know, these beef burgers are probably a better kind, but we never stopped eating it for very long.

Also discussed was the rationale that food scares have now been around for long enough to have persuaded people that this disproves the immediate risks in terms of individual vulnerability. As a result of this accumulation of scares relating to specific foods people spoke of reacting less strongly (in terms of behaviour modification) to more recent food scares than they had in the past. They appear to develop an apathy towards food risk which was justified as due to the number of previous scares, all of which were deemed to have been publicised as likely to have a more widespread impact that had actually occurred.

> DG: It did with the beef you know with the mad cow disease? But we don't eat a lot of red meat anyway so it wasn't a big problem but I think I probably didn't buy it for a while and we ate more chicken. But then with the chicken no, I didn't stop buying it.
> LB: *Why not?*
> DG: Well I'm just getting to the point now where I think that nothing ever really comes of these things in the end.

The fatalistic approach

This history of time-limited, acute responses to suddenly elevated risks associated with a specific foodstuff (which are perceived to fade away over time without the anticipated degree of effect ever really materialising), has led to a large number of the people we spoke to becoming relatively unconcerned about the potential risk to their family. We have termed this approach as 'fatalistic', which refers to discussions in their accounts where people often spoke of choosing to take a 'sensible' approach and not allowing their families' shopping and eating habits to be affected by the next temporary shift in media attention. Although aware of the risks associated with food scares, in particular these accounts display a belief that a lack of action is justified by the fact that events are in some way pre-determined, that is, they accept the risks but do not believe that they are able to influence the impact:

> JB: no, I think I'm quite sensible with that I mean I didn't stop eating beef when the mad cow scare was on, I didn't stop eating eggs when they had the salmonella. Obviously it makes you think about things and you're a bit more careful in perhaps your choices. And making sure that you buy you know, good cuts of meat and things like that. But no, I'm not easily put off by that.

Trust and authority

This fatalistic approach was often coupled with a trust or belief in 'authorities', namely the government and the food industry to do the right thing, and ultimately to manage the risks on the family's behalf. For example here, DG speaks of how her belief that government regulation would not allow 'unsafe' food to be sold enabled her to justify continuing to purchase chicken and serve it as a family meal, despite what she may have seen or heard in the media referring to the then-current bird flu scare in the UK:

> DG: …then when the chicken thing came in we didn't stop buying chicken we carried on. I thought if it was that bad then they wouldn't be selling it.

This reflects the consensus that, in complete contrast to the government and other accepted experts, the media were definitely not to be trusted, with accusations of the media 'blowing everything out of proportion', appearing in many accounts. This opinion was summed up for many in the phrase 'scaremongering' which was present in a number of interviewees' accounts in terms of their opinions of the media and how they choose to represent food risk, as this quote demonstrates:

> AO: not really to be honest I'm not into all that scaremongering.
> LB: *is that how you see it?*
> AO: yeh. I think I do yeh. I think they're quite often isolated incidents and then it just gets all blown up out of proportion in the media and everything.

Trivialising risk

Others demonstrated a slightly different approach to managing food risk. It appears that in order to rationalise the risks around food and allow them to go about their 'normal' family lives without having to worry about every item of food they consume, people tend to trivialise the potential risk. This opinion was based on an individual's own experiences of food scares, and a lack of individual impact on them or their families, which had led them to minimise the risks they perceive. One interviewee in particular talked about being able to joke about risks, possibly as a way of dealing with them:

> JD: Oh yeh, like the bird flu thing. Erm, well we're of the ilk of, we make a joke about things like that. And one of the things my husband says is like oh, that's good that because we'll be getting some cheap chicken.

Long-term habits

Another way in which trivialisation of food risk was justified was a belief that sticking to long-term habits and learned family behaviours was protective. This perhaps has some association with the fact that rapid technological change is most associated with risk in these accounts and that therefore habits which have not changed for years are conversely seen as safe:

> AO: Well I mean it took them so many years to find these things out that we'd have eaten it anyway if we were going to eat it we'd have eaten it when we were young. So if we were going to get it we would have already got it anyway, so stopping eating it now isn't going to

make any difference I don't think. That's probably stupid but it's what I think.

Discussion

The aim of this chapter was to explore how parents perceive and make sense of the risks associated with food and eating and how this affects the food choices we make for our families. Analysis of these data revealed that families generally take either a fatalistic or trivialising stance in relation to food risk and talk primarily of the risks associated with farming and industrial practices. Fatalistic families are realistic about the risks associated with food consumption but take minimal action as they believe that events are pre-determined. They therefore accept the risks but do not believe they can influence the outcome. Those who trivialise food risk play down the associated risks due to a perceived lack of individual impact. These responses in relation to food risk go some way to developing our understanding of how people manage everyday risks as they attempt to provide their families with a healthy, safe and varied diet.

Our interviewees spoke primarily of the technical risk associated with food and focused on the food scares which have been attributed to changing farming and industrial practices. Food safety experts believe that the public under-assess the risk associated with some microbiological hazards and over-assess the risk associated with other hazards such as BSE (De Boer *et al.* 2005). Our results confirm their perceptions, as there was no mention of food poisoning in our interviewees' accounts, which all centred on the risks associated with food production techniques.

It has been shown that experts consider the potential severity or harm from an event as well as the probability of it occurring (Slovic 1987; Frewer 1999), whereas laypersons focus on qualitative aspects of risk: whether an event can be controlled, avoided or easily understood (Covello and Johnson 1987; Pidgeon and Beattie 1998; Bennett 1999). Many of these accounts display a belief that the family has little control over technological food risks, and that without resorting to extreme diets that the risks cannot be entirely avoided. This therefore may explain why many of our interviewees chose to rely on 'authorities' to manage the risk and were fatalistic in reference to the potential threats.

These accounts therefore can be said to confirm the two dimensionality of food risk perceptions defined by Leikas: scariness and likelihood (Leikas *et al.* 2007). Leikas showed that food risk perceptions generally form two dimensions: scariness (the level of risk) and likelihood (the relative chance of any individual being affected), and that the interrelationship between these two dimensions may depend on the nature of the risk. It is a reduction in the perceived likelihood of being personally affected by a food risk which, over time, has led to a decline in the perceived scariness. This may explain why our interviewees said they were less affected by current food scares than they had been in the past.

De Boer found that experts are of the view that the media have the ability to improve awareness and knowledge about food risk issues but believe that the media tend to communicate information that is misleading (DeBoer *et al.* 2005). This was demonstrated in the media distrust frequently mentioned here. There is also the argument that consumers display behaviour patterns and make choices that seem irrational or illogical or at least inconsistent with expert opinion and scientific knowledge (Verbeke *et al.* 2007) as they often demonstrated poor connections between the perceived risk associated with a specific food safety concern and its actual risk. Many of our interviewees' accounts made very little differentiation between specific risks, and opinions were based on an accumulation of previous food scares from which no personal problems were encountered. There is also evidence to suggest that this generic distrust, and a believe that the media tend to communicate information that is misleading, extends to professionals as well as laypeople (DeBoer *et al.* 2005).

Assessing consumers' perceptions of risk related to food safety and the impact this has on family food habits can be used by policy-makers and legislators to inform programmes and policies to manage food safety risks and maintain public confidence in the food supply (Rosati and Saba 2004), and by food safety specialists to develop effective education and risk communication programmes (Blaine *et al.* 2002). In this case, our families have focused on the technological risks and the transient nature of the perceived risk. This may explain why issues such as food hygiene were not discussed and indicates that messages around safe food preparation, which have a greater likelihood of exposure for the family, need to be constantly reinforced in the public sphere in order to compete for attention with the perceptions of scariness which affect people's interpretations of food risks. More transparency and understanding of perceptions of risk may help to provide better explanations of the decisions parents make when dealing with and interpreting food risk for their families.

Part III
Family Meals

7
Myths of the Family Meal: Re-reading Edwardian Life Histories

Peter Jackson, Sarah Olive and Graham Smith

This chapter uses evidence from the Edwardian period in Britain, immediately prior to the First World War, to challenge present-day myths about the decline of the 'family meal'.[1] Defining a 'family meal' is, of course, no easy matter and raises thorny issues about the distinction between families and households. But the term generally refers to members of the same (usually nuclear) family eating a meal together, sometimes in the presence of other (non-family) members of the same household. As is now widely recognised, 'family' is itself a falsely monolithic concept (DeVault 1991: 15), its taken-for-granted character belying the diversity of family forms. In what follows, we take a performative approach to defining 'family', where the preparation and eating of food plays an active role in the constitution of family life, rather than approaching 'family' as a pre-formed social unit who happen to take some of their meals together. Indeed, as others have argued, 'a "family" is not a naturally occurring collection of individuals; its reality is constructed from day to day through activities like eating together' (DeVault 1991: 39).[2] Like DeVault, we argue that the preparation and consumption of food plays a crucial role in 'doing family', a practice that involves complex forms of social organisation and highly gendered patterns of paid and unpaid work.

The chapter begins by reviewing the current evidence of decline, arguing that we are experiencing a 'moral panic' based on a partial and exaggerated interpretation of the evidence.[3] We then examine some evidence from the Edwardian period which reinforces the notion of a contemporary moral panic. Rather than family meals being in steady decline over the last 100 years, we argue that the 'family meal' as a venerated social institution has long been asserted as an ideal by society's moral guardians while its observance in practice has always been more variable.

Myths and moral panics

Throughout this chapter, we are using the term 'myth' not in the commonly-accepted sense of a demonstrable falsehood but in the more specialised anthropological sense of myths as stories that circulate within society, providing a moral commentary on the appropriate conduct of social life (Cohen 1969). In anthropological work of this sort, assessing the truth or falsehood of these stories is not as important as understanding the way that myths serve as a kind of social charter. A similar approach is taken by Hobsbawm and Ranger (1992) in their historical analysis of the 'invention' of tradition and by Samuel and Thompson (1982) in their account of 'the myths we live by'. Like Samuel and Thompson, we are interested in myths as narratives that shape collective experience and in understanding how memory and tradition are culturally re-shaped and re-cycled to make sense of the past from the standpoint of the present. Like them, too, we see myths as a way of structuring memory and exploring experience, and we understand myths as windows on the making and re-making of individual consciousness, memory and experience as well as on the reproduction of social or collective memory and more public forms of consciousness.

We argue that myth plays a key role in the articulation of contemporary 'moral panics', where the identification of a 'folk devil' (illegal immigrants, football hooligans, single mothers...) serves as a convenient scapegoat, held responsible for a variety of social ills whose causes are usually more complex and intractable. In criminologist Stanley Cohen's (1972) original analysis, the media (newspaper journalists and television reporters) played a key role in identifying the appropriate 'folk devils' and in the articulation of a 'moral panic' that served the interests of society's moral guardians, almost irrespective of the actual evidence. In a typical moral panic, the empirical evidence is ignored or exaggerated, used selectively or wilfully distorted. Gossip and rumour proliferate, described by Shibutani (1966) as 'improvised news', filling the vacuum created by a lack of verifiable information. In what follows, we wish to argue that the alleged decline of the 'family meal' can be analysed in these terms. While it may be difficult, in this case, to identify a specific 'folk devil', responsible for causing the perceived problem, the proliferation of poorly-informed public debate about the issue and the disregard for solid evidence, equates to a contemporary moral panic. We begin with current debates and then consider what light historical evidence from the Edwardian period might shed on these issues.

Current debates

According to chef and food writer Richard Corrigan, 'It's so important that we sit around the table with our families for a proper meal at least once a week...There's a reality in the saying that the family who eat together, stay together...Sunday is a very important day to me, and Sunday lunch is a big part of that – it's sacred' (*The Independent on Sunday* 11 June 2006). Such views are commonplace and represent a form of 'received wisdom', based partly, we argue, on a misreading of the past that makes an important contribution to a wider public history of 'better times' – a point we return to in the conclusion. The normative language of 'proper meals' and 'sacred' family time demonstrates that these debates are morally and politically charged.[4] Those who fail to live up to the implied standards of proper eating are failing to perform 'family' in the socially-approved manner and are cast as 'folk devils' in Cohen's (1972) evocative term. Nor is Corrigan alone in his emotive assessment of the decline of the family meal. Restaurateur Oliver Peyton calls the Sunday meal a sacred thing, while chef Jean-Christophe Novelli describes Sunday lunch as a great tradition which it would be 'sacrilege' to lose (*The Independent on Sunday* 5 March 2006). These comments are all cast within a Christian rhetoric, comparing family meals to Sunday worship and implying that Sunday lunch is comparable to Holy Communion. Other commentators have focused on the role of family meals in the promotion of cohesive communities and active citizenship, acting as a kind of 'social cement' or an opportunity for 'bonding', where families can sit down together and chat about the day's events (Margaret Ryan, BBC News On-Line, 2 October 2006). The decline of family meals has also been linked to recent increases in eating disorders, childhood obesity, drug abuse and alcoholism.

Writing as part of *The Independent on Sunday*'s 'Sunday Lunch Campaign' (5 March 2006), Jonathan Thompson refers to Sunday lunch as a 'centuries-old tradition' that is now in rapid decline. Thompson reports that 'As recently as a generation ago, British families sat together for a meal nearly every day, but today a quarter of us don't even have a dining table'. Thompson paints a nostalgic picture of happy family life, based on clearly demarcated gender roles, with 'mother, cheeks flushed, carrying the rib of beef, leg of lamb, or joint of pork to the table as father stands by, sharpening the carving knife'. These representations of the role of food in the reproduction of harmonious family life are, we argue, based on dubious evidence invoking extravagant comparisons with simplistic understandings of medieval feasting and impressionistic vignettes of cosy Victorian domesticity. The historical evidence regarding family mealtimes and the current sociology of family eating is far more complex.

We start our examination of the historical and sociological evidence with Anne Murcott's (1982) seminal account of the social significance of the 'cooked dinner', based on observations in South Wales. In that paper Murcott described the essential components of the meal (meat, potatoes, vegetables and gravy) and demonstrated how it is socially defined as a 'proper' meal *par excellence*. Murcott shows how the preparation and presentation of the 'cooked dinner' among this group of young mothers in South Wales followed certain rules and rituals. A 'cooked meal' was a fairly elaborate affair, prepared just once a day and usually on only three or four days a week. Eaten in the evenings on weekdays, on Sundays it was generally served sometime after mid-day and ideally eaten by all household members at the same time. 'Cooked dinners' should be prepared from fresh ingredients. They should be hot, not cold, and served up as a plateful, with the gravy added last. With few exceptions, the cooking was regarded as women's work, symbolising 'the home itself, a man's relation to that home and a woman's place in it' (Murcott 1982: 693).

As Director of the ESRC's research programme, *The Nation's Diet* (1992–98), Anne Murcott subsequently wrote more widely on eating practices in contemporary Britain, challenging the popular assumption that the 'family meal' is in terminal decline and questioning the evidential base on which many social commentators seemed prepared to rely (Murcott 1997).[5] While a 'family meal', eaten together with family members sitting round the table at the same time, may be an ideal to which many people aspire, Murcott argued, there is a big gap between actuality and aspiration. She concluded that the idea of the family meal is 'redolent of ideology, social prescription and ideals' (*ibid.*: 38). The ideal to which she refers was subject to variations by gender, age and class, all of which, Murcott argued, 'start to break up an image of sharing at the dinner table by reflecting internal divisions of status and power in the domestic group' (*ibid.*: 44). The ideal-typical model of the 'family meal', Murcott concludes, is mainly shared by members of middle-class and (respectable) working-class families. Murcott concludes by speculating that:

> Those who are most likely to express anxiety about the possible disappearance of families eating together are those whose own social origins are the source of an allegiance to middle-class values and the middle-class valuation of family meals (*ibid.*: 44).

This is precisely the point that Cohen (1972) makes in his argument about the articulation of moral panics by the self-appointed guardians of good taste and propriety.

More recently, Alan Warde and colleagues have provided a systematic account of eating practices across Europe as part of a wider study of changing consumption patterns, based on an analysis of time diaries for the period 1975–2000 (Cheng *et al.* 2007). In the British case, they conclude that the evidence for an overall decline in 'family eating' is equivocal. While there is definite evidence of a shift from set mealtimes, with a common pattern of three meals a day at relatively fixed times, to more varied patterns, including a proliferation of informal eating occasions and casual snacking (see Figure 7.1), the actual amount of time that families spend eating together appears not to have changed significantly over the last 25 years, particularly if the increase in eating outside the home is taken into account (cf. Warde and Martens 2000). In particular, Cheng *et al.* argue that while there has been an overall decline in the amount of time people spend eating and drinking at home (from 71 minutes/day in 1975 to 56 minutes/day in 2000), this pattern of generalised decline is not confirmed by their analysis of the episode data which measure the duration of eating events, where the evidence shows 'remarkable stability' since 1975 (2007: 47).[6] They also note that the decline of eating and drinking at home has been compensated by a rise in eating and drinking outside the home, from an average of 11 minutes/day in 1975 to 25 minutes/day in 2000. Much of this time is, of course, spent in family groups. While tendencies towards temporal fragmentation are noted, counter-tendencies were also found which the researchers interpret as evidence of the resilience of family eating practices to external pressure. Cheng *et al.* conclude that while eating out may substitute for eating at home to some extent, it does not cause a radical transformation in patterns of home-based eating and drinking. Indeed, 'eating remains a sociable and collective practice, despite shifting temporal pressures which make the coordination of eating events within social networks more difficult' (*ibid.*: 41). Moreover, the stability of the episode data implies

136 *Myths of the Family Meal*

Figure 7.1 Changing mealtimes, 1961–2001

% eating or drinking, in or out of home, by time of day, all day

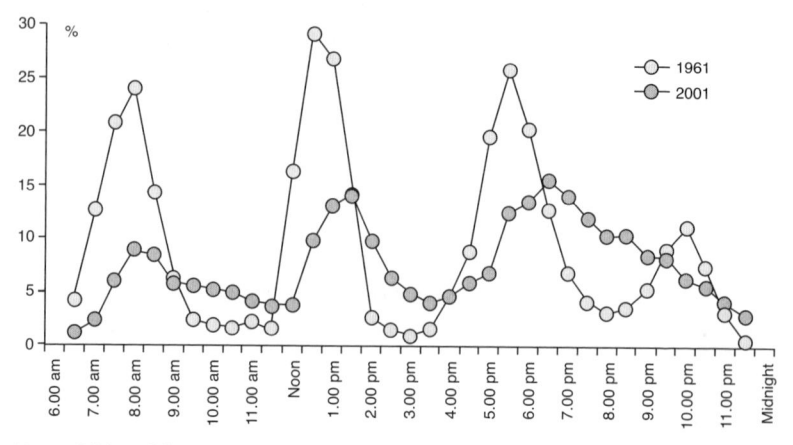

[Chart showing percentage of people eating/drinking by time of day, comparing 1961 and 2001, from 6.00 am to Midnight]

Source: Cabinet Office (2000a)

that the form of domestic meals has not dramatically altered since 1975: *the family meal persists* (ibid.: 55, emphasis added).

Based on their contemporary ethnographic evidence, James *et al.* (forthcoming) argue that the symbolic importance of 'eating together' in their case-study households (which include families from a socially deprived inner city area, a multi-ethnic inner city area and an affluent suburb) has lost none of its potency across the generations even if it is now less frequently achieved in practice (see also Chapter 4). On the basis of all this contemporary sociological evidence, then, there is support for our argument that the decline of the 'family meal' is something of a myth. In order to assess longer-term trends, we turn now to some evidence from the Edwardian period.

Edwardian evidence

Our analysis of Edwardian eating practices and family mealtimes is based on a re-reading of existing archival evidence, focusing on a selection of the more than 400 life histories that comprise 'The Edwardians' collection. The interviews were collected by Paul Thompson and a team of interviewers during the early 1970s using a lengthy interview schedule. Interviews lasted for up to six hours and followed a broad life-course trajectory covering childhood and schooling, work experience and social life, marriage and parenting. Thompson himself used these interviews to write *The Edwardians* (1975) and *The Voice of the Past* (1978) and the data have been subject to extensive re-analysis, facilitated by the availability of the 'Edwardians On-Line' digital archive (http://www.qualidata.ac.uk/edwardians/about/online.asp). Our own analysis of this material focuses on questions about families and food as part of the 'Families Remembering Food' project which aimed to answer four research questions:

- What is the place of food in people's memories of family life?
- How have social constructions of 'the family' and memories of family life changed over time?
- How do gender, ethnicity and social class impact on the different inter-connections between family and food?
- What methodological considerations do researchers face when reusing oral history archives?

There is an extensive literature on the politics and practice of re-using secondary data, particularly in the context of oral history research (Bornat 2003; Mason 2007; Perks and Thomson 2006). Our own work supports the practice of re-use, provided that the data are adequately (re)contextualised and that the dialogical nature of life history research is sufficiently understood (Jackson *et al.* 2008).

In this chapter we have not attempted a systematic analysis of the entire Edwardians collection. For a more general overview of the material, readers are directed to Paul Thompson's (1975) own analysis which includes a chapter on 'sustenance' and a separate section on 'leisure and drink'. The original data collection and analysis aimed to include a representative sample of British society. There was a clear attempt to get a balanced cross-section in terms of the gender, location and social status of the interviewees. Of the 449 interviewees, almost half were male (222) and half female (227). The project had a nationwide emphasis, although large numbers of interviews were conducted in particular cities including London, Bolton, Salford, Keighley, Liverpool, Oxford, Guildford and Glasgow. The collection captures largely working-class experience, although a few interviewees were members of the middle-classes – a group that were relatively small in the early 1900s. The occupational class of interviewees in the collection, from most to least common, was semi-skilled manual (86), clerical and foremen (52), employers and managers (47), unskilled manual (28) and professional (23). One hundred and seventeen interviewees were not classified by occupation. It is also important to note that the lives of the upper classes can be glimpsed through the voices of former servants that are part of the collection.

In our own analysis, in this chapter, we have used the material in a rather different manner, presenting detailed information on a small number of case-study families, comparing three interviewees' recollections of their domestic routines. To facilitate comparison, we have selected three families who all worked in the same industry (textiles) and lived in the same region (West Yorkshire) at approximately the same time (the early 1900s). While there are obvious limitations to what can be established on the basis of an analysis of just three families, we do not base our argument on their statistical representativity or otherwise. Instead, we have employed the kind of inferential logic that Clyde Mitchell (1983) advocates as the epistemological basis for effective case analysis. As Mitchell argues, the point is not to try and generalise from a handful of case studies based on a flawed notion of *statistical inference*. Rather, case studies are better suited to a form of *logical inference* where even two or three cases can demonstrate, for example, that a particular social institution (such as the 'family meal') is not universally practiced. In the present case, our analysis reveals the importance of class differences between the families as well as variations by geographical location (rural versus urban) and family size. While we draw attention to the differences between the three families, we would also note that we could have chosen examples that offered greater contrasts.

We recognise that gender relations, working patterns, domestic routines and mealtimes were contingent upon local circumstances and that there were more pronounced regional differences in the past. So, for example, in the 1900s in places where large numbers of married women worked, such as in Dundee, there were large numbers of female headed households as well as outlets where hot meals and snacks could be purchased (including tripe and pie shops and buster stalls) (see Smith, 2007). We would also note that there were wide class differences. So, for example, there were families living in extreme poverty in the 1900s, often with dependent children and ageing relatives. These people, along with a larger group of working-class families, simply would not have had the space to hold large gatherings. One of Thompson's interviewees, for example, recalls that the younger children sat on the floor to eat, while the parents ate at a small table. The rest of the family were fed at a 'second sitting'.

The three families we have chosen all come from the same region in which gender relations were relatively similar. Although their diets were different, the difference was not as pronounced as would be the case if we were to compare across Britain. So, for example, the diet of fishing communities was quite different from that of isolated rural dwellers. And all three families not only described themselves as respectable, but are remembered as valuing respectability.

In comparing the three families, we draw attention to several key themes: the impact of people's working lives on their domestic routines; contrasting family mealtimes; and gender and domesticity. Having presented the evidence we will return to our discussion of the contested nature of the 'family meal'. We begin, though, with brief vignettes of the three families, focusing in each case on a single interviewee.

Born in 1902, *Hilda Ogden* grew up in Thwaites, a village on the outskirts of Keighley, near Bradford in West Yorkshire. She was her parents' only child. Her father was a wool sorter at the local mill while her mother, who had worked as a seamstress before marriage, kept house. At the age of 12, Hilda started working half-time in a woolen mill. The Ogdens' rented house had three bedrooms. The kitchen, with its gas oven, was used primarily for cooking, although in summer, when the weather was warmer, they would dine in there rather than in the living room. In terms of sourcing food, they kept hens and grew fruit and vegetables. In addition, relatives with a farm supplied them with game: 'My grandfather and grandmother had a farm at Ripon and – any rabbits or pheasants; they used to send them on. We always had plenty of anything like that'. Thus, despite her father's modest place in the hierarchy of mill life, Hilda's family ate relatively well. Their eating practices were characterised by separate mealtimes and their domestic situation including a significant contribution by Mr Ogden to the housework.

Born in 1890, *Edith Speight* was raised in Keighley. Her elder brother died in infancy, so she grew up as the eldest child, with two younger brothers. Her parents had busy and varied working lives. Her mother had worked in a paper mill and as a weaver before marriage. Afterwards, and in addition to looking after her own family, she kept house for two uncles. Edith's father was a twister in a woolen mill, although at one stage her parents ran a fish and chip shop. She followed her parents into the mill at age 12. The Speights rented their family homes until Edith's mother purchased a house from a builder. Their kitchen was equipped with a fire, gas ring and coal oven. However, it was not large enough for the whole family to eat in, so they dined in the living room. In terms of food provision, they had easy access to dairy products as her father kept hens and their uncles kept a cow: '[We had] two quarts a day at least. So – we were brought up on plenty of milk'. In spite of this, domestic life at the Speight's was marked by elements of hardship, ranging from Edith's mother being over-burdened with housework to the constraints placed on meals by the low wages her father earned.

A retired company director, *Ronald Walker* was born in Leeds in 1902. His father had worked his way up from clerk to director of a firm of wholesale clothiers. Ronald describes his father's ascent of the social ladder:

> He'd had a grammar school education but he'd had to work from early on all his life and he was a man of some erudition, but he'd done it himself and I think he felt that if he'd had a better opportunity he would have been a professional man himself, and he was pleased that professional people regarded him as worthy of their steel and he could cope with them and live socially with them on that level, and it pleased him

His mother, however, originated from a country district near Leeds and had, Ronald thinks, 'a better background' than her husband. Although she never undertook paid employment, she worked as a volunteer and maintained a busy social schedule attending 'at home' days with her circle of friends. The Walkers owned a large house in Harrogate with a bathroom and two bedrooms for the servants as well as a small holiday house in Bridlington. Unlike the other families considered here, they had a dedicated dining room, although the children sometimes ate tea in the nursery or kitchen which was equipped with a gas ring and range. The servants also ate in the kitchen, except for the nanny who ate at the table with the family. In contrast to working-class rural families, the Walkers purchased all their food supplies. The Walkers' domestic routine was very much characterised by their social status as wealthy 'city dwellers'. Family members had little or no involvement in growing, preparing and cooking their meals. Household tasks and mealtimes were clearly differentiated (with the possible exception of the nanny) by each person's gender and status as parent or child, master/mistress or servant.

Working lives and domestic routines

Despite pronounced differences in the domestic lives of our three Edwardian families, there are common themes which cut across their individual narratives. For example, each interviewee made references to their father's working routines in their account of everyday meals. Hilda and Edith both recall the specific timing of mill breaks which governed their father's and sometimes their families' meals. Breakfast at the Ogden's saw their father getting his eggs and bacon first, before going out to work, while Hilda and her mother ate together before leaving for school. Mid-day 'dinner' was eaten at 12.30 during Hilda's hour-and-a-half break from school when her father, too, would return from the mill. Hilda describes the family as 'good meat eaters' and reels off the weekly routine of dishes:

> It was something different every day. I know on Thursday it was always meat and potato pie and – usually steak and chips or fish and chips on a Friday...we'd have cold meat on a Monday, but I – a roast on Sunday, yes. Cold meat and – meat and vegetables on a Monday.

Evening 'tea' was focused around either fruit or meat dishes.[7] As at breakfast, the family ate at different times. Hilda and her mother ate first, after school had finished, while her father ate at quarter to six upon finishing work. Although both the Ogdens' and the Speights' mealtimes were determined by the rhythm of mill work, the form and content of their meals differed. For the Speights, breakfast consisted not of a fry-up but of homemade bread and jam or porridge, with milk or cocoa rather than tea. Like the Ogdens, dinner was eaten between 12.30 and 1.30 when the mill workers had their break. Edith's father would either return home or her mother would deliver his portion to the mill. Edith comments: 'When he worked at Vale Mill – me mother used to walk from here and take him his dinner. Aye. That were her running up and down...I think about it many a time, I don't know how she lived as long as she did'. This interweaving of the generic mill timetable and the timing of domestic mealtimes occurs in several more interviews with ex-mill workers in Keighley and is readily generalisable (cf. Hareven 1982; Rotenberg 1981). In this way, then, domestic routines can be seen to be heavily dependent upon the rhythms of family members' working lives, especially the male 'breadwinner'.

Family mealtimes

The timing of most meals in these interviews is presented as contingent upon and determined by the public world of work rather than the private world of family life. Mealtimes are dynamic: changing as fathers change jobs, or as the children grow up and commence their own working lives. Moreover, they are presented in a matter-of-fact way as occasions for re-fuelling. The exception to this is the mid-day meal which is presented, by middle-class families at least, as constant, stable and symbolic of family life. It is the only meal which all three families ate together at least on some occasions.

At the Walkers, the children ate breakfast without their parents. Ronald stresses, however, that lunch was 'a *family* lunch', a 'substantial Victorian sort of stodgy meal'. He recites the regular weekly pattern of each day's dinner:

> A bit of hot joint on Sunday, cold on Monday, stew on Tuesday, sausages Wednesdays, boiled cod – hateful stuff –...plus in winter we had lots and lots of soup and plus a stodgy pudding of some sort, you know the old stodge.

Tea was eaten separately by the various family members. The children ate a high tea in the nursery, kitchen or dining room, while their mother usually took tea out as part of her social calls, returning to a cooked evening meal with her husband. The children in Ronald's family ran on a separate domestic routine, overseen by their nanny, which was largely independent of their parents' comings and goings. The Walkers' domestic routines are recalled as having been determined not so much by family as by household – the family *and* its servants: a cook, a general maid and a nanny. Blurring the boundaries between family and servants, Ronald describes his nanny as doing 'a mother's work' of teaching them to read and write.

'Dinner', as constructed by these families, also highlights the contrast between male and female, social and domestic roles in these Edwardian families. Dinner is predicated on the ability of their fathers to return home from work: men must opt out of their public role and opt into a domestic one (man of the house, head of the table). Rather than switching between public and private role, the mothers (or cooks) must intensify their existing domesticity: their organisational and culinary skills must enable a meal of several courses to be presented and consumed within a small window of time. This leads us to a wider consideration of the relationship between gender and domesticity in these narratives.

Gender and domesticity

In spite of the difference in their socio-economic status and their urban or rural background, the three mothers in our case-study households are, to varying extents, responsible for similar household tasks such as making clothes and feeding the family. The only woman with a public role, after marriage, in these interviews is Ronald's mother who was engaged in charity work. Notably, she is also the woman least engaged in domestic duties and routines. In contrast, all the fathers in these families had a public role, which arguably shaped their contribution to domestic work in the home. There is, however, great diversity in the domestic roles of the three fathers. Hilda's father had the greatest involvement in the day-to-day running of the house, making his own breakfast, lighting fires and washing up. In addition, he is described as taking on occasional childcare responsibilities, even instructing his daughter in cooking. Hilda also recalls occasions when her father would style her hair before putting her to bed:

> If mother went out of a night, of course I had long hair then you see, and – and he'd either put it in curls you know, the wrapped curls or – what they used to put up, you know, pieces of rag and wind it round, or he'd put it in plaits. Mother always knew that me hair would be different when she came home...because he – he just did what I wanted him to do.

Such contributions to the household chores do not represent the mainstream of fathers in 'The Edwardians' interviews. For instance, Edith and Ronald's fathers did no housework and had minimal contact with their children despite their disparate occupations and social standing. Edith describes her mother as doing 'nearly all the work': 'she got up at half five in the morning and she were last in bed at night'. Apart from cooking and cleaning, she also sewed and knitted; making dresses and shirts for her extended family. Edith describes her father as more interested in choir practice than chores such as painting and decorating: 'He didn't do a lot of repairs...He'd happen put a few nails in but – he weren't a right – handyman that way, he liked to go to choir practice, see, and he were a tenor'. In addition, he is portrayed as too tired to spend time looking after his children. Rather, he would help in the fish and chip shop or look after his hen run. Edith thus constructs her father as too tired or too busy to engage with a domestic role. In contrast, Ronald's parents' division of household labour is framed in terms of his father's clear ideological beliefs about gendered roles. His father had no involvement with the housework. Ronald says, 'He would have no part of it at all. He was the old fashioned type who thought that it was women's work'. Edith's father's domestic role is depicted as contingent upon practicalities, such as working hours, while Ronald's father's non-participation is portrayed as allied to his sense of masculine identity. These interviews, therefore, construct women's domestic roles as coherent across family and social class. Conversely, men are shown as having individualised domestic roles, even where they explain them with reference to broad, gender stereotypes.

Conclusion

In this chapter we have argued that current debates about the alleged decline of the 'family meal' are based on questionable sociological and historical evidence. The proliferation of these debates despite the absence of firm evidence, we argue, amounts to a contemporary moral panic. While the pattern of regular 'family meals' may be fragmenting, the overall time that families spend eating together, both inside and outside the home, has remained remarkably constant since the 1970s despite 30 years of social change, including increased female participation in the paid workforce, changing domestic technologies and the rise of 'convenience' food. The mythologising of the weekly 'Sunday lunch' has become a mainstay of the popular media but, our evidence suggests, was only ever observed in some households, in some places, some of the time. It exists more as a venerated social institution, upheld by society's moral guardians, than it does as a regular, widely shared, social practice. The gap between aspiration and actuality is, as Anne Murcott (1997) argued some ten years ago, as wide as ever.

Our re-reading of the Edwardian evidence adds further to this argument, confirming that there has been no clear-cut or widespread decline in familial commensality over the last 100 years. Specifically, we have examined the food practices and memories of three West Yorkshire textile families, with different class backgrounds. From this discussion we have argued that the 'family meal' – in the sense of a universal, regularly practiced, stable event – is one of 'the myths we live by'. Our re-reading of these interviews demonstrates that mealtimes were flexible and contingent, with the partial exception of the mid-day meal which families spent together insofar as circumstances permitted. A close examination of family meals does, however, reveal a good deal about changing gender roles and domestic responsibilities, about changing attitudes to domesticity and changing constructions of childhood and family life.[8]

Our three cases demonstrate difference even in the same region amongst families with broadly similar values. As already noted we could have chosen families that had even greater contrasts. The logical inference of our argument is that there were even greater variations in how people organised their mealtimes and how they performed family than is suggested by the evidence reported here. Such a finding further challenges the construction of a public history of the family meal as a mainstay of a stable, less differentiated past.

In Edwardian times as now, we suggest, family mealtimes and domestic routines were highly contingent on other practices, mainly taking place outside the home. The 'family meal' may have been venerated by some families as a (middle-class) ideal. But the ideal was rarely attained in practice. Where 'family meals' did take place among our Edwardian families, it usually occurred on weekdays at mid-day and on Sundays, a pattern that was largely dictated by the demands of paid employment outside the home. We would suggest that current domestic practices need to be investigated with equal rigour to establish more definitive evidence before the ideological assertion of a general decline in the 'family meal' is accepted as fact.

8

Food as a Medium for Emotional Management of the Family: Avoiding Complaint and Producing Love

Joseph Burridge and Margo Barker

Introduction

Key studies within the sociology of food have explored the gender division of labour in the family and household, observing the construction and persistence of asymmetrical power relationships between men and women within the domestic context of food provision (DeVault 1991; Charles and Kerr 1988; Murcott 1982, 1983). Several other contributions to this volume have continued to explore these themes with a similar methodological approach. This chapter adopts a rather different route, examining some of the ways in which that domestic context is constructed in cultural representations of the work of feeding a family. In so doing, it follows those such as Parkin (2006) and Warde (1997) by focusing upon the content of women's magazines, and developing a nuanced understanding of the environment of food provision as constructed in such material.

In her book *Food as Love*, Katherine Parkin (2006) identifies several key themes running through the content of food advertisements in the American women's magazine *Ladies Home Journal* throughout the twentieth century. These themes include: the consistent construction of 'food as love'; recurrent praise for women preparing it; simultaneous attributions of power and subservience in relation to food provision; and the significance attributed to female responsibility for the health of the family, specifically children. This chapter explores issues connected to some of Parkin's themes, and one of the key 'principles of recommendation' for food that was identified by Warde (1997) – a connection between food and the giving of 'care'.

Our analyses draw upon material extracted from a corpus of women's magazines (*Woman's Own* and *Woman and Home* – henceforth *WO* and

WH respectively) collected by the 'Food Provision and the Media' project within the *Changing Families, Changing Food* research programme. The chapter concerns a rather interesting way in which the social environment of food provision tends to be constructed in relevant magazine content. It explores three interconnected things often constructed as being at stake when food is prepared (by a woman) for others:

- The construction of food as a tool for pursuing the happiness of others, and ultimately their love.
- The way in which the environment of food provision is constructed as potentially hostile – with the potential for complaint and food refusal to occur.
- The configuration of the environment of food provision as one in which food is used as a medium for the emotional management of the family, and its members.

With all this in mind, we turn first to discussing some notable ways in which the environment of food provision has been understood previously. Then follows a set of methodological reflections, before an analytic section where observations are offered on some tendencies in the magazine content, with two interesting instances discussed in greater detail. This is followed by a section noting some observable changes over time in the relative frequency of relevant content. The chapter concludes with a summary which restates that all of this can be usefully understood as the construction of food as a medium for the emotional management of the family.

Sketching the environment of food provision

The environment in which food provision takes place has previously been understood in multiple ways. It is usually considered to be a place in which the family as an institution undergoes constant (re)construction, and one in which gendered power relations are expressed, and reconstituted in an everyday fashion (DeVault 1991: 54–55; Charles and Kerr 1988: 17). Key studies in these areas have explored the injustices of the persistent gendered division of domestic labour when it comes to responsibility for preparing food, and the relative cultural expectations made of men and women with regard to food provision.

In her pioneering work in this area, Murcott (1982, 1983) observed the important connection between domestic femininity, social organisation, and the production of the 'cooked dinner' as a normatively expected part of family life. She identified the differing positions of family members *vis-à-vis* the routine performance of this work, noting that: 'Men – and children – have meals made for them as a matter of routine: but for women it is a treat' (Murcott 1982: 691; Murcott 1983: 85). The 'cooked dinner' has a key relationship to gendered household structure, since it 'symbolizes the home itself, a man's relation to that home and a woman's place in it' (Murcott 1982: 693). It has tended to reinforce an ideology of a male breadwinner and a female homemaker, or 'agentic man and nurturant woman' (DeVault 1991: 95) with a woman located in the role of 'server and provider' (Charles and Kerr 1988: 229) for men and children alike.

Key studies such as those of Charles and Kerr (1988) and DeVault (1991) built upon the foundation laid by Murcott, and explored various aspects of female responsibility for food provision, including the extent to which care through food is constructed as a 'natural' component of the gendered self (DeVault 1991: 119; also see Bugge and Almås 2006; Lupton 1996), and an index of worth (Charles and Kerr 1988: 218). Although most of these studies are now rather dated, more recent accounts such as Short's (2006: 78) work on cooking practices note that food preparation is still something which men can opt into, but women have to opt out of. A degree of qualitative asymmetry therefore persists in cultural expectations about gendered responsibility for food provision.

These studies also bring to light an important aspect of food provision which has tended not to undergo direct consideration elsewhere – the significance of the reception given to food prepared for others, and how such feedback can impact upon the decision-making process that precedes purchase and preparation. Importantly, Murcott, Charles and Kerr, and DeVault, all identify the possibility that unpleasant negative responses can ensue upon receipt of a gift of food. Murcott (1983: 86) describes a conservative tendency amongst her respondents in relation to the reception of food. The possibility of 'adverse and discouraging remarks' in response to food they prepared resulted in women sticking to what they knew worked, rather than experimenting. For Murcott (1982: 691) when it came to accommodating the desires of others, 'compromise' tended to mean the selection of food 'according to his, rather than her, likes and dislikes'. In their work, Charles and Kerr also identified a tendency for women to prioritise the needs and desires of others (Charles and Kerr 1988: 63; Lupton 1996: 59) such that their responsibility for food provision is actually a 'responsibility without control' (Charles and Kerr 1988: 59). Women 'bring the fruits of their work to table, offering them up for the approval of a (usually male) other' (DeVault 1991: 234). Such approval can, of course, be withheld, and initially, the process is very much one based upon 'trial-and-error' (DeVault 1991: 62; Charles and Kerr 1988: 69) that unfolds while a relationship develops.

When it comes to food provision, there is an apparent 'need for the end product to be appreciated' (Charles and Kerr 1988: 68), and evidence of enjoyment – as positive reinforcement – is itself taken as evidence of the woman's specific importance to the family – her ability to care which accommodates the individual preferences of family members (see Murcott 1982: 692; DeVault 1991: 85). Positive feedback demonstrates the success of the giving of care, reaffirming and reconstituting familial bonds, and providing evidence of love.

This generalised 'aiming to please' is also brought about by a need or desire to avoid *negative* sanction, which potentially undermines those very bonds. Negative reception, in the form of complaint and refusal, is reported as deeply upsetting (Charles and Kerr 1988: 92), and Charles and Kerr (1988: 72) even discuss the angry and violent rejection of food, including plate-throwing in several cases. Such outright food refusals, and other less drastic negative responses, feed into and impact upon the range of things a woman is willing to try – a process through which she learns how to please her man (Charles and Kerr 1988: 40). Discussing one of her respondents, DeVault (1991: 157) argues that those occasions on which a family member complains about cooking impact upon her practices: 'The possibility of such criticism becomes part of the context in which she plans her work'. The context of food provision is therefore two sided with regard to the reception of food that is prepared: the pursuit of positive responses *and* the avoidance of negative ones are key goals to be realised through feeding work.

Some similar arguments are made as part of social scientific analyses of textual sources such as recipe books and magazines. Of course, as already mentioned, the connected issue of 'care' is itself one of the main 'principles of recommendation' observed by Warde (1997), standing in an antonymic relationship to 'convenience'. Writing specifically on recipe books published in the 1950s, Jessamyn Neuhaus notes the way that something akin to the marital bargain identified by Murcott (1983: 87) and DeVault (1991: 144) permeates such texts. She observed a strong 'connection between husband-pleasing cooking and marital stability' such that:

> a woman's work was never done. Even after a woman obtained a husband, her culinary skills remained a critical part of her attractiveness.

Keeping a husband, in many of these texts, was often a matter of providing a good meal or having the perfect drink ready when he came home from work (Neuhaus 1999: 538).

The implication was therefore that failure to please through cooking might fundamentally undermine the stability of the marriage – demonstrating insufficient attention to caring activity.

In her analysis of 300 adverts drawn from various magazines, including *Woman's Own*, Winship (1980: 16) focuses upon the ideological construction of femininity through the figure of the housewife in the 1950s. Her account includes the identification of a tendency towards the representation of a service role – the 'hostess' – for the family and for guests. Here 'mothering', as a process, consists largely of 'providing appropriate commodities for children' (Winship 1980: 19). To some degree we might postulate that her textual material from the 1950s resonates quite closely with the conclusions of key studies from the 1980s – although that is certainly not to postulate some causal relationship between the two.

Parkin's (2006) more recent textual analysis of advertisements from *Ladies Home Journal* also identified a range of interesting patterns relevant to the understanding of the environment of food provision at stake here. Her central thesis is that a fairly consistent trajectory of magazine advertising throughout the twentieth century was to construct female accountability in the kitchen (Parkin 2006: 6). The focus of advertisements for food was a woman's presumed role as a care-giver (*ibid*.: 222) such that 'women should serve food to demonstrate their love of their families' (*ibid*.: 4). Part of this generalised advertising project was directed at fostering insecurity in women – prioritising men's preferences – and portraying poor cooking as problematic for the continuation of marriage (*ibid*.: 158).

Food provision was constructed as having the 'ultimate goal of pleasing men' (*ibid*.: 54) – part of a more general promotion of primary concern with men's happiness (*ibid*.: 135), and perfectly in keeping with DeVault's (1991: 95), and others', observations about the 'womanly' servicing of men through food. Moreover, advertisements sometimes 'suggested that it was acceptable for men to be angry and disappointed' (Parkin 2006: 143) with the food provided, and Parkin discusses several examples which make such suggestions (*ibid*.: 136, 138, 142–143). So, similarly to the more ethnographic evidence, both the positive and negative social (and psychological) consequences of food provision emerge fairly clearly – specifically in terms of the impact of any feedback received.

In light of all of this, it is certainly worth exploring the construction of the environment of food provision in British women's magazines. Following some brief methodological reflections, the remainder of this chapter goes on to discuss some observable regularities in the corpus of magazines assembled as part of the *Changing Families, Changing Food* programme.

Methodological reflections

The project from which these analyses are drawn explores the construction of the gendered responsibility for food provision. Part of this involved considering the range of ends, purposes, and functions offered when it comes to magazine content relating to food provision: what are constructed as the things that can be achieved by the purchase and preparation of food? Clearly these ends are varied, and include obvious candidates such as achievement of a balanced or healthy dietary intake, or the pursuit of weight loss, as well as the socialisation of children.

A particularly interesting and recurrent possibility, which forms the basis for this chapter, is that food has considerable importance in the project of managing the emotional responses of family members. In this material, that tends to mean a male partner of the woman who is assumed to be preparing food, or children, or, much less frequently, dinner guests. The rest of this chapter explores several dimensions of this possible function of food, building up to some conclusions about how this constructs the environment of food provision within a family context.

The chapter is based predominantly upon consideration of regularities evident in materials drawn from a corpus of 2544 magazines articles, adverts, recipes and editorials taken from 144 issues of *WO* and *WH* published between 1940 and 2006. Analytical attention here is centred firmly upon those materials in which a recipient and a response were identified directly – content which constructs a likely subjective response (either positive or negative) from the recipient of food. So, the claim that a food recipe 'is delicious' was excluded, whereas claims centred on recipients – such as 'he will be impressed' or 'they will love its taste' were deemed suitable for inclusion.

In what follows, nothing is intended to suggest that the emotional management of the family is the only, or even the primary, function attributed to food in these texts, or in society more widely. Standard disclaimers also apply regarding the nature of the claims being made. This analysis is clearly in the realm of cultural representations, many of which are economically-tinted because of the proportion of the materials that are made up by advertisements (70.2%). There are no direct claims made about what people do in their everyday social practices, although a resonance with more ethnographic literature is identified. The purpose of considering these materials is to explore the attributed role of feedback in the construction of the environment of food provision, in order to explore what this demonstrates about cultural expectations regarding responsibility for food provision in Britain.

Producing 'love' and avoiding complaints

Considering the entire corpus, 14.9% of all articles contained at least one direct reference to the reception of food, coupled with a recipient. In *WH* this represented 14.8% of the total material, whereas in *WO* the corresponding figure was 14.9%. Some temporal shifts are explored in the section on secular trends below, but here we offer some observations, and explore a couple of examples in some detail to illustrate the argument about the environment of food provision that is constructed.

So, how is it that the issue of the reception of food enters into the magazine material in this corpus? Well, a considerable amount of relevant content involves claims that the recipients of certain products would appreciate them if they were purchased and prepared. Very often this proceeds by something approximating the claim that 'they', 'the family' or 'the children' will 'love it' – thereby approximating the process that Parkin (2006: 30) labels the 'touting' of various products' 'love value'. So, for example, and advertisement feature for Black-Vel-Vit drink claimed that the 'whole family will love it' (*WH*, November 1962: 138), while one for Unox Luncheon Meat (*WO*, 8 November 1956) declared that 'Your children and menfolk will love that rich spicy taste'.

Some adverts even approximated Parkin's (2006: 39) claims more closely by promising that 'serving particular foods would earn [women] love from their families' – stating boldly that if you provided the product: 'They love you for it!' (Sun Maid Raisins, *WO*, 2 November 1966: 93–95) or 'They will love you for it!' (Lyle's Golden Syrup, *WH*, November 1962: 105). Alternatively, the reader was incited to 'Show them you love them with Atora' (*WH*, March 1971: 84). Importantly, though, this sort of explicit call to demonstrate love is much less frequent than one might expect given Parkin's emphasis upon it in the US context. Nevertheless, 'love' is constructed as potentially entering into food provision in *at least* three possible ways. These are: the woman's demonstration of love through providing the product, the recipient's love of the product, and the recipient's love of the woman as a response. Something of a love triangle, but one heavily mediated by commodities.

Other promised responses are rather less intense, yet involve positive appreciation of some type. These often involved the recipients of food acting in some way so as to make their happiness or pleasure empirically available to the provider. For instance, such evidence emerges through the production of smiles in response to the food (Quaker Wheat, *WO*, 13 July 1940: 26); the issuing of requests for more of the same (Little Miss Muffet Junkets, *WO*, 2 June 1944: 14; Jus-Rol Potato Croquettes, *WH*, September 1973: 103); or provision of a conventional 'Thank You' (Harris of Calne Minced Steak, *WH*, April 1961: 70; HP Sauce, *WO*, 20th July 1940: 5). Other such responses include the presence of a glint in the eye of family members (Ovaltine, *WH*, January 1954: 61; Birds Custard, *WO*, 12 December 1950: 36), or others way of indicating recipients' 'delight' (Wall's Ice Cream, *WO*, 9 October 1949: 36) – perfectly in keeping with Warde's (1997: 137) account. Some advertisements even managed to combine several of these into one, with an advert for Paxo Stuffing (*WO*, 8 December 1955: 43) distinguishing itself in this regard, and even managing to rhyme: 'See the family's delight as they savour every bite – hear them pay you, with good reason, compliments upon the season!'

Not all of this is centred vaguely upon 'them' or upon 'the family' in general. The possibility that food provision might be directed at the pleasing of men specifically does recur throughout much of the content invoking feedback. This is especially the case in the earliest material – from the 1940s well into the 1960s. This includes reference to men as a general category of people to be pleased, other references to 'your man', your husband and/or son, and various fictional characters populating advertisements. So, a recurring advert for Lea & Perrins framed the product as 'a condiment to please men' (*WO*, 28 December 1950: 25; *WO*, 8 February 1951: 4). An advert for Betty Crocker Cake Mix was constructed as helping those women 'out to please the men in your family' (*WH*, December 1962: 36), whereas a feature on 'Making the most of expensive meats', by Marguerite Patten, was introduced with the heading: 'Looking for a meal to please a man [...]?' (*WO*, 21 August 1965: 18–19).

In the content concerned directly with men, several rather more negative responses also feature, ranging from an asserted refusal to deviate from a chosen brand (Bovril, *WH*, January 1954: 72), to the problem of general 'faddiness' (Batchelors Beans, *WO*, 18 October 1956: 48; *WO*, 1 November 1956: 43), and the provision of derisory comments about a woman's lack of cooking skills (McDougall's Flour, *WH*, December 1954: 5; Shippam's Tinned Foods, *WH*, May 1963: 75).[1] All of these use such negativity as a point of rhetorical contrast – as part of the construction of the product depicted, or recipe offered, as a solution to the apparent problem of needing to please people through providing food.

It is clearly the case, therefore, that both the positive and negative responses identified in the work of Murcott, Charles and Kerr, DeVault, and Parkin have a clear presence in this material. It is important to note, however, that magazine content featuring men in all of these sorts of ways is far rarer after 1970, and almost disappears completely after that point. There are two exceptions to his, and we will dwell briefly upon one of these from 1981 (see Figure 8.1) because it connects up in interesting ways with some observations made by both Charles and Kerr (1988) and Parkin (2006).

This advert is for Heinz Ravioli, and is striking in its visual depiction of the man concerned – the intended recipient of the food, who acts, of course as an index for husbands in general. He is placed in a baby's high chair, and the smile, or glint in the eye, that is so often used to indicate contentment with food is most certainly absent from his face – he looks rather less than pleased.

There are many potentially interesting things that could be said about this advertisement. It clearly involves a degree of infantilisation. The male recipient is visually constructed as childish – a big baby – even as it is claimed that it is hard to believe that he was once a child. We could also ask whether or not it constitutes a relatively early example of 'irony' in representing gender relations? But, rather than conduct a comprehensive analysis of all of its facets, we will restrict our comments to those most pertinent to the matter at hand.

The situation that is constructed here, is one in which the man (husband) longs for food he was apparently given as a child – the pleasures of his lost youth, including the ravioli that women are constructed as giving to their children. His frustrated desire to reconnect with that past is constructed as problematic to the extent that the future offered once he is given the product is portrayed as one in which he will feel 'better'. According to the advert, providing Heinz Ravioli is the solution to his eyes going 'misty at tea-time', and will allow him to enter a second childhood. Now, the nuances aside, this is a fairly clear example of food constructed as having a role to play in

What does a man have to do to get ravioli?

This may be hard to believe, but your husband was five once.

And that may well have been when he had his last taste of Heinz Ravioli. (Haven't you wondered why they all go on and on about their mother's cooking?)

Now, while you're feeding your own kids on Heinz Ravioli in Tomato Sauce, or Heinz Ravioli in Beef and Tomato Sauce, the man in your life may well be turning a plaintive eye back to the pleasures of his lost youth.

And when you think of those succulent pasta envelopes crammed with best chopped beef, in a mouth-watering sauce, no wonder his eyes go misty at tea-time.

So the sooner you treat him to a tasty, filling meal of Heinz Ravioli, with perhaps baked potatoes and green beans, the better he'll feel.

It's high time he got into his second childhood.

HEINZ Ravioli

Make a meal of it.

Figure 8.1 Advert for 'Heinz Ravioli', *WO*, 21 November 1981: 58. Reproduced with the permission of H.J. Heinz Company Ltd.

the emotional management of the family – the husband's psychology being clearly portrayed as open to alteration through the medium of food, as purchased and prepared by his wife.

Another notable feature here is the mention of the man's mother – the individual previously responsible for pleasing him through food, and a figure that often seems to hover in the background in relation to food provision. Charles and Kerr's (1988) interviews identified the mother-in-law as a figure often invoked in talk about a woman's ability to please her man through cooking. Those occasions where a partner said something like 'Why don't you cook it like my mother does?' were particularly troubling to women, and it was seen as a key moment if and when their partner expressed a preference for their cooking over their own mother's (Charles and Kerr 1988: 70). Parkin's (2006: 136–137) material also features several uses of 'the mother' as a figure of contrast. In Figure 8.1, the man's mother is, however, not a point of comparison in terms of the relative quality of her cooking, but in terms of the types of food she prepared for the husband figure when he was a child. Things are a little softer here than in most of Parkin's examples.

Where magazine content makes claims about men's positive responses to meat products, as they do in several instances here, it is not hard to connect this to long-standing cultural associations between meat and masculinity or virility (Charles and Kerr 1988: 77; Lupton 1996: 104; Fiddes 1991). It is notable also that several of the advertisements discussed above are also for sauces, soups, gravies and flavourings – traditional accompaniments for meat – which is also interesting in relation to the construction of family unity through food.

According to Murcott's account of the 'cooked dinner', gravy is the fourth element supplementing a portion of meat and two vegetables. Gravy: 'not only links together the previous three separate components and translates them into a coordinated whole, it also emphasizes that this coordinated whole, the cooked dinner, is indeed a plateful' (Murcott 1982: 683). By flowing over all of the components of the meal, gravy connects them together and transforms them into a coherent whole. We wonder whether an argument can be constructed that, in these texts, gravy is also being portrayed as providing a similar function in cementing the family together through their appreciation of food provided by the mother.

In Britain, between 1983 and 1999, Oxo gravy cubes were advertised on television with a series of over 40 adverts featuring the 'Oxo family', including actress Linda Bellingham. For many years, a family would be shown sitting around a table in semi-chaotic but loving excitement, busily attending to their individual activities, before being united in quiet anticipation of the thick brown liquid oozing over their plates. This line of thought – the association between gravy or sauce and family unity – has a certain resonance with some of the magazine material, but it would be taking interpretative liberties to make any strong claims about such matters.

We now turn to another advertisement in some detail, this time an older advert for Bird's Custard, from the 1950s (Figure 8.2). This is not because we think that Custard is somehow 'gravy for desserts' – making a dessert into a bowlful – but because it neatly distils some of the important issues that we believe to be at stake in this material. It contains content relevant to the construction of both positive *and* negative responses to food that is prepared.

What is at stake here, again, is this conception of reception or feedback that we have been mobilising. The advert is actually quite complicated, involving several sections, and some sequential art, which features rhyming text underneath it. It is closely tied to the ending of rationing and the renewed availability of certain products (Burridge 2008), and constructs its central female character as ignorant of this. At the start of the story she is unaware of the renewed availability of Bird's Custard. Because of this she is providing food, some of which is poorly received by her family – as we are shown in picture 2 in Figure 8.2, and told in the accompanying text, via a piece of lyrical wizardry: 'her firsts won praise that rocked the rafters, but everyone condemned her afters'. She is successful in receiving positive feedback ('praise') for her first course – with rafter-rocking being hard to eclipse. This contrasts sharply with the reception afforded her desserts, which are 'condemned'. Indeed, in picture two you can see a refusal on the part of her family to accept the dessert she has prepared – and we are supposed to believe that this is because she is not using Birds. She is shown in the next picture wiping tears from her eyes while 'a little bird' lets her in on the news of Birds' renewed availability. This ultimately leads to the 'happy family' picture number four – replete with members smiling approvingly, in appreciation, as the protagonist stands centre-stage, proudly displaying the newly acceptable custard. She can now avoid negative, and achieve positive, feedback when serving dessert, and 'watch the family's delight' when she does so. The asserted payoff from the effort required for the product of a happy family, indeed one of the 'happiest' is constructed as most definitely worth it. All of this preceding discussion has made clear the specific ways in which the environment of food provision as constructed in women's magazine content. In a substantial portion of the material in the corpus, this environment is shown as a context in which pursuit of positive reactions, and avoidance of negative responses, from the recipients of food are key. Food provision is therefore shown to occur in an

158   Food as a Medium for Emotional Management

She thought she was up-to-date...BUT

1. She still thought
Bird's, she thought, was hard to find,
Took *any* custard, didn't mind.

2. And so
Her "firsts" won praise that rocked the rafters,
But everyone condemned her "afters".

3. Then someone told her
"Things are different in the shops —
You *can* get Bird's. Just *ask*. It's tops!"

Moral: The days when the best hid under the counter are *gone!* To-day, shopping's different. All you need to do to get creamy, smooth, golden Bird's Custard is *ask* for it by name. That's no trouble, but just watch the family's delight when you serve Bird's. Isn't it worth it? You see, custards *are* different and Bird's is the custard with the formula and flavour to make all your sweet dishes the *best!* The happiest families have thought so for over 115 years!

4. Modern Mrs.! Happy family!
She acts upon those friendly words,
Invariably *asks* for Bird's.

Smoother! Creamier!
Best-ever flavour!

BIRD'S CUSTARD POWDER

How to make this Bird's tested recipe
COCONUT CUSTARD PIE
2 pints Bird's Custard (double thick)
2 oz. Margarine   2 oz. Desiccated Coconut
Line a pie plate or dish with short pastry, bake and cool. Make Bird's Custard (double thick, remember) and while still warm beat in margarine. When cool beat again, adding desiccated coconut. Spoon into pastry case and decorate. See how deliciously the flavour of the coconut mingles with the creaminess of Bird's Custard.

Remember – custard is always better when it's Bird's Custard

Figure 8.2 Advert for 'Bird's Custard', *Woman and Home*, January 1954: Back Cover. Reproduced with permission of Premier Foods

environment in which food has a role to play in the emotional management of family members. Although a very different type of material – textual representations often with an economic imperative – these

Trends

Having established, qualitatively, the range of issues that we see as interconnected, it is worthwhile considering briefly some very general observable temporal shifts in the proportion of materials containing relevant claims about the reception of foods. It is, of course, notoriously difficult to make claims about temporal change in relation to advertising, due to the ephemeral and ever-shifting form of the genre (Cook 2001: 222), and the same problems occur in relation to other similar material. Nevertheless, some general trends have already been mentioned, anecdotally, in the previous section – specifically, much less emphasis being placed upon men, and upon negative reception from the early 1970s onwards. It is also appropriate to consider the proportion of content that involves some form of feedback – to see if there are any noticeable changes over time: has the relative incidence of such material shifted? Given broad (although uneven) changes in the relations between the sexes over the last half century, we might expect material of this type to decline in its regularity, if not disappearing completely.

Figures 8.3 and 8.4 report percentage of adverts and articles, categorised by decade, which contain material of relevance involving the recipient of food and a response.

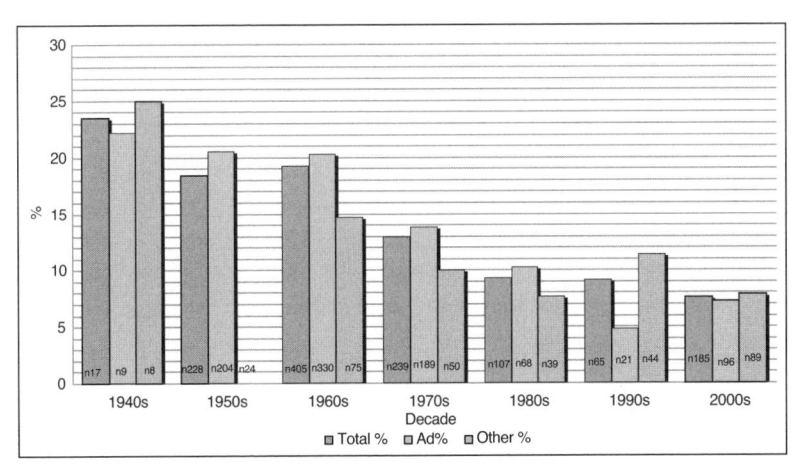

Figure 8.3 Percentage of material featuring feedback (recipient *and* reception) in *Woman and Home* by decade (n=base numbers)

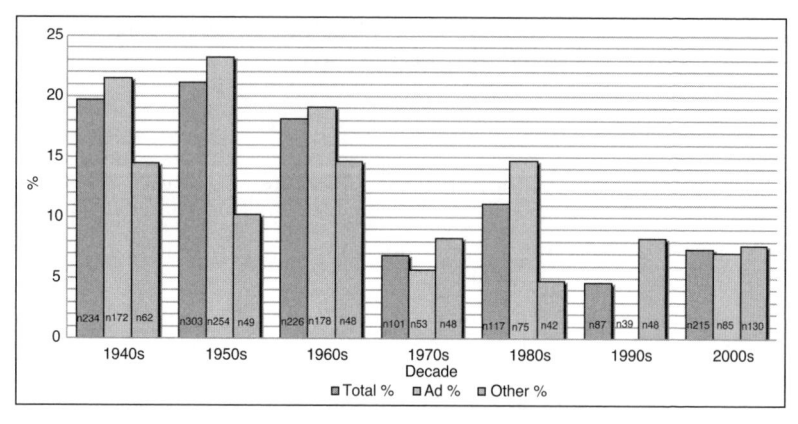

Figure 8.4 Percentage of material featuring feedback (recipient *and* reception) in *Woman's Own* by decade (n=base numbers)

As can be seen from these Figures, there is a clear trend of a decline in proportion of advertising and articles which feature feedback and reception of food. Adverts and articles featuring food reception decline from approximately 20% of content in 1940s and 1950s to approximately 5% in 1990s and contemporary magazines. The fall is particularly marked between the 1960s and 1970s. The same effect has been observed in a specifically quantitative analysis of similar magazine content (McNeir and Barker, unpublished observations), which documented that food claims incorporating "pleasing others" were particularly prevalent in 1950s and 1960s magazines. The observation also fits broadly with the decline in the incidence of 'care' as a principle of recommendation for food between the 1960s and 1990s, observed by Warde (1997: 158, 176–177). How can we account for this apparent general decline?

Firstly, as part of the successful spread of some core feminist principles, there may well have been a decline in the acceptability of assuming that responsibility for food provision falls upon women who fulfil domestic tasks for men. If this is the case, then advertisers and magazines may be less likely to rely on materials which construct such a situation as normative and expectable, for strategic reasons.

Secondly, there does seem to be a more general refocusing of the attention in such magazines over the period in question. Winship (1980: 14–15) identifies a movement from emphasis upon the woman as a mother/housewife, in the 1950s, to one in which, by the 1970s, she was constructed as more of a mannequin/narcissist (Warde 1997: 198). The increasing emphasis upon "lifestyle' matters results in the content of these types of publication becoming rather more self-directed. The emergence of concerns such as slimness centres attention much more upon the body and the consumption of the individual woman reader rather than upon her family.

Thirdly, there is arguably an increasing differentiation and multiplication of the various ends and purposes associated with the provision of food – leading to a greater set of competitors for advertising and article focus. Although nutrition-related coverage in advertising in *W&H* and *WO* fell from the 1950s, the prevalence of nutrition advice in articles rose exponentially from the 1970s onward (McNeir and Barker unpublished observations). Whilst health concerns have always been an issue in these materials – receiving attention throughout the period under study; in more recent magazines these are increasingly differentiated with a greater range of specific issues constructed as being necessary to balance as part of food provision work. There has been varying emphasis over the time period in question on specific nutrients for health, such as omega-3 and polyunsaturated fats – avoidance of additives and advocacy for low calorie products, and including a dilemmatic imperative to balance pleasure and health for children (Burridge forthcoming). However, this is not often framed in terms of feedback – the issue is more how to coax children to doing what is best for them, and although their pleasure is a concern, there is much less emphasis upon them empirically manifesting 'delight' in response.

This does not necessarily mean that food provision becomes a merely technical activity rather than a labour of love (Warde 1997: 131), but rather that a wider range of issues are potentially salient to the activity itself. The problems and incompatibilities offered by these empirical materials (along with a usually commercial solution) are certainly no longer restricted to the antinomies identified by Warde (1997). Arguably women's magazines now construct an ever-increasing set of practical problems to be confronted and resolved by women – an expansion of the range of valued ends to be pursued, combined with a rather more loose sense of what ends and purposes are in tension with one another, and how they are to be balanced. For example, in contemporary material health and convenience can be seen to be set against one another, and contrasted for rhetorical effect. All of this means that there is less space for some of those concerns previously given attention – such as feedback and family unity in the more 'traditional' sense. In addition, in the case of advertisements specifically, there may also be a wider recognition of changes in family structure. These changes might make automatic reference to the categories associated with a 'nuclear' family, something that may alienate potential customers, by failing to fit with the realities of their lives. Hence there is less of an emphasis upon husbands, and their responses, as identified in the previous section.

Having made these general comments, it is important to acknowledge some exceptions to the trend and, where possible, account for them. There are two rather striking, and possibly anomalous, 'zeros' which merit discussion – among *WH* editorials, recipes and articles, in the 1950s and *WO's* adverts in the 1990s. In the former case, the base number of editorials, recipes and articles is small (n=24); corresponding material is also relatively low in *WO* at this time (10%), and it could be interpreted that this represents a degree of sensitivity about the widespread loss of life suffered during the Second World War – with magazines refraining from assuming specific family structures out of respect for the consequences of War. However, in both magazines, family feedback features heavily in advertising – in over 20% of the material, which undermines this suggestion considerably. In the latter case – that of *WO* advertising in the 1990s – it is also notable that the proportion of advertising featuring feedback in *WH* is also at its lowest level of 4.8%. We might postulate that this represents the relative success of the impact of feminism at this time, soon to be undone somewhat by a 'backlash' and then the spread of 'irony' in the early twenty-first century (Jackson *et al.* 2001). In addition, this connects to the point already made about family structure, and the potentially exclusive and alienating consequences of assuming a specific configuration of family members are involved in the receipt of food. As Warde (1997: 137) put it, by the early 1990s, references to the family were increasingly rare since the: '[c]o-resident family no longer provides the quintessential legitimation for home cooking'.

This leaves us with a definite sense that these concerns are still present in women's magazines, but to much less an extent than in the 1940s and 1950s. Using food to manage the emotions of family members is rather less commonly represented in contemporary magazines, and takes a slightly different form. Nevertheless, it is still a component – one of many – of the ways in which the work of food provision is constructed, and deserves attention in those contexts in which such issues are discussed and analysed.

Conclusion: food and emotional management of the family

This chapter has used material from a corpus of women's magazines from 1940 to 2006 to explore one facet of the construction of gendered responsibility for food provision, specifically, the portrayal of the reception of food, and the significance of feedback given. This has been explored in connection with key studies of the gender division of labour (Charles and Kerr 1988; DeVault 1991; Murcott 1982 and 1983), and of studies also examining the food content of women's magazines (Parkin 2006; Warde 1997) noting connections and differences between their findings and aspects of the magazine content in the corpus assembled by the *Changing Families, Changing Food* programme.

The chapter has identified the phenomenon of feedback, and the way that it seems to construct the environment of food provision as one in which women are portrayed as using food as a medium to manage the emotions of their families – avoiding complaints that result from disappointment, creating happiness, and ultimately family unity and love. We have documented some of the recurrent ways that this is present in magazine content by constructing familial responses to the food that is prepared, and elaborating this in relation to two particularly interesting examples.

Some observations have also been made regarding observable changes in the relative occurrence of relevant content, and tentative explanations offered for the shifts that can be observed. Some minor fluctuations undermine the smoothness of the apparent decline in proportion of magazine food content featuring feedback – the positive and negative reception of food by the recipient. Nevertheless, overall, the process is certainly one of a generalised decline, and the two magazines seem to converge at around 5% in both adverts and other content in the early twenty-first century.

Food may or may not *be* love, but at times it has certainly been implied that it can be heavily involved in the creation of happiness. It has been constructed as something that is provided in a context in which both positive and negative feedback can be forthcoming, with the implication that this should enter into the purchasing and preparation decisions that women make. Women have therefore been presented with the notion that they are not only responsible for food provision, but that they are also responsible for managing the emotional responses of family members through the medium of food. Whether or not they have always taken on that responsibility, and the techniques used to negotiate it, comply with it in practice, or resist, are questions that require a rather different type of data, but are certainly worthy of detailed exploration.

Acknowledgement

We would like to thank Julia Harkness at Premier Foods for her help in facilitating copyright clearance. We would like to thank Julia Harkness at Premier Foods and Nigel Dickie at Heinz for their help in facilitating copyright clearance, and Lynda Matthews for her help in assembling the corpus of magazines.

9
The Governing of Family Meals in the UK and Japan

Takeda Hiroko

Introduction: the 'governing' of family meals

The term 'food policy' internationally subsumes a number of policy areas including food supply, food safety, public health, environmental management, animal welfare, agriculture and trade (Lang *et al.* 2001; Cabinet Office 2008b). Naturally, agents and institutions involved in the political process relating to the regulation of food are multiple, being located at different levels of the national, international and local governance systems as well as in both the public and private sectors (Lang *et al.* 2001; Harrison *et al.* 1997; Flynn *et al.* 2003).

The governing of family meals is, therefore, one of many items on the political agenda of national food policy. At the same time, it can be argued that it occupies a crucial strategic position where interactions between individuals' acts and the government's (direct/indirect) interventions are clearly observable. National food policy cannot bring about outcomes without being complemented by the everyday practices of food consumption. In other words, food policy is meant to be practised by individuals, and in this manner, links individuals with a multitude of governing bodies and organisations including the nation-state. Put another way, food policy is a part of a 'food discourse' that exercises disciplinary functions over individuals (Coveney 2000; Lien 2004) – it is a food discourse that is prescribed and endorsed by *institutional political power* while being practised by *individuals*. As one recently-published UK government report emphasises, therefore, the national government is required to work with, not only the food industry but also consumers, namely, individuals who make decisions over food (what they eat and how they eat it) on an everyday basis. In particular, issues such as food safety and improvement of dietary health are profoundly embedded in individuals' habitual and cognitive processes and hence the national government 'encourages cultural change' among individuals (Cabinet Office 2008b: 47):

> The future food system will be sustained by consumers who understand food, how it is produced and how to prepare it. It will sit in a society where learning about food is as much part of growing up as learning to cross the road. The gap between how people think as citizens and act as consumers when choosing what to eat will narrow (*ibid.*: 36).

Along with schools, the family is the primary site where individuals' behaviour patterns and understanding of food are constructed. Thus, the governing of family meals needs to be quintessentially a part of the national food policy that aims at improving the state of health of the populace. Indeed, historical research has shown that the national governing bodies paid attention to the everyday practices of organising family meals and even implemented measures to improve those popular practices. For example, influenced by Foucault's discussions of governmenality and 'biopolitics', Donzelot has illuminated how the modern family as a social and private unit has been linked with other social institutions and organisations (school, hospital, and social service) and through this nexus, the modern national and local governments, in cooperation with professionals (doctors, teachers, social services and counsellors, for example), intervenes in the everyday lives of individuals and *vice versa*, shaping both individual everyday life and subjectivity in a way that is compatible with liberal capitalism. The improvement in nutrition for children (and hence the improvement of their health and body strength) was vital to this process. For this purpose, support networks for mothers at home, in which health and medical professions and social services took part, was organised, and mothers obtained relevant skills and knowledge of domestic work including good practices of meal organisation and cooking (Donzelot 1997). That is to say, the family has been functioning as an arena where state political measures intersect with individual conduct. In this very sense, and contrary to the conventional idea of the private-public divide, the family is a 'political' unit.[1] Today's food policy directed at family meals is, therefore, a contemporary version of such 'biopolitical' arrangement of government in which the family is located as a political unit.

It is worth noting that extant studies on 'biopolitical' arrangements of governing also have identified some points of transition in terms of the state-individual relationship from the earlier models in the eighteenth and nineteenth century in Western Europe via the Welfare State to the governing strategies of contemporary advanced liberal democracies (Burchell 1996; Rose 1996). In particular, as the process of the upgrading of the national governing system incurred by globalisation and neoliberal political reforms progresses, the following five elements of the biopolitical arrangement of governing have become strengthened and accentuated, shifting the ways in which the family functions as the political unit from what Donzelot delineates in his work.

Individualisation

In his examination of the early form of liberal government to the neoliberal type of government, Burchell identifies the promotion of an 'autonomisation of society' as a technology of neoliberal government. Neoliberalism tends to encourage organisations and individuals to foster capacity for an independent and autonomous conduct 'that pursues a competitive logic' (Burchell 1996: 27–28). The theme of individualisation has been elaborated further by Dean. He points out the importance of citizens being 'self-governing individuals' in contemporary liberal democracies (Dean 2007: 61). These citizens are the capable life-planners who develop and manage one's identity as a reflexive project in a cosmopolitan context while competently understanding and autonomously mediating various risks in their life. With these self-governing citizens, 'cultural governance', 'that is, the attempt to govern the individual through his or her ethical culture' (Dean 2007: 78) becomes possible.[2] It is noteworthy, however, that individualisation is incoherent at the level of society. Therefore:

> We need, I have suggested, to understand how identities are formed as ideals for certain social strata engaged in particular social and political practices and come to act as educative mechanism for others – both the life planner and the cosmopolitan individuals are fitted out for different social groups and purposes (Dean 2007: 78).

Enterprise

When Burchell points out that the autonomisation of society values a particular type of independent individual conduct, he discusses this point by making reference to the idea of economic 'enterprising' (Burchell 1996: 27). The term 'enterprise' became a part of the social lexicon in Thatcherite Britain, being presented as the core norm of the 'new Britain'. It refers to an individual attitude 'striving to maximize its own advantage by inventing and promoting new projects by means of individual and local calculations of strategies and tactics, costs and benefits' (Rose 1992: 145; see also Heelas and Morris 1992). The enterprising self is therefore a rational subjectivity that tries to amplify and maximise one's 'own power, happiness and the quality of life' (Rose 1992: 151). This kind of subjectivity is the premise for the successful implementation of a type of government using advertising techniques that became more common from the 1960s onwards, as exemplified by the anti-drink driving campaigns, especially at Christmas (Miller and Rose 2008).

Responsibilisation

The enabling and enterprising self is also a subjectivity that manages various risks competently. The neoliberal form of governing requires individuals to deal with risks in a particular way and O'Malley observes here the proliferation of 'prudentialism' (O'Malley 1996: 199–202). According to O'Malley, this involves the following three related changes:

> ...the retraction of socialized risk-based techniques from managing the risks confronting the populace; their progressive replacement through the extension of privatized risk-based techniques; and the articulation of this process with the strategic deployment of sovereign remedies and disciplinary interventions that facilitate, underline and enforce moves towards government through individual responsibility (O'Malley 1996: 199).

In other words, through the responsibilisation of individuals, 'security becomes the responsibility of private individuals, who through the pursuit of self-interest, and liberated from enervating reliance on the State, will participate in the creation of the new order' (*ibid.*: 201). In this sense, the 'prudent subject' within the neoliberal governing system 'enters "partnerships" with public authorities' (e.g. the police), or 'becomes the "customer" – literally or figuratively depending on the degree of marketization' (*ibid.*: 203).

Social stratification

These enterprising, active, capable and responsible individuals, however, only represent one side of the populace living in today's industrially advanced capitalist countries. Rose has pointed out the 'logics of incorporation and exclusion' behind this picture of contemporary citizenhood (Rose 1996: 59). In order to understand this logic, Rose urges us to turn our attention to the languages of 'empowerment' observed in the administrative terminologies in which unemployed people have become 'job seekers' and homeless 'rough sleepers'. He argues:

> ...the disadvantaged individual has come to be seen as potentially and ideally an active agent in the fabrication of their own existence. Those 'excluded' from the 'benefits of a life of choice and self-fulfilment are no longer merely the passive support of a set of social determinations: they are people whose self-responsibility and self-fulfilling aspirations have been deformed by the dependency culture, whose efforts at self-advancement have been frustrated for so long that they suffer from 'learned helplessness', whose self-esteem has been destroyed (Rose 1996: 59).

From a different theoretical position from the governmentality school, Bauman also discusses the selection mechanism of the national and international population with reference to individuals' financial and consumptive capabilities and fitness. Through the gaze of Big Brother (in both senses of Orwell's novel *1984* and the contemporary TV show), the 'unfit' is identified and nominated, and once excluded, there are only narrow chances to return to the world of the 'included' through re-education, which Bauman calls, the recycling process (Bauman 2004: 131–133; see also Bauman 2005).

Relationships with expert knowledge

The aforementioned four points, individualisation, enterprise, responsibilisation and social stratification tend to place an emphasis on individualism: an autonomous and competent subjectivity acts responsibly in order to strive to better their own lives. Nonetheless, as Dean has pointed out, this individualism is not 'pure'. Rather, 'it is something constructed with the help of experts and has an institutional face' (Dean 2007: 67). In one of his earlier books, Rose has explored the role of various experts and professionals (counsellors, career advisors and so on) in the contemporary process of constructing subjectivity in which indices and criteria set by professionals are constantly made reference to, and in this sense, individual identity is inherently enmeshed with a multitude of social discourses (Rose 1999).

Beck's thesis on the Risk Society is suggestive for understanding the increased importance of the role of professionals who have knowledge and expertise that is mobilised to anticipate, calculate and hence try to eliminate risk that poses the possibility of serious and irreversible damage (Beck 1992, 1999; Lupton 1999). Yet, scholars like Luhmann and Ewald, among others, have pointed out the fundamental instability of professional knowledge and expertise as the tool of managing and taming various risks, since professional knowledge and expertise is characterised by constant development and progress, and new knowledge and technologies introduce new areas of untamed uncertainty (Luhmann 1993; Ewald 2002; Yamaguchi 2002; Ōsawa 2008). This means that the act of making references to professional knowledge and expertise is an open-ended process, which will be continuously updated and re-examined without being confirmed. In other words, an individual is required to construct his or her subjectivity as an individual in constant exchange with professionals and institutions to which those professionals belong.

Going through the five points of transition in the updated biopolitical governing system through globalisation and neoliberal political reform discussed above, what can be understood is that the 'object/subject' of biopolitical governing has become an autonomous, competent, responsible and enterprising individual who enjoys and appreciates the services offered by professionals. This has led to the alternation of methods and techniques of governing, as exemplified by the use of advertising and marketing tactics that suggest the cost and benefit of a particular type of behaviour to customers-cum-citizens.

As discussed earlier, today's food policies in the UK and Japan still acknowledge that the family occupies a crucial strategic position where state measures intersect with individual conduct and, on this understanding, the family is located within the political process of governing food. Simultaneously, the discussion on the updated biopolitical governing arrangement suggests that individuals within the family are now expected to organise their acts in accordance with a different set of values and normative standards. But how is the new governing arrangement that places an emphasis on a particular type of individuality supposed to operate in the everyday lives of families? In order to understand these questions clearly, we will below explore recent developments of food policy in the UK and Japan and, in so doing, discuss the ways in which the state-individual relationship and the role of the family in the political process are envisioned in these documents.

The UK and Japan governments and family meals

Food policy in both the UK and Japan has undergone a process of substantial change in recent years, though on a slightly different chronology. The attempts by the UK government preceded those in Japan for a multitude of reasons that will be discussed below. This is why the British case, along with EU policies, was referred to and examined by Japanese food policy-makers and experts when BSE raised the degree of public and political attention to food policy in the early 2000s.

UK food policy: 'retailer-led governance system'

Extant studies on food policy in the UK identify a watershed for the post-war national food policy in the early 2000s when a major institutional change, namely, the establishment of the Food Standard Agency (FSA) and the Department for Environment, Food and Rural Affairs (DEFRA) was implemented (Marsden *et al.* 2000; Lang *et al.* 2001; Barling and Lang 2003b; Flynn *et al.* 2003; Lang and Rayner 2003). There are a number of reasons why food and food policy, which 'have long records of causing political difficulties, yet continue to be seen as fairly marginal in public policy and national politics' (Barling and Lang 2003a), increased its presence within the British national political agenda around that time. Firstly, a series of food scares and crises (additives, pesticide residues, salmonella, *E. coli.* o-157, BSE and Foot and Mouth Disease to name but a few) from the late 1980s onward significantly eroded consumer confidence in food (Flynn and Marsden 1992; Lang *et al.* 2001). Secondly, the nature of the food system in the UK also underwent changes. While the decline of the farming sector that conventionally influenced the food policy-making process continued (Flynn and Marsden 1992), major food retailers recorded substantial growth, increasing their dominance in the food market (Harrison *et al.* 1997; Marsden *et al.* 2000; Flynn *et al.* 2003). Thirdly, the further involvement of the European Union (EU) in the British domestic policy-making process 'raised the profile of food issues' (Marsden *et al.* 2000: 13) through the harmonisation of agriculture and food policy at the European level. These factors all taken together exposed the policy deficiencies caused by gaps and contradictions between the national framework of governing food and the contemporary food system, and the institutional changes were implemented in order to recalibrate and update food policy.

In their examination of Labour's food policy since 1997, Barling and Lang describe it as 'reluctant', being an outcome of negotiations between 'public demands for food safety' and the 'economic requirements of being competitive in a liberalizing international economy' (Barling and Lang 2003b: 9). On the one hand, food and farming crises certainly provided a political opportunity for reviewing and reformulating food policy and through this, institutional reform was realised. On the other hand, the environment for food policy-making for Labour was constrained by a number of factors. To start with, the Labour government inherited a 'flawed food policy with some serious problems in agricultural, environmental, health and social policy terms, generating substantial economic costs due to inefficiencies (some recognized; others externalized and less readily recognized)' (*ibid.*: 9) from the Conservative government. According to Barling and Lang, the Conservatives' food policy was characterised as 'self-regulative' rather than 'de-regulative' (*ibid.*, 2003b). In addition, the Labour administration had to comply with the liberalisation of international agriculture trade prescribed in the GATT Uruguay Round's Agreement on Agriculture (AoA) and the Common Agriculture Policy (CAP) of the EU in circumstances where the EU's prerogative over food policy was expanding (Marsden *et al.* 2000). Finally, Labour's approach to food policy is also framed by their political stance of adopting the 'Third Way' in which private actors (in particular, agents in private business and civil society) play a more significant role in the governing process and, in turn, national and local governments bear smaller responsibilities, in comparison with the classical social democratic system of governing based on the Keynesian welfare state model (Giddens 1998).[3] All in all, Barling and Lang argue that Labour's food policy 'has exhibited a tough pro-GM, pro-US, pro-trade, pro-market position, all the elements of which stem from a core commitment to international competitiveness and narrowly defined market efficiency' (Barling and Lang 2003b: 17). This is exemplified by the FSA's approach to food safety that is described as 'a consumerist, market-based approach to many issues of food safety advice, often stressing the role of individual preference and choice, as opposed to a more fundamental, structural assessment of food safety and the food system' (Barling and Lang 2003b: 11–12).

Marsden, Flynn and Harrison also observe the emergence of a 'private-interest style of regulation' through the institutional reform carried out from the 1990s (Harrison *et al.* 1997; Marsden *et al.* 2000). In this style of governing, the government engages in the 'governance' of the food system in tandem with other international and domestic agencies (public and private, from WTO and EU via food retailers and producers to NGOs) as well as consumers. It is 'governance' as distinguished from 'government', in terms of its hybrid, flexible and networked structure

(Smith *et al.* 2004).[4] Yet Marsden *et al.* further point out that major food retailers, who enjoy a high proportion of concentration in terms of food grocery shopping in the UK, are required to exercise, and indeed have exercised, the leading role in the food regulatory system, and hence names a new governance system as the 'retailer-led governance system' (Flynn and Marsden 1992; Harrison *et al.* 1997; Flynn *et al.* 2003; Marsden *et al.* 2000). That is to say, the reality of the 'private-interest approach' of food policy is conditioned by the retailer-dominated structure, casting some doubt over the notion of 'empowerment' of consumers through the new institutional setting. Indeed, the other side of the highlighted role of major retailers is a relatively marginalised positioning of consumer groups in the UK (Marsden *et al.* 2000). According to Marsden *et al.* the limited presence of consumer pressure groups in the food regulatory process, despite mounting concerns over food safety, is compensated by the competitive space of food retailers. There, food retailers are in 'battle to attract and legitimate consumer "loyalties"' (*ibid.*: 92) and in so doing, strive to offer food of the appropriate quality and price for their targeted customers. Customers, in turn, secure food at the preferred quality by purchasing it from the shops they select. Or, more precisely, as Marsden *et al.* have pointed out, given the 'hierarchy' of food retailers (determined by prices that tend to correspond to food quality) in Britain, 'those people who are likely to be most concerned about the quality of food have freedom to purchase it from the retail outlet of their choice' (*ibid.*: 72) and therefore, there is no need for them to join consumer pressure groups.

Comparing these recent developments of food policy in the UK with those of Australia, Caraher and Coveney argue that 'the underlying philosophy [of UK food policy] was and still is that of neoliberal economics' (Caraher and Coveney 2004: 59). According to their assessment, UK food policy has achieved self-sufficiency by obtaining 'cheap food from a global market' (*ibid.*: 594), but, in so doing, failed to address and deal with structural issues such as the externalised costs of cheap food (health problems, environmental impact and the like). Rather, the UK government tends to 'focus on individual behaviours, such as increasing the consumption of fruits and vegetables' (*ibid.*: 594). Most of the initiatives are downstream, 'encouraging local communities to set up self-help projects often to do skills acquisition'. These attempts are, however, not supplemented by 'projects which focus upstream on the food supply chain' (*ibid.*: 594–595). Consequently, 'the focus on skills may divert attention from the determinants of food poverty by offering short-term solutions to long-term problems and diverting attention from the real causes or determinants' (*ibid.*: 545).

Indeed, Ellaway and Macintyre examine food shopping patterns of different social groups, and argue that there are even some adverse effects of the retailer-led governance system of food that focuses on individual behaviours. According to them, the lower social groups, which tend to have less spending power and car ownership, 'may be more likely to shop locally for bread and milk', as they do not have access to a car to get to supermarkets that are often located outside of the town. This means that these people are excluded from 'advantages of lower prices and wider range of foods' offered by supermarkets while the price of basic foodstuffs such as bread tends to be higher at corner shops (Ellaway and Macintyre 2000: 58). Yet, simultaneously, it is the lower social groups that are most vulnerable in terms of health due to poor dietary practices (Philip *et al.* 1997). In this sense, the retailer-led governance system of food misses its crucial target.

Still, one of the most recent government reports seems to maintain the stance of the retailer-led governance system of food (Cabinet Office 2008b). In the executive summary, for example, four government's strategic policy objectives (a) fair prices, choice, access to food and food security through open and competitive markets, (b) continuous improvement in the safety of food, (c) the changes needed to deliver a further transition to healthier diets and (d) a more environmentally sustainable food chain) are set. And the report continues to say that 'government action to realize this vision and these strategic objectives is needed in three areas; (i) active engagement with consumers; (ii) working in partnership with the supply chain; (iii) leadership by example' (Cabinet Office 2008b). The government role in food policy is further elaborated in Chapter 3 of the report, entitled 'Future Food Policy: Vision, Strategic Priorities and Approach'. There, the role of the government in the UK food system is specified as:

- to correct market failures where they arise (the food economy may be distorted by market failures caused by poor information, imperfect competition, the failures to price externalities and the under-provision of public goods)
- to ensure that social equity is safeguarded. Generally, this will be achieved through the tax and benefit system, but special measures may be needed in some cases to ensure that the more vulnerable in society have adequate access to nutritious food. (Cabinet Office 2008b: 38).

While admitting the harms that 'market failures' may cause, the report still regards 'well functioning, open and competitive markets' as 'the best means of securing fair prices for consumers and fair dealing along the supply chain' (Cabinet Office 2008b: 68). Such effective use of the market in the food governance system needs to be supplemented by 'enabled consumers' who can make informed choices of food and their diet. For this purpose, the government plays a catalytic role, in cooperation with business, by providing appropriate and integrated information through consumer 'social marketing', as exemplified by the FSA campaign on reducing salt intake and the NHS's 5-a-day campaign, and other means like food labelling (Cabinet Office 2008b). With such governmental support, consumers' decision-making abilities are improved, and the cultural and behavioural changes regarding food consumption among people are facilitated.

The role of the family in such a retailer-led governance system of food is not straightforward to see in the government report, except through the mention of the family as the site where 'cultural capital, attitudes, values and aspirations' are fostered (Cabinet Office 2008b). Yet the FSA's survey that explores eating habits of different social groups suggests, among many others, the following points:

- 86% of the respondents agree with the statement 'parents should be strict with children and make them eat healthily'.
- 71% of women agree with the statement that 'they tried to encourage other people to eat healthily whenever they could', in comparison with 54% of men.
- Women with children are more likely to encourage others to eat healthily, indicating that 'having a family at home has strong influence on likelihood to encourage others to eat healthily' (FSA 2002: 11).

Family meals organised through appropriate choices made by enabled and considerate consumers (who are more likely to be women), therefore, still play the vital role for the retailer-led governance system of food to be implemented effectively. For families who tend to display 'problems' and vulnerabilities in terms of food hygiene and healthy eating practice, the government provides support measures, as illustrated by the Healthy Start initiative that is directed at low-income and disadvantaged families (in particular, women and children in unemployed families and pregnant women under 18 years old) (Cabinet Office 2008b: 39). In this sense, meals organised by individuals within the family are expected to function as a marker that demonstrates a set of individual qualities (the level of responsibility, consuming power and knowledge) and individuals are categorised into different groups accordingly, identifying those who need surveillance by the government.

All in all, the retailer-led food governance system certainly underscores empowered, independent and enabled consumers. In cooperation with food retailers that form a highly organised, competitive market, the government provides these consumers with support to 'encourage cultural change' among consumers, while exercising more disciplinary measures against vulnerable groups in society. Yet in this system, some structural issues such as the externalities of the current food system or social divisions created through differences in purchasing power are obscured and left behind, and this in turn brings about new deficiencies in the governing system. The role of the family, too, seems to be blurred. The retailer-led food governance system still relies heavily on the gendered practices within the family, whose rationales are quite different from those of market behaviours (Folbre 2001). Nonetheless, a wide gap between these two types of acts is not addressed clearly.

Japanese food policy: fostering 'human power'[5]

The Japanese government embarked on serious efforts to carry out policy reforms and institutional changes of the food regulatory system after the first domestic case of BSE was officially announced on 10 September 2001. This does not mean, however, that the BSE case was the first challenge for the food system in Japan. Rather, the Japanese state has faced a long series of food scares throughout the post-war period (accidents caused by manufacturing failures, industrial pollution, food additives, food poisoning such as salmonella and *E. coli.* o-157, to name but a few), while its food sufficiency level has kept falling continuously, recording 40% in 2003, in comparison with the British figure of 70% (Ākaibu Shuppan 2008: 4–5). Furthermore, prior to the 2001 BSE 'discovery', the Japanese government in fact received a warning from the EU of the risk of BSE infection through meat-and-bone meal (MDM) imported from the UK, Denmark, Italy and Ireland in the period between 1980–99 that had been identified as the cause of the outbreak of BSE in Europe (Murakami 2004).

Still, public reactions to BSE were initially moderate, overwhelmed as they were by the shock of the 9/11 attacks. Popular concerns over BSE only exploded when the mass media reported that Yukijirushi Shokuhin, a large food production/trade company, intentionally mislabelled imported beef as domestic beef to apply for compensation under the buyback system then in place. This led not only to the bankruptcy of the long-standing Yukijirushi but also profound scepticism among the populace over the national food safety policy including the labelling system (Yoshida 2005). The government's handling of the initial case did not appear to go well, either, with misinformation being fed to the public in terms of the way in which the infected cows were disposed of. A report published by a special review committee on the BSE issue in 2002 clearly condemned the government for a multitude of deficiencies observed in Japan's food regulatory system (Murakami 2004).

Corresponding to the assessment of these governance deficiencies, some institutional reforms were introduced from 2003–5. Firstly, the Basic Law for Food Safety was promulgated in 2003, and, as a result, the Food Safety Commission was established within the Prime Minister's Office. This institutional and administrative enhancement to govern food safety was supplemented by the legislation of the Basic Law for *Shokuiku* (literally translated, 'Nurturing through Eating') in 2005, whose purpose was to promote the campaign of *Shokuiku*, an enlightenment activity over healthy eating lifestyles initially started by some food enthusiasts in the 1990s, as a national movement.

Takemoto Toshihiko, who was a senior bureaucrat of the Ministry of Agriculture, Forestry and Fishery (MAFF) and in charge of the special review committee on the BSE issue under the MAFF Minister Takebe Tsutomu, recalls that the reform process for realising the institutional changes was facilitated by an amalgam of political opportunities. To start with, the Japanese government was at that time led by Koizumu Jun'ichirō who enthusiastically pressed forward drastic political reforms, being assisted by neoliberal economic advisors. As a result, the extant administrative and economic structures underwent a great deal of transition in order to make Japan's political economy more competitive from 2001–5. Secondly, Minister Takebe was seeking a way to impress Prime Minister Koizumi by implementing drastic measures of political reforms, in particular, after the initial dealing with the BSE case had disappointed many Japanese people. Thirdly, the national agriculture policy was also in the process of a thorough review at that time (Takemoto 2008). In order to respond to the requirements set up by the WTO/GATT regime of international agriculture trade in the mid-1990s and reorganise Japan's agriculture sector more competitively, the Food, Agriculture and Farming Village Basic Law was established in 1999 (Shōgenji 2008; Shibata 2007; Sasaki 2008). As a result of the Basic Law, the Cabinet approved the Food, Agriculture and Farming Village Basic Plan in the following year, and the Second Basic Plan was set up in 2005. These policy changes in the agriculture sector were meant to achieve the efficient and stable management of the agriculture industry, and, in so doing, the level of income for individual agriculture producers could be raised to the average standard of workers in other industries. For this purpose, measures to stimulate enlargement in the scale of farming by concentrating farm lands on competent producers were introduced. Still more importantly, the policy changes implemented since the late 1990s in agriculture suggest a shift in the policy-making perspective from producers to consumers (Takemoto 2008). The consumer-centred policy-making is, as observed in the UK case, the mainstream approach in the food policy of industrially advanced countries, and the Japanese state also has taken on board this global trend in the context of Koizumi' neoliberal reform agenda.

The Basic Law for Food Safety and Food Safety Commission were designed by referring to European models, in particular, the EU's EFSA and the British FSA. The main mission of the Food Safety Commission was to provide scientific analyses of food risks and provide relevant information based on its research activities. The basic standpoint of the Basic Law and Commission is that there is no 'zero-risk' food. The risk assessment by the professionals of the Commission is passed onto the Ministry of Health, Labour and Welfare (MHLW) and MAFF to set up policies, regulations and administrative systems to deal with the risks identified by the Commission. In addition, the information as regards risk assessment conducted by the Commission is released to the public through the 'risk communication' process. Besides the numerous publications on different food-related risks and online materials including homepages, the Commission organises public meetings in which anybody can participate and ask the professionals of the Commission questions. In 2005 and 2006, topics such as BSE, residual pesticides, methylmercury contaminated fish, imported soya beans and genetically modified foods, were discussed in the public meetings organised by the Commission and sub-regional authorities across Japan (Naikakufu 2006; Matsunaga 2005; Inubushi 2005).

On the other hand, the Basic Law for *Shokuiku* legislated in 2005 and the national *Shokuiku* campaign based on the Basic Law attempted to disseminate a wide range of knowledge of foods and public health, from nutrition via healthy eating and cooking to food education for children, among Japanese people. As the First White Paper on *Shokuiku* states:

> It is an urgent task to promote the *Shokuiku* campaign as a nationwide movement in which all Japanese people autonomously participate in and play a lead role. In so doing, each Japanese person

independently acquires pertinent and proper knowledge and a decision-making ability that enables them to voluntarily practice a healthy lifestyle with healthy eating (Naikakufu 2006: 20).

The political concerns over the national medical and social security expenses resulting from unhealthy diet practices, in particular, obesity, certainly fuelled the process of incorporating the *Shokuiku* campaign into the national political system. Simultaneously, in order to achieve the objective of the 'autonomously-organized healthy eating lifestyle', risk assessment and communication of food-related risks appear vital. For individuals to self-sufficiently organise their own healthy lives with healthy eating, it is important to reach an adequate level of 'risk literacy' that helps in independently understanding, analysing and, in so doing, avoiding various food-related risks. By providing information regarding food and healthy eating as well as risk assessment conducted by the Committee, the *Shokuiku* campaign contributes to building this risk literacy and makes individuals enabled agents to organise their eating in an appropriate manner (Naikakufu 2006). In other words, the *Shokuiku* campaign is an educational device for the Japanese state to turn individuals into autonomous agents to organise their everyday meals – or in the buzz term that can often be found in government documents on political reforms at that time, 'individuals who possess '*human power*' (*ningenryoku*) (Hatae 2005: 107–108). The state provides information and administrative support, but in the framework of the *Shokuiku* campaign, it is individuals who actually bear responsibility for making choices in relation to food matters. As far as the government documents suggest, food policy in Japan has made a shift towards the consumer-focused approach in which individuals are located as the responsible agent of managing food matters in everyday life, and the government engages with these enabled consumers of food. Put another way, in the new food regulatory framework based on the Basic Law for Food Safety and *Shokuiku*, the role of the government has mostly been reduced to the managing of the basic administrative infrastructure of disseminating information, with the individual consumer being left with the task of choosing food.

Simultaneously, it needs to be noted that the institutional changes taking place in the 2000s were contextualised by the structural constraints that the Japanese government was facing. Firstly, Japan's trade-oriented industrial structure was sustained by a large proportion of overseas agriculture imports to compensate for the trade surplus earned through exporting high valued high-tech products. Indeed, some agriculture products, for example, beef and citrus fruits, have been used as bargaining tools in the trade conflicts with the US. This has in fact made it increasingly difficult for the Japanese government to deal with BSE cases since the infection in the US was reported in 2003. The Japanese government soon placed a ban on the import of beef from the US until 'product safety is ensured' like other recipient countries (South Korea and Russia, for example) of beef from the US. The US government responded to these measures by exercising political pressure on the Japanese government and politicians to lift the ban, and hence beef imports from the US, once again, became a highly political matter. In the end, the decision to partially remove the import ban was agreed between the Japanese and the US governments in 2004 and the 'scientific' BSE risk assessment made by the Food Safety Commission was referred to in the process of negotiation. Yet this government decision was severely undermined as a number of the members of the special committee on prion contamination, which released BSE risk assessments in response to the request made by the government prior to the 2004 decision, started to publicly express their frustration over the political nature of the decision-making process. One member of the special committee testified in the Japanese Diet (parliament) that the special prion committee was abused by the national bureaucracy that tried to push the agenda of lifting the import ban, while the other stepped down from his role relating to risk communication in the Food Safety Committee. Both are leading experts in scientific research on prion in Japan. Far worse, soon after the import of the US beef restarted, specified-risk materials (SRM) were detected at the customs, and the ban was immediately brought back. The havoc surrounding US beef significantly impaired the credibility of the Food Safety Committee (Aonuma 2008).

Furthermore, while the new institutions to secure food safety became crippled by politics, due to the state of the retail industry in Japan, the market did not work in the way the British 'retailer-led governance system of food' did, not being able to benefit from its editorial and adjusting functions through competition. To start with, the period in which the institutional reform of food governance progressed in Japan was profoundly marked by severe economic setbacks, which in turn was translated into destabilisation of employment and pay stagnation. In response to the macroeconomic doldrums, household spending decreased from the 1990s to 2000s, and, in particular, food-related expenses went down by 15% (from 1.1 million yen in 1992 to 0.851 million yen in 2005) (Iimori 2007: 36–37). The total sales turnover of supermarkets also fell from the late 1990s to the 2000s. The sales of foodstuffs remained almost flat from 80.69 trillion yen in 1997 to 84.59 trillion yen in 2006, despite supermarkets' efforts to increase their sales by extending opening hours (Ākaibu Shuppan 2008: 8–9). In addition to this, the food retail industry in Japan is still highly fragmented. According to the Japan Chain Store Association website, they have 72 member companies that exceed turnover of one billion yen or run more than 11 branches.[6] The term 'chain store' here subsumes not only department stores and supermarkets but also so-called 'convenience stores'. The total turnover of convenience stores (first appearing in Japan in 1969) was recorded as 7.4 trillion yen in 2005. Unlike supermarkets, convenience stores tend to be located in the urban environment, often within office buildings or train stations, and sell packaged and processed food or fast food rather than raw ingredients (Ākaibu Shuppan 2008). In contrast to the poor performances of supermarkets in the 1990s and early 2000s, convenience stores persistently and exceptionally expanded their presence in the retail sector (Dawson and Larke 2004). Seven-Eleven Japan is the largest among all the convenience store chains, making over 2.5 trillion yen and running over 12,000 franchises across Japan in the year of 2007, and there are nine more convenience store chains whose turnovers exceed 100 billion yen (Nihon Keisai Shinbun, morning edition, 23 July 2008). According to a survey conducted by the Cabinet Office, 56.7% of male respondents aged 20–29, 49.5% of male aged 30–39 and 43.6% of female aged 20–29 frequently buy foodstuffs at convenience stores. Women in the older generations are reported to shop less at convenience stores, but 14.7% of women in their 30s and 10.8% in their 40s still buy foodstuffs at convenience stores frequently (Naikakufu Shokuiku Suishinshitsu 2008: 25). As such, in comparison with the British case where the 'big four' supermarkets claim clear dominance, the degree of market concentration is smaller, while competition between different types of shops is harsher in Japan.

In the political and economic circumstances of the 1990s and early 2000s in Japan, the straight introduction of a form of food governance that is closely linked with market functions, as in the retailer-led food governance in the UK, encountered a number of structural problems. Thus, when the Japanese government in the 2000s tried to shift its approach of food policy to a more individual-cum-consumer-oriented direction by implementing the *Shokuiku* campaign, it was required to seek an alternative path to make this shift. Indeed, the two government White Papers on *Shokuiku* published in 2006 and 2007 only spare three and four pages, respectively, to the role food retailers, traders and producers can take in the national *Shokuiku* campaign through their promotional activities. Instead, the White Papers pay more attention to school and the family as a locus of *Shokuiku* activities. As a result of the Basic Law, schools are now obliged to instruct pupils about healthy eating lifestyles and the government distributed specially-designed materials for this purpose. More importantly, in the latest 2007 White Paper, the family is clearly located at the centre of the national *Shokuiku* campaign among other agents such as schools, the food industry, food producers, public health organisations, food experts, voluntary organisations and national/local bureaucracies. The White Paper claims:

> Shokuiku activities undertaken by parents or guardians at home are at the centre of the implementation of the national Shokuiku movement. In particular, Shokuiku activities directed at children will make a great deal of impact on their mental and physical developments and their personality formation. They will be the basis on which children foster sound bodies and minds and rich human qualities (Naikakufu 2007: 20).[7]

On this understanding, the White Paper details how family practices such as eating dinner together closely relates to a desirable eating lifestyle of children (*ibid.*: 15). Carers of children are expected to make efforts to practise a sound and healthy eating lifestyle along with improving their own knowledge of food (*ibid.*: 20), and social and administrative organisations such as schools, nurseries and public health centres are to provide support for families to practise good eating habits (*ibid.*: 22). Importantly, in practice, nurseries and schools often bear a surveillance and disciplinary role in identifying parents (mainly, mothers) whose skills of meal organisation appear problematic and, in so doing, re-educate them. These educational institutions are often used to hold training sessions in cooking for mothers and children, but as one of the organisers spelled out, the real purpose of these activities is to retrain 'incompetent' mothers (Ebihara 2003). In this sense, the 'enlightenment' national *Shokuiku* campaign that emphasises individuality and autonomous subjectivity contains a blunt normative pressure about what these individuals should be.[8]

Conclusion

Reading through the UK and Japanese government documents relating to the revision of food policy in the 2000s, the direction of policy changes certainly suggests that the operation of the revised food regulatory system assumes a particular type of subjectivity. In both the UK and Japan, individuals are now expected to be enabled, independent and responsible consumers of food who have relevant knowledge and hence competently understand and manage food matters and healthy and safe dietary practices. Those enabled consumers tend to strive for optimising their everyday lives. The government supports those consumers, in cooperation with other organisations such as food retailers and schools, by playing a galvanising role via the provision of information. For this purpose, scientific and professional government organisations, for example, the FSA in the UK or the Food Safety Commission in Japan, have been set up, and consumers are now exposed to a multitude of channels of information on food and dietary matters. Yet, not all individuals are able to take advantage of this enterprising, consumer-oriented food regulatory system. The two governments have thus implemented special measures to manage those vulnerable groups of people, and, in this way, food has become an index of social stratification. All in all, the subjectivity suggested by the revised food regulatory system in the UK and Japan in the 2000s can be understood with reference to the aforementioned five points of the upgrading of the biopolitical arrangements, namely, individualisation, enterprising, responsiblisation, social stratification and strengthened relationships with expert knowledge. In other words, the food regulatory system was recalibrated in a way to fit the 'governing strategies of advanced liberal democracies' under the national governance system influenced by neoliberal ideas both in the UK and Japan.

Despite these commonalities, the role of the family in the new food regulatory system in the UK and Japan appears different, with the stronger presence of food retailers in the UK governing system on the one hand and an emphasis on normative pressure in Japan on the other, suggesting some variation in the governing strategies of 'advanced liberal democracies'. The organised, competitive market in the UK functions as a medium to bridge measures implemented by the state and individuals via market forces. Individuals are encouraged to behave as good and wise consumers, and, in so doing, the state's intervention is neutralised, successfully avoiding the stigma of being a 'nanny state'. The role of the family through gendered family practices in the food governing system is also obscured, despite its centrality. In contrast, in Japan, without the high degree of concentration of food retailers but with structural distortion of the food market, the state-citizen relationship looks more straightforward with the government exercising strong normative pressure on the organisation of family meals.

All these points suggest that policy changes relating to the governing of family meals in the UK and Japan offer us a valuable lens through which to view the transition in the state governing system from the 1990s to 2000s. One important point to be noted here is that the governing strategies of advanced liberal democracies take different forms, influenced by historically contingent situations. In this very sense, neoliberalism is never single. What we need to examine is neoliberalisms operating in different industrially advanced counties.

Part IV
Family and Community

10
Eating In Time, Eating Up Time
Megan Blake, Jody Mellor, Lucy Crane and Brigitta Osz

> *Eating, apparently a biological matter is actually profoundly social* (DeVault 1991: 35).
>
> *Thus discussion around the timing of meals at weekends are not only necessitated by the facts of family living...but they also constitute a family set, a range of people whose projects and timetables need to be taken into consideration* (Morgan 1996: 141).

The fact that a woman's role within the family has been thought to be that of primary care giver coupled with increased expectations that women will participate in the labour force, has led some commentators to argue that there has arisen a care deficit in today's society (Putnam 2000; Hickman and Crowley 2008). This care deficit is being held responsible for a number of perceived social ills including rises in obesity and the decline of the traditional family due to women's lack of time and therefore inability to produce 'proper meals'. This narrative can easily be critiqued along a number of dimensions. For example family is understood as a fixed category within which certain individuals (e.g., mother, father, child) are responsible for certain roles, rather than considering the family as a set of individuals engaged in a particular set of social practices (DeVault 1991). Likewise, care is expressed as an outcome rather than as the basis or motivation for engaging with a particular set of practices (see Schatzki 2002 for more on emotion, motivation and practice).

Many scholars have pointed out the usefulness of examining social relationships through food. For example, Deborah Lupton tells us:

> Food consumption habits are not simply tied to biological needs but serve to mark boundaries between social classes, geographic regions,

nations, cultures, genders, lifecycle stages, religions and occupations, to distinguish rituals, traditions, festivals, seasons, and times of day (1996: 1).

Curtin (1992) likewise tells us that personhood is structured by food; however, the literature concerning family and food tends to focus overwhelmingly on a single and largely mythologised family eating event: the 'family meal' (Bell and Valentine 1997). This focus means that attention is diverted from other engagements family members have with food, at other times of the day that may also offer other, perhaps more practical and more easily accommodated, opportunities for all family members to engage with the work of 'doing family' as well as offer windows into the ways that family members engage with non-family-focused practices. Finally, the emphasis on time poverty of dual-career households, while acknowledging the constraints of objective time, fail to engage with existential time, which structures social practices (Schatzki 2005).

This chapter takes up these critiques and enlists recent conceptions of social practices as a way to understand how families are created and recreated. Specifically the chapter focuses on the timing and placing of food-related activities in the daily life of parents in households. By examining accounts of food-related activities provided by household members in the UK and Hungary we reveal the spatio-temporal contexts of those food activities and consider how food-related activities are part of the practices that facilitate family life or are constructed by individuals as something else. The chapter concludes that while eating is an activity done by people every day as they go about their lives at home and at work, certain spatio-temporal contexts mark out food-related activities as part of the social practices that make up family life and help to determine what or how much is eaten. When family members consider food-related activities that are not contextualised within the specific time-space contexts of family life, food practices take on other meanings which, in turn, influence what and how much is eaten. As a result, the ways that food activities are or are not part of family practice has implications for healthy eating. The chapter also concludes that while there are specific differences in the practices of the UK and Hungarian examples, there are also a number of important similarities that point to ways family members all engage with the care work that helps to constitute families. Understanding food practices as they are situated within and outside of family practices should also contribute to ongoing European and national level policy efforts aimed at improving diets in two countries where there are high rates of diet-related illnesses and obesity (UK adult obesity is 24% and in Hungary the rate is 18%, WHO 2002).[1]

Practice, time and family

Schatzki (2002) defines social practices as an organised nexus of actions that are made up of doings and sayings that hang together in what he refers to as an assemblage. The elements that help structure both the organisation of actions within an assemblage and the practice itself are (1) a shared notion of the ends or projects that should be pursued according to some socially recognisable set of rules and norms (e.g. the family or the family meal); (2) a practical understanding of how to achieve these ends (e.g., the ability not just to do the tasks but also an understanding of when it makes sense to do so); (3) the spatial and temporal context within which the ends are being pursued; and (4) a willingness and desire on the part of the person to pursue a particular set of ends (see also Hägerstrand's (1982) concept of 'thereness', Simonsen (2007) for a discussion of emotion, and Rouse (2007) for more on normativity). Not only are practices embedded, constrained, and enabled by the space and time within which they are enacted, but individual projects themselves are similarly embedded, constrained, and enabled by time and space. Hägerstrand (1982) argues that project realisation involves not only human time, but also a corresponding appropriation of things and room or space within which to complete them and, as a result, interdependencies arise between the person pursuing the project and the things, including other people, required to pursue this project. The materiality of this means that to pursue a project, a person must be co-present with the tools and so forth needed to pursue that project. The broader social context within which the project is being pursued will help to structure more specifically how an individual will choose to pursue that project (Hägerstrand 1982; Schatzki 2002). For example at one time and in one place meals may be cooked over an open fire (e.g., in the modern day while camping for example, or in a prior era because no other technology was available for cooking), while in another they may be cooked on a range cooker. This also means that as changes in circumstances occur, the ways that people pursue projects will also change over time and across space (Hägerstrand 1982). Moreover, when considering social practices time should be considered as both an objective measure (e.g., sequential time) and as the experience of past, present and future (e.g., existential time) as it relates to family practice.

According to Schatzki (2005) the two broad concepts of time that matter to the way we can conceptualise and understand social practices are objective time and existential time. Objective time concerns before and after or succession and can be considered in absolute terms (e.g., time of day, year) or relative terms (e.g., before the Roman Empire or after the stock market crash). This conception of time, while it can be rooted in human understanding, is independent of any one particular human and has a degree of uniformity in that it shares a similar relationship across group members (e.g., clock time). The second concept of time, existential time, is rooted in human experience of being in the world and is centred on the way that individuals make decisions about what course of action to take now based upon their own understanding of the past coupled with their intentions for the future. This time is profoundly human time as it is rooted in human experience and existence and shapes human being in the world (Heidegger 1962). This second form of time as it is located in the materiality of everyday life (in space and place) are key axes around which family processes should be developed; past relationships shape and influence future relationships (Morgan 1996). Likewise DeVault (1991) points out that family practices are rhythmic, in that they require a repeated performance day in and day out. This repetition provides the basis for establishing and maintaining families as it creates opportunities for mutual recognition by combining both the existential time of the actor with the more shared objective form of time that is conjured up through the regularity and predictability of this action (Simonsen 2007; Lefebvre 2004). While there is some research concerning the role that memory has in giving meaning to food (e.g., Sutton 2001), and a ready acknowledgement of evidence that people feel they have little time for cooking and eating in a modern world (DeVault 1991), there is actually relatively little research that explores these two interconnecting dimension of time as they pertain to eating and feeding.

Feeding and eating in and beyond the family in Hungary and the UK

The following discussion derives from research conducted with families in both Hungary and in the UK. Between 2006 and 2007 we conducted repeat interviews with all female partners in eight households in both contexts. We also conducted interviews with five male householders in Hungary and three male householders in the UK. In Hungary participants lived in a small city located along the southern border of the country, while in the UK participants lived in a town in Yorkshire located on the edge of two cities. These locations were chosen because they and the participants were known to at least one member of the team. Extensive everyday knowledge of the study sites was important as it enabled a greater level of contextual knowledge than would have been possible otherwise. Familiarity with participants enabled a trusting relationship early in the research process (see Blake 2007 for a discussion of friendship and its relevance to ethics in this research), that proved to be particularly useful in the Hungarian context. However, the unfamiliarity of other team members with both the contexts and the participants, enabled a fresh perspective on the 'familiar' and offered a degree of triangulation regarding our observations of everyday life. Households were selected based on where they were positioned in the life-course, and included a younger family with no children, younger families with small children, middle-aged partners with older children and households where the children were now adults. In all the households, both Hungarian and UK, both female and male partners were employed, or if they were retired, they had been employed.

Each participant was interviewed over two or three meetings and interviews covered topics such as regular and favourite foods, the pattern of food in daily life, entertaining, and special meals, provisioning, and if it was completed by the participant a food diary (all the Hungarian and about half of the UK participants completed food diaries). It is evident from the accounts of both the Hungarian and British participants that the timing of food is an important component of how they relate to food. Our participants conceptualised food time in a myriad of ways including duration, volume, frequency, biological time, immediacy, remembered time, and cycles, and the importance of this timing is linked to how individuals conceptualise the eating episode in the first instance. So, for example, is this food moment concerned with feeding the family, or is it just feeding oneself, or perhaps entertaining others?

To illustrate these points and the ways that time and time-space help structure food and family life, the following discussion is drawn primarily from two families, both of whom are dual-career households with middle-aged parents and primary school aged children. These two families were selected on the basis of their demographic similarity, but this case study approach also provides the concrete and context-dependent knowledge necessary for understanding practices in everyday life (for a review of the value of case study research see Flyvbjerg 2006; for the need for context dependent knowledge see Hägerstrand 1982 and Schatzki 2002). Both partners in both households participated in the interviews. First we introduce each family and provide a discussion of eating and cooking by household members. The discussion then turns to examine how food projects are also family projects by paying careful attention to the ways that adult family members perform feeding work. What is striking about these two cases is that while there are distinct differences in the detail of the accounts, there are some strong similarities in the household narratives that include the importance of feeding healthy meals to family members, which involves careful timing in terms of not just sequencing but also existential time. Indeed, it is this temporal contextualisation provided by existential time that helps to give definition to family feeding and which is also often missing from individual eating. In each account we consider the relationships between time and food as they are situated within family eating and feeding and then how these relationships between time and food are reconfigured when eating does not concern family. We then turn to the idea of the family meal, something expressed in both accounts, but performed in ways that are different from an idealised, but nationally specific construction of the family meal.

The Hungarian family

Tamas (aged 40) and his wife Kati (also 40) have two children, Lesco (aged 10) and Dora (aged 6). Both Tamas and his wife Kati work full-time. Kati works at the University, while Tamas has a job that frequently takes him out of the city where they live, but still enables him to be home in the evening. Both children attend school. Lesco goes to primary school and Dora attends the Kindergarten near the primary school (five minutes walk away), both of which are very near Kati's workplace. This family, like many urban Hungarians, live in a flat.

This family provided a lot of description regarding their regular household pattern. The parents arise at about six thirty in the morning. Kati makes breakfast and they eat together, then Kati does the washing up. While Kati makes the drinks (both tea and coffee for both the adults and hot chocolate for the children) and assembles the breakfast (which includes toast and ham or liver paste, some red pepper or tomato, plus an additional half slice of bread with jam, Tamas gets the children up and ready for the day. The whole family leave the house at about seven forty-five. The children are dropped at their respective schools at about eight in the morning. Kati arrives at work shortly after and Tamas goes onto his work.

During the working day, Tamas will eat lunch usually having a cooked meal in a restaurant. The children eat three pre-paid meals at their respective schools: Elevenses, lunch, and afternoon tea. Elevenses and tea involve bread, a yogurt drink, and something else such as a piece of fruit, and a piece of cake. Lunch, traditionally the main meal in Hungary, is a larger hot meal that is supplied to the schools by a catering company who supplies all the school meals in the city. Kati says that the children are beginning to request foods that they eat at school be also prepared at home, which means she is having to learn new dishes such as how to cook lentils and kolrabi. Despite the fact that Kati grew up in a family where lunch was the most important meal, unlike Tamas whose family gave equal importance to both lunch and dinner, Kati does not usually eat lunch. Instead she will grab a pastry and eat it at her desk or forgo lunch altogether as she is often busy and she finds lunch becomes sidelined.

> I don't have lunch regularly, as we have a cooked meal for dinner at home. That is why I just rush out to the shop or to the bakery and I buy something for myself...Mainly I have lunch at the department and I eat my pastry sitting in front of the computer. I prefer eating with company than alone, but that takes one hour and if I eat by myself then I can eat in only a few minutes. I keep postponing, I delay it. [I say] I'll just do that before it and it is half two or three in the afternoon and I notice I am so hungry that I am close to having a headache. However I don't go then [to get lunch] because I leave my workplace around four or four-fifteen.

As this quotation illustrates, unless there is some social purpose to her eating, it can easily become sidelined. During her workday, Kati's time is a resource to be used wisely. She must complete her work and as a result her working schedule is constrained by the demands of her family.

After work Kati meets the children at school and is either collected in the car by Tamas or, if Tamas cannot collect them, they either take the bus or tram home or take a taxi, arriving home just before five. Kati then goes to the gym for exercise between five and six in the evening. If Tamas is home he watches the children, if he is not then they relax and watch TV for the hour she is away. Between five and eight or eight thirty Tamas works at home in his office typing reports or talking on the telephone. Three days a week he will go for a run while Kati is at the gym. During this late afternoon early evening period, Lesco and Dora may have a piece of fruit with a small sweet such as a turorudi, which is a chocolate coated cheese finger, that Kati keeps for them to eat. There is also a bowl of sweets from which the children can help themselves. Kati described the children's snacking in the following way:

> If I offer them fruit, they don't consume that as self-service. They only eat fruit if I wash it and if I slice or peel it. They don't eat fruits spontaneously, I have to give it to them in their hands. Sweets, including Turorudi they consume in a self-service way. They ask for the Turorudi but they help themselves to the candy from the bowl. They can control themselves and I know this because I can see how quickly the bowl becomes empty.

While the more healthy snacking requires an obvious expenditure of time for Kati as she must prepare and then put the food 'in their hands' even the self-service food demands her time and attention as she must make sure it is available and also monitor how quickly it is eaten.

At about seven or seven thirty the children have their evening meal, which if it is the beginning of the week are leftovers from the food Kati, like the other Hungarian women we spoke to, prepared on the weekend for their main meal at lunchtime on Sunday. If no leftovers are available she cooks what she called 'fast dishes' such as scrambled eggs with onions and salami and a bit of ketchup with thin sliced ham on the side and raw vegetables such as pepper, tomato, cucumber and onion and cheese or sausages with raw vegetables and cheese. Occasionally they may have chicken nuggets. They never have ready meals because, according to Kati they take too long to prepare. While the children are bathing Kati and Tamas will eat a light meal of salad with a yogurt dressing and more of what the children have had. They also have a beer with their dinner, which is poured into a glass.

Later in the evening, after the children have gone to bed Tamas will then watch television or play on the computer, while Kati cleans up the dishes from the evening meal and prepares for the next morning's breakfast by getting the cutlery and breakfast plates out and getting the coffee and tea ready. Once the children are in bed, Kati starts some laundry and Tamas gets everything ready for his work the next day. Sometimes they will have a sweet snack before bathing and going to bed, but not always. At about ten in the evening they go to bed and read or watch a film together before falling asleep at about eleven or twelve.

Before moving on to discuss our Yorkshire family we would like to highlight how objective and existential time figure importantly in this family's narrative as elements that help to make this family. What is evident from this account is the amount of time-specific effort required from Kati to feed this family during the week, when she has had a full workday to contend with as well. Not only does it take time to prepare the two meals that she takes responsibility for, but she must provision for these meals, usually on Saturday and she must cook extensively on Sunday to provide the leftovers that are eaten on Monday, Tuesday and Wednesday. However by cooking extra food at the weekend, she is able to make time for herself to go to the gym, which she values. There is also a careful sequencing of feeding events that have a rhythm and regularity to them which operate at both a daily scale but also at the scale of the week. This ordinary family feeding is ordered and structured by the planning, provisioning, and cooking activities that she performs. One must not assume, however, that she is doing this performance on her own and in isolation. While Kati does the vast majority of the practical feeding work in this family, certain elements are facilitated by Tamas. For example, while she is preparing the breakfast, he takes responsibility for getting the children ready for the day and makes the beds. Moreover, in order for these feeding events to be successful, they require the co-presence of the other family members.

Existential time is also very evident in this narrative. Food is clearly a key aspect of the family work that Kati does. Kati's actions are the result of her and Tamas's shared desire to produce and maintain their family in a way that is healthy so these actions are intentional and directed at others and are shared. They also are linked to their own past experiences of family, but do not slavishly replicate these past traditions. Instead, new traditions, such as the family breakfast, are forged. Family food traditions serve two key purposes. Firstly, they help to produce the boundaries between what constitutes this family and previous families experienced separately by the adults. Secondly, this ritualised eating provides order to daily life while at the same time ritualised meals like this family's breakfast helps to produce what Sutton (2001) refers to as 'prospective memories'. Prospective memories are future memories to be recalled by Tamas and Kati after their children have left the home, but they will also be remembered by Lesco and Dora as they start their own families. This memory work helps to create family continuity over time and through changes in household composition (Morgan 1996).

Kati also talked about the enjoyment of cooking for her family in ways that combine both objective and existential time. Kati said she loved eating but doesn't enjoy having guests as she feels compelled to cook more elaborate and traditional food that she is less confident making and which requires more time than she feels she has. She does, however, enjoy cooking for her family:

> If I have time I like to stay in the kitchen. I can say the kitchen is my favourite place in the flat. If I had more time I might like having guests more. I am happy if somebody likes my dishes. I have to say, I enjoy feeding the family.

Kati gets satisfaction from making food that she knows her family enjoys and will eat and is willing to accommodate their preferences and desires. This may involve making food she knows they like such as the scrambled eggs described above. Her egg dish, which she refers to as 'my mother's method' differs from what her children referred to as the 'simple style' of just scrambled eggs that they are not so enthusiastic about. She is willing to cook hot meals at dinner time, which is not her tradition but instead is more the experience and preference of her husband. She is also willing to compress her time getting ready for work in the morning in order to facilitate Tamas's desire for a family meal at breakfast, a tradition she does not indulge when Tamas is away from home.

Finally, Kati and Tamas's accounts of their working days are telling. Kati's rather limited engagements with food are in stark contrast to her intensive engagements with food at home. Her daily time-space rhythms move her into and out of family life. While her work day is bracketed by caring activities concerning her family, her focus while she is at work is not on her family. As feeding work is not an important or regular part of that effort, it holds little of her attention. As a result she often grabs something quickly or eats nothing at all, both of which are not ideal from a health point of view, but understandable given that her ordinary relationship with food is one concerned with maintaining others and when these others are absent food is also largely absent. Tamas, on the other hand always eats a hot lunch. Tamas has very clear ideas about food and feeding and his preferences are for the traditional meat stews that his father cooked when he was young.[2] He does no cooking and is instead used to being fed regularly by either his parents or Kati and as both lunch and dinner were important meals in his family, he continues to eat a cooked lunch from a restaurant, or if he is pressed for time he has two grilled chicken salads at McDonalds. Thus for both Tamas and Kati, their roles within the family help to structure their eating when they are not at home.

The Yorkshire family

In the Billing household there are five family members: Lucy and David (both in their lower 40s) and Sally (age 10), James (7), and Will (4). David works part-time as a senior executive director for a telecommunications firm, which means Tuesday and Wednesday he is in Paris, Friday he is in the nearby city, and Monday and Thursday he is a stay at home dad. Lucy has recently finished a health professional degree at university and works in a nearby town on Monday, Tuesday, and Thursday.

In contrast to our Hungarian family, eating within this household is managed around the various home-work schedules of both partners and includes direct contributions from each. This sharing of responsibility introduces quite a bit of variation within the week, but this pattern is consistent from week to week and it is the weekly cycle that both Lucy and David tended to describe when we asked them about their 'normal day'. David takes responsibility for the household evening cooking on Monday and Thursday and shopping on Monday, while Lucy cooks on Tuesday, Wednesday and the weekend days. Lucy's mother lives about a half hour away and quite often comes on Tuesday to be with the children and cooks a meal for them as this is the day that both David and Lucy work. Friday they have 'Pizza Night' which involves making three pizzas: cheese and tomato, mushroom, and pepperoni. David likes the pepperoni, Lucy likes the mushroom and the children tend to eat tomato and cheese, although the eldest child will also eat pepperoni. There is also a salad and wine for the adults. Importantly, while a ritual meal in this household, it is not necessarily eaten together:

> I have it on Friday night so it [marks] the end of the working week, a bit of a treat. I like having it at home, sitting at my kitchen table. We've had pizza on Friday night for years. We do it now with the children and they also like to have pizza on a Friday night. They complain if they don't get it. Sometimes I like to get the children into bed and then when everything is quiet, just to have it then...it is like a ritual (David).

For David this meal is a treat to celebrate the end of the working week and he views it as a way to recreate the idea of home as respite from the world (for more on home as respite see Johnston and Valentine 1995).

While both Lucy and David say they try to eat together with the children during the week, the breakfast meal is the one that is most consistently eaten as a family as David only misses the family breakfast on Tuesday and Wednesday mornings, when he is away. The evening meals tend to be less collective either out of choice as described in relation to 'Pizza Night', or because of both partners' work schedules. David eats in restaurants on Tuesday when he is Paris and on Wednesday he has a late meal that Lucy has left for him in the microwave. Likewise he often prepares a plate for Lucy to eat on Thursday after she returns from work. With the exception of Friday, either parent will eat with the children if they are at home between five and six, which is when the children eat.

> I like to cook when I have got time. When I have not got time I find it a chore. It's better now, we try and all eat together, as much as we can. Whereas when the children used to eat earlier and then David and I would eat later and it did become a real chore and I just felt I spent the entire evening cooking. But now we eat together, and perhaps we don't have as many exotic things like we used to have because I know the children don't particularly like them. It is easier because we only have to do one meal and we all eat it. This is partly a conscious decision because it means less cooking but partly because I do like us to all sit down together as a family. I think it's quite important (Lucy).

David is less enthusiastic about sharing the evening family meal than he is about the shared breakfast as he preferred it when he and Lucy ate later in the evenings. He says he also finds the timing of shared family dinner to be too early in the day as he feels it 'runs into' lunch. This running into he puts down to the way the children's schedules structure the time in the afternoon.

> I make my lunch [about 1pm]...and then the children will come home from school [3pm] and then we will have a drink and a biscuit when they get in and then before you know it, by the time I've persuaded somebody to do their times tables or spellings then it is time to make the tea (David).

For David, the early meal means that not only is there no time to do other activities in the afternoon, which makes him feel as though his day is shortened to just the morning. Likewise, the early meal means that he gets hungry at about eight in the evening, and as there is no formal meal scheduled at that time he finds that he eats biscuits rather than something more healthy, which he then feels guilty about.

For both Lucy and David, lunch is shaped by both their working and domestic schedules. When they are both at home (together or separately) they will fix a light meal such as a sandwich and a piece of fruit. When at work, Lucy will go to the nearby Morrisons and buy a salad or sandwich for lunch. She feels she has enough time for this because lunchtime is scheduled into her working day at the hospital and is taken by all the staff in her unit. David's work is task focused, rather than scheduled like Lucy's. As a result, he has a certain amount of work to complete each week while he is in Paris if he wants to avoid extending his working week beyond the three days he is paid to do.

> I'm working extremely hard because I do a full-time job fundamentally in three days. I have to manage it and it is a real balance. I start early and finish late to get everything done to catch up with everybody else who's been in for five days…I'm trying to cram so much work into three days it's very unlikely that I will have lunch at all or I will nip to the machine and buy myself a can of Coke and a little bag of tiny cakes. If I am really busy I won't have anything at all. I don't eat with the others because I object to the time it takes to walk six or seven minutes to the canteen and then you sit or queue up and before you know it you've lost an hour. I know that will put pressure on another part of my day and then the potential for spillover into days when I am not at work is even greater.

Like Kati, David forgoes lunch because it is not particularly facilitated by his employment and it has little purpose in his life. Instead, he views lunch at work as something that has the potential to interfere with his home life.

There are some particular, time-related differences in the feeding and eating activities of this UK family that distinguish them from the Hungarians. For instance they cook on a daily schedule in order to introduce variety and as a result there is a reluctance to use leftovers as a way to save time. There is greater involvement of the male householder's time in the actual provisioning and cooking work of the household than was the case in the Hungarian family. But, there are also some striking similarities. Feeding work is viewed in both households as important to family life as it helps to create the parameters or boundaries of the family as well as contribute to the memory work that helps family to endure. Individual feeding of adults is given time if there is enough and after everything else has finished. Children, are often framed in the food and family literature as either powerless recipients or active agents in determining what is eaten through their refusal to eat certain foods or their demands for certain items. But as both households' narrations show children also have agency by their very co-presence as their needs and schedules are accommodated by and within their parents' own understandings of what a family is. It is this understanding and these parents' willingness to act on them that are expressions of care making food practices the outcome of the intention to care.

Family meals in the UK and Hungary

For quite some time researchers have argued that the 'family meal' is something that has achieved mythic proportions in the public consciousness (DeVault 1991; Murcott 1997, Chapter 7 this volume). Indeed, this normative ideal is promoted in the public consciousness through the efforts of advertisers while at the same time government officials lament its decline. Murcott (1997) likewise points out that the 'family meal' is something researchers have taken for granted when trying to understand recent declines in social cohesion and children's health, while at the same time there is little evidence that family meals have been the most prevalent form of eating since industrialisation. What is apparent is that the idea of a family meal, whether practised in actuality or not, has strong currency in the public consciousness and sets the parameters for what counts as family eating as well as what families should strive to do as illustrated in Lucy's comments concerning the importance she gives to eating together (DeVault 1991).

In our study the spectre of the family meal was present in the Hungarian and British households where there were children living at home. In both geographical settings commonly held conceptualisations of an idealised notion of the family meal involved a particular form of food. In the UK and Hungary the family meal involves serving 'proper food' that is hot, cooked food. However, while in the UK the traditional discourse of the cooked meal resembles the description provided by Mary Douglas's (1972) account of a meat and two sides, in Hungary the proper meal involves three courses starting with a hearty soup followed by a meat dish with accompaniments (salad, pickled vegetables), or a vegetable dish accompanied by meat or meat stew, or goulash followed by a dumpling dish. The third course is cake and/or fruit. The meat dish can be something similar to what one might find in the UK such as a roast ham with roasted vegetable, but it also equally might be some organ meat (liver, tripe, lung, heart, brain) with a hearty vegetable sauce. According to Kati these sauces are quite time consuming to make and she only makes them during holidays when she has 'four or five days to cook'.

These understandings of the proper meal also carried with them very definite notions about how the food should be prepared and served. David provides a discussion of this preparation:

> The idea that you put in the effort in order to make something nice particularly for the children... notso much for your wife I suppose...[laughter] but nevertheless, you'd like to think that you're giving them a good meal and healthy food and that sort of thing and so...so I think that's part of it as well. And so there's a sense of, you know, if you do that you do, you're playing your part in doing a good job for them and looking after them.

For David, cooking food for children ideally involves not just throwing something together quickly, but taking time and care over the act of preparation. Likewise Kati revealed that the table must be laid with cutlery. In her household, when a 'proper' meal is prepared – usually at the weekend – this main meal will generally involve two courses initially – soup followed by a main dish – then after the table has been cleared and the dishes washed, coffee and cakes are served. Coffee for the adults, and cakes for both the children and the adults. In Hungary the 'proper' or main meal is thought to be traditionally served at lunchtime, with a lighter, cold meal served at dinner time (although as Tamas and Kati's account shows a hot meal may also be served at dinner).

While there are clear shared notions about a proper family meal in both the UK and in Hungary, each geographical context has its own particular variation. What is also shared across these two contexts, however, is that the ideologically 'proper' meal is not necessarily produced regularly. In Hungary, almost none of our families produced these 'proper' meals during the working week as most did not eat lunch at home. If parents ate, they ate at work, while children also tended to eat their lunch at school. Likewise, our UK families frequently found that the various schedules of household members made it difficult to produce the time-intensive dishes that comprise a proper meal at times other than on the weekend. David even went so far as to describe how this roast meal was prepared while he was growing up, but then argued that in his family 'such a production' was not necessary or even desirable:

> Despite the fact that we both came from families where Sunday lunch was the norm, there was something about knowing the effort

and the complaints of your mother who had made it and did nothing on Sunday but cook as far as we could make out.

Learning about Sunday lunch is not just what the ideal is, but also the time involved in the production of that ideal and recognising that it could be rejected. This rejection does not represent a lack of care, but quite the contrary, it is an expression of the care David has for Lucy. While Kati does make the Hungarian equivalent of the Sunday lunch, it also serves the time-saving job of producing leftovers that are then eaten through the week. Our two accounts also show that a family meal may be more easily accommodated within household schedules if it is the breakfast meal because that is the meal most easily accommodated into the complex of family time schedules. David and Kati both illustrate that a certain amount of ambivalence can arise toward the requirement of co-presence at family meals that must be scheduled early enough to accommodate children's daily routines or which cuts into the limited time available to get ready for the day.

Concluding thoughts

In this chapter we have drawn on practice theory and its particular sensitivity to the ways that individuals have intentions about the activities that they pursue, which are rooted in context-specific normative understandings about how those practices should be pursued. We have argued that while these normative understandings are socially recognisable, individuals also engage with these norms in ways that are practical for their own circumstances. Thus individuals may not act in ways that replicate exactly these normative understandings, but which are intended to achieve similar ends. Key to this understanding is a dual conceptualisation of time that encompasses objective and existential time.

Specifically, in the chapter we have examined the ways that parents in two dual-career household in two differing geographical contexts engage in two types of food engagements. The first type, concerned with the ordinary feeding of the family, is readily identifiable as a project in that they are purposeful (Hägerstrand 1982). The accounts of these projects demonstrated how food and feeding are used intentionally by parents to create future memories of family, demonstrate family cohesiveness and caring relationships, and also to define a particular group of individuals into a specific family that is recognisably separate from other groups organised as families. The motivation of our participants to engage with the specific and time intensive family food practices that were part of their regular routines was their care for their children and sometimes their spouse. The second type of food engagements concerned lunchtime at work. It was apparent from the accounts that participants' attachments to these engagements as projects was much less and is demonstrated by their willingness to forgo lunch if it was inconvenient or impinged upon other activities such as work or even future family engagements.

What is clear from this is that initiatives aimed at reducing diet-related health problems should consider how eating is attached to particular projects in ways that include not just the purpose of a particular food project, but the strength of that relationship. Linking healthy eating to caring, for example, may improve the ways that parents feed their children (and was expressed as such by our households), but without enabling a conceptual link between food and, for example, success at work or that healthy eating by adults contributes to healthy families, there is likely to be little change in the eating practices of adults when they are not engaged with 'doing the family'.

Finally, we considered how participants engaged with the normative idea of a proper family meal. In both geographical contexts, the notion of a proper meal, to be fed to family members was clearly defined and readily identifiable, although it was configured differently in each context. Despite this clear definition, in all our households and as described by our two cases, family meals are practised in ways that do not always resemble this trope. In our two families, for example, breakfast was more easily accommodated into their schedules than other meals. This meal, rather than the Sunday lunch, became the ritualised representation of the family and enabled the regular identification work involved in creating and maintaining these two families. If family circumstances change such that it makes it difficult to accommodate this particular meal it may be abandoned because of the embeddedness of this meal in the daily schedules of household members and its relationship to practicality. It is likely, however, that another solution will be provided as the shared meal is held as being important by parents. What this tells us is that while it may appear that there is a 'care deficit' that is measurable in the decline of the traditional 'family meal' in truth as long as parents continue to care for their children and for each other they will endeavour to invent ways of practicing family that are suitable to their situation because of the importance of ritual in this process. Thus, policies aimed at low income families should focus less on reproducing normative notions of eating and feeding and emphasise instead the ways that family cohesion and care may fit within the specific conditions of each family's circumstances.

Acknowledgements

We wish to thank the participants in both the UK and Hungary for giving so much of their time to us. It is clear that time is precious and in short supply in these families and we recognise their participation as a gift of friendship. We would also like to thank the editor, Peter Jackson, for being patient with us as we struggled to complete this chapter amidst the pressures of other work obligations as well as demands on our time by our own families.

11
Making Healthy Families?

Trish Green, Jenny Owen, Penny Curtis, Graham Smith, Paul Ward and Pamela Fisher

Introduction

If you try to give too much information it doesn't work...and, you know, you have to bear in mind there are some communities that have very, very limited diets already. I mean, you know, they wouldn't know what an aubergine looked like in some communities. Particularly in [this town] (Karen/Manager/Primary Care Trust).

The people that come to us do definitely benefit and they do need it, eh, I would say they're very typical of people who do need interventions (Sadie/Practitioner/Community Food Worker).

I'm not a silly person I know what is healthy, I already know that...it isn't about that, and it was more...somewhere to go in the evening for, for me...I've not done that for a long time (Ingrid/lone mother/four children).

Certain geographical areas and neighbourhood types have come to symbolise patterns of ignorance, lack of opportunity and 'poor lifestyle choice' in public discussions of family food practices. The media, reporting recently on the activities of one of the UK's 'celebrity' chefs announced: 'Jamie Oliver to teach the poor how to cook 'the basics' in town [Rotherham] where mums opposed his school dinners campaign' (*The Daily Mail* 28 March 2008). Concern about diet and about contemporary eating practices is therefore widespread. An increasing public focus on diet and health is not surprising: in England the number of obese children has tripled in 20 years. Ten per cent of six year olds are estimated to be obese, rising to 17% of 15 year olds (Zaninotto *et al.* 2006). While current concern about childhood obesity is usually expressed in terms of *what* children eat, implicit in contemporary discourses about health is also a critique of *how* they eat. While the 'what' is subject to scientific debate among for example, nutritionists and members of the medical profession, discussion of the 'how' has often been dominated by prejudice, myth and unquestioned assumptions which are grounded in notions of appropriate – and inappropriate – forms of parenting and family life. At the same time, while the development and direction of food policy has been well described (see, for example, Lobstein 2002, 2008), the delivery of food-related interventions at a local level has not. In this chapter, we therefore explore the ways in which ideas about 'family' have been understood and communicated through recent government-funded interventions about food and health in the UK. These interventions have been high on public health and 'social inclusion' agendas in recent years, and they span public and private spaces: examples range from the funding of individual Community Food Educators to advise individuals in their own kitchens, to educational programmes such as '5-a-day' and 'Cook and Eat', usually targeted at low-income communities and delivered in Children's Centres and other community venues.

We shall argue that the ways in which issues of diet and health are addressed, in policy and practice, tell us a great deal about how particular family forms and relationships are currently understood, and how they are valued or marginalised in specific contexts. Following a discussion of the background to our research into family, food and health, we concentrate on four overarching themes that emerged from our study: the relationship between food knowledges, diet and inequalities; the emergence of a new form of 'public kitchen'; concepts of healthy family practices; and gendered patterns in food and health interventions. Drawing on qualitative research carried out in four sites in Northern England, we focus both on policy and professional perspectives, and on the accounts of the family members who are on the receiving end of food-related classes and interventions.

Background: family, food and health

Social research about families has traditionally adopted either a structural or a functional approach. While a structural approach emphasises the identification of different types of family, as defined by social positions or roles, the functional approach offers a way of looking at activities that family members do together, in order to meet their needs, within a context of mutual responsibility (Cheal 2002). While this latter approach facilitates an examination of the different roles and distribution of tasks within families, including food provision and consumption, it tends to stress positive benefits while leaving unanswered questions as to *why* families may work well or badly in particular ways.

More recently, in response to the perceived shortcomings of both functional and structural perspectives, Christensen (2004) has proposed an 'ecocultural approach' focusing attention upon family practices in everyday life (Cheal 2002; Morgan 1996, 1999; Silva and Smart 1999). From this perspective, 'family' cannot be conceptualised as a static unit but as an aspect of social life that is constructed in and through multiple practices and processes. With its multi-dimensional approach, the ecocultural model takes account of the fact that families have varying levels and forms of socio-economic and cultural resources at their disposal. Factors such as social networks, employment, financial resources, time and the moral and cultural meanings that underlie and influence practices are considered important. In this perspective, 'families "are" therefore...what families "do" and this matters more than institutional definitions of "family"' (Silva and Smart 1999: 11). Importantly, the ecocultural approach defines all family members, including children, as agents who play a part in creating (or undermining) relationships, as well as family health and well-being. This 'ecocultural' perspective informs our discussion of food interventions and family life below.

In recent years, family food practices have become the site for contending sets of ideas in relation to risk, responsibility, health and 'inclusion'. Since 1997, new ideas of personhood (Giddens 1998) have underpinned an ideology of responsible citizenship (Du Gay 2000; Munro 2004; Newman 2000). The effective citizen, from this perspective, is the one who is able to manage her or his biography by anticipating and dealing with the risks and opportunities associated with late modernity: notions of risk are heightened and individuals are increasingly expected to seek out and use expert bodies of knowledge (Beck 1992; Lupton 1996, 1999). The social inclusion of particular groups (such as the elderly, people with disabilities, those from minority ethnic backgrounds or from economically disadvantaged communities), is sought through the privileging of notions of independence and individual responsibility. Citizens are expected to take advantage of all opportunities – particularly in education, training and employment – to acquire the necessary human capital for full and active citizenship (Poole 2000). Indeed the welfare subject has been recast, as

Fiona Williams succinctly puts it, 'from *passive* to *active*' (2002: 504 original emphasis).

Issues concerning diet and health also come under the rubric of individual responsibility, as government health policies discursively construct the public's health within a framework of rational choice. This emphasis was exemplified by the UK Conservative government in the early 1990s: '[health education] can enable people to make informed decisions about their health and that of their families' (DoH 1992, cited in Keane 1997: 173). It has been reiterated more recently by New Labour: 'the opportunities are now opening up rapidly for everyone to make their own individual informed healthy choices which together will sustain and drive further the improvement in the health of the people of England' (DoH 2004: 19). The interventions we discuss below were a product of the *Choosing Health* policy and its linked documentation.

Although there is some continuity over time in the health policy rhetoric of different governments, both Conservative and Labour initiatives have been characterised by a pronounced shift in focus away from the family as a unit, and towards the individual as the vehicle for change. Indeed, as we shall illustrate in our discussion below, the individual is now accountable for improving both their own and others' family food and health practices. In consequence, the 'strong families' of New Labour's Britain are now made up of 'healthy individuals' making the right choices in the marketplace with respect to food, health and well-being. In this way, the family has acquired an 'assumed' presence, positioned as it is between the individual and the community; a positioning that creates a tension within policy discourses that we shall examine later in this chapter.

In our discussion, we also identify the ways in which food-related initiatives are a component of the government's drive to regenerate 'failing' communities and to promote community cohesion and social inclusion. As Ling (2000: 89) suggests, social inclusion is being attempted through the 'colonisation of identity', as those seen as marginal, or as dependent in some way, are drawn into compliance with dominant values. This has the subsidiary effect of marginalising still further those who are perceived to resist. Moreover, those given responsibility for interpreting policy at the point of delivery are trained and managed within a dominant paradigm of acceptable eating and health practices, via their immersion in policy discourse and concomitant practice guidelines. The *Choosing Health* document, for example, states that 'the changes needed to deliver the policies in this White Paper will only occur if the right people with the right skills are in place to deliver them and if barriers to change are broken down' (DoH 2004: 18). In this account, changes to specific features of the nation's health are only achievable via recourse to the input of specific practitioners, who are charged with *changing* individual food and health behaviours (Yeatman 2003: 125). The understanding is that these changes will be adopted and implemented within the home, thus impacting on the food and health practices of the wider family. In this respect, a diverse range of high-profile initiatives about food, including both government-led and celebrity chef projects to educate consumers, underscore the ways in which buying, preparing and eating 'healthy' food is associated with dominant notions of responsible citizenship.

Our overall aim, was to see what we could learn about prevailing ideas of 'family' and 'healthy family' by examining current examples of policies and community-based interventions related to food and health. We identified four research sites, in which we carried out qualitative research. Seventy-five in-depth, semi-structured interviews were undertaken with the three groups involved in healthy eating interventions: managers, practitioners (who included graduate-trained professionals and non-graduate support staff) and family members. Seventeen participant observation visits were also carried out in the four research sites. Our research cohort was predominantly White British and the majority were women. We did not specifically sample for class.

Our investigation addressed both the practical application and the experience of food and health-related community interventions. As such, our enquiry was threefold: firstly, we asked how those charged with the responsibility for planning food-related public health initiatives and those charged with delivering interventions understood 'healthy family'. Secondly, we considered how family members views accorded with these and with understandings of 'healthy family' that are scripted into public health policy. Finally, we considered whether the ways in which these differently positioned actors understood 'family' had implications for the ways in which issues of food and health are being – and should be – defined and addressed. Although different interview schedules were, of necessity, used for our professional and family interviewees, each participant was asked to describe and illustrate her/his understanding of 'healthy family'. It should be noted that the study was focused on participation rather than non-participation with government-directed programmes. The subject matter thus warrants further exploration into why members of the public choose *not to* engage with the food and health-related initiatives currently being promoted. All interviews were transcribed verbatim and participants' quotes are presented here as such. Below we elaborate on some of our main findings.

Food, diet and inequalities

Families on low incomes, and disadvantaged neighbourhoods in general, have been prioritised as the recipients of educational and health promotion initiatives about diet. Commonly, resources are directed at the provision of information about budgeting and healthy eating, through classes or poster campaigns or other familiar health promotion channels. However, a broad range of research suggests this may be misdirected effort, since people on low incomes generally take a highly responsible attitude towards budgeting and purchasing food. Unsurprisingly, budgetary constraints take precedence over issues of taste, cultural acceptability and healthy eating (Dobson et al. 1994; Dowler 1997). When under financial pressure, people either economise on food by buying cheaper or different items or by omitting meals altogether. A study conducted by DEMOS in 2002 (Hitchman et al. 2002) showed that people went to enormous trouble to seek out the best bargains and tended to avoid experimentation on the basis that this might be costly, for example if children refused to eat new types of food. In a study for the Joseph Rowntree Foundation, Dobson et al. (1994) showed that children received more of their preferred foods, such as burgers and chips, in low-income families, as this was seen as less likely to result in waste. Family members were aware of the fact that they were eating food that was less than optimal in nutritional terms, and also that poverty excluded them from the consumer choices available to others. Rather than adopt innovative eating habits, people living on low incomes tend to adopt cheaper versions of conventional eating patterns. In our study, as the following quote from a manager indicates, there was some recognition that the facilities available in a given area would be a deciding factor in a family's ability to eat healthily. Nevertheless, the emphasis in several manager and practitioner narratives still reflected government policy, by placing the responsibility for making healthy choices with the individual:

> 'Choosing Health' really demonstrates strongly that we have to help equip people to make the choices themselves…public health practitioners and professionals…aren't there to tell people what they should and shouldn't be doing. We're there to simply provide them

with the information to then equip them to help them make those decisions (Belinda/Manager/PCT).

Many of our family participants were keen to inform us, however, that they did not lack cooking skills or 'know-how' regarding healthy food and eating practices. This is not to make a judgement about how our research participants ate, in practice, but rather to raise questions about the ways in which the food and health knowledges of some members of the public are currently represented in the public domain, both through policy channels and in media discourses. Indeed as Ingrid said: *I'm not a silly person, I know what is healthy. I already know that.* However, as she further explained regarding her community: *it's an area where money dictates an awful lot of what you eat.* Living on a tight budget thus directly affected what could be bought in the supermarket, as Karla, a married mother of two informed us: *I chuck in the buy-one-get-one-frees that we want, which are usually rubbish food [...] if organic food was cheaper, I would buy that, but it's not and I think that's disgusting.*

Participants' experiences sit uneasily, then, with the recent televising of celebrity chef campaigns calling for supermarkets to stock only organic/ free range chickens and other such produce, and to engage members of the public in learning the cooking skills that they have not learned from their parents. Some managers and practitioners shared this acknowledgement of the importance of understanding local resources, when planning and health interventions; this provided a contrast with the emphasis on individual responsibility illustrated above:

> If you're talking to people about how to change lifestyle you've got to know what's achievable for that group, so you've got to have some local knowledge as well, which no policy can tell you. Eh, so, for instance, if you're going to a group and say, you know, you need to buy these fruits, vegetables or whatever [...] you need to be able to tell people where they can get those things from ... and similar with exercise, you know, it's alright to say, go and do this, this and this, but you've got to know how they can do that locally, and so local knowledge is very important for implementing the programmes (Sharon/Community Dietician Services Manager).

> Education is key and clearly people won't change their diet unless firstly they know that would be a good thing and they understand why. It's not the only thing, because there are issues about availabil-

ity of food. There are wider cultural issues to be addressed in some areas, you know, things like work patterns for some people are very important in determining what they can eat and when (James/Manager/ Primary Care Trust).

As these interviewees intimate, national policy cannot capture the full range of local contexts; it is left to practitioners – the 'street level bureaucrats' (Lipsky 1980) who translate policy into local practice – to mediate between national frameworks and neighbourhood-level complexities. A number of managers and practitioners commented on the material constraints facing the communities where healthy eating initiatives were underway:

I've been to certain areas and when I go and do a workshop I try and call in and buy some fruit and veg or some fruit on the way, and there have been groups, places where I have been to, where it was impossible to buy any fruit, 'cause there just wasn't any available without driving 4 or 5 miles to another part, 'cause there was just nothing in the local shops...there's food deserts, food poverty, in some part of [the city]...so with the best will in the world, you can't [have] a healthy diet (Sadie/Practitioner/Community Food Worker).

When they want to getting a big shop [done], I found that quite a lot of our families on low incomes will have a taxi to the Asda, which I think is a real shame...where the Asda is actually situated from here is literally five minute drive in the car, but there's no direct bus service from here, or even from the [estate] to a large supermarket...and when they've got a few children with them as well...it makes it even more hard (Nellie/Practitioner/SureStart).

[This estate] especially, is so isolated. It's very cut off with, eh, a big dual carriageway, so no access to shops. And the shops they have got, the corner shops...are really expensive and not very good quality fruit and vegetables (Linda/Practitioner/Cook and Eat).

We see here, therefore, that practitioners are being funded to implement healthy eating as an everyday family practice, when they are aware that many of the people they are working with cannot easily access affordable and appropriate sources of food. As their statements show, there is a growing tendency for many services and amenities, including major food retailers, to be located on the edge of towns, and out of easy reach of public transport. This also raises concerns about access to genuine and affordable food choices (Charles and Kerr 1988; Dowler and Caraher 2003). Many family members confirmed that poor local services and amenities severely limited options for making healthy shopping choices:

> There used to be a lovely little fishmongers [here], at the side of the library up the little ginnel and, oh, they sold everything, yeah, that was a lovely little shop...it went years ago (Ellie/lone mother/two children).

> There isn't the Morrison's bus now...there used to be...you could just hail and ride, you don't have to get to a proper bus stop...if I ever want to go to Asda's I'd have to catch the 37 and, oh, it's miles and miles, I'd never make it (Ingrid/lone mother/four children).

To summarise, then, many professionals acknowledged that low incomes and poor local amenities strongly influence family members' ability to act on 'healthy eating' messages. This does raise questions about the purpose and scope of these interventions, and it is to this issue that we now turn.

A new 'public kitchen'...?

> '[Food is] private, in that it is stored and consumed in the domestic domain' (Dowler and Caraher 2003: 58).

Healthy eating classes are reportedly in place to meet a perceived gap in culinary skills and to impart information. In some important respects, these programmes make the domestic family kitchen – and the practices associated with it – open to scrutiny and intervention in the public domain. This is not the first time that private kitchen practices have been the focus of public and professional surveillance (see for example Charles and Kerr 1988). However, we do suggest that these interventions represent new examples of a 'public kitchen space', with implications that need examining in their own right.

As we have already indicated, the women we interviewed who attend programmes such as 'Cook and Eat' can for the most part already cook and also know what healthy foodstuffs are. They are not attending out of a perceived need for education or information. This does, of course, raise another set of questions: are these programmes simply not an effective way to reach those who might genuinely lack information about food and health? Or are there fewer people who consider that they need this kind of intervention than government policy suggests? These are important questions, identified by our study, but beyond its scope to answer. What we can consider, on the basis of our study data, is what else might be 'going on' in the publicly-located domestic kitchen of healthy eating interventions. Participants' narratives offer some substantial insights here:

> Some of them haven't been out and accessed anything much before, and they get out, they access a course, find that they really enjoy it. They're getting out of the house; they get a bit of time away from the children, and the Cook and Eat stuff has always been really popular (Nellie/Practitioner/SureStart).

> I was giddy when I came back the first day, eh, it was just, eh, 'cause I'd done it for me…I'd done something for me that was solely mine and nobody could share or have a comment on…they couldn't make a comment on that because I was away from everybody and I was there and nobody could say a word, and I liked that (Lizzie/Family/partnered/three children).

Evidently, locating the domestic kitchen in a public place offered a space in which feelings of well-being were nurtured and where needs entirely different from those related to culinary competence were being met. Several of our family participants described their attendance at cooking classes as 'me time' so that paradoxically, time spent in another kitchen space outside the home was experienced as time for the self; as 'leisure' rather than 'labour'. In order to evaluate these and other respondents' narratives, Elspeth Probyn's analysis of 'choice' and what she terms the 'rearrangement of *feel* of the material' provides a useful metaphor:

> Representations of choice are not simply about the opportunity to change our lives, but may more modestly simply allow us to 'feel differently' [about] the affective implications of the images of choice as they circulate within the material structure of our lives (Probyn 1993: 138).

Indeed, without improvements in incomes and in access to local amenities, for example, there might be nothing else on offer in the public kitchen of healthy eating interventions but a *change* to the way those attending cook and eat and other food-related initiatives can *feel* about their material circumstances. It was certainly the case that a narrative of local/community empowerment ran through several of our practitioners' accounts, alongside an explicit awareness of the pressure to meet government health targets:

> In the long run, you know, you're empowering people to take more control of, of health and getting involved and having a say, eh, in their community in, in health. And in the long run then, you're you know, you're reducing health targets. (Beth/Practitioner/ Development Worker).

Our data also evidenced that healthy eating interventions provided managers and practitioners with an alternative, or double-edged, schema. For example, the civilised and civilising notions that underpin the practice of sitting down at the table to eat a meal often informed aspects of public health workers' practices. Although many interviewees acknowledged that ideas about 'healthy food' can change – for instance, many recalled cooked breakfasts or hearty teas from childhood, which seemed 'very fatty' to them in present-day terms – the core idea of sitting down together to eat and talk was a consistent reference point that evidently formed part of the rhetoric of the healthy eating intervention. Indeed, as one practitioner told us: *I make that a very important part of 'Cook and Eat'* (Linda). Interestingly, or perhaps more surprisingly, this practitioner worked in one of the more disadvantaged localities we investigated. Family interview data from this site reveals how affording a dining table, or indeed having the space for such an item of furniture, was not always possible. Nor did it fit in with everyone's ideas about how to 'do' family:

> Obviously, when you got your own place you think, well, can't be bothered to use a table. You just use your knees. Or when you've got kids you just, eh, do what they wanna do (Vaughan/Family/ estranged from his wife and three children).

Nevertheless, eating around the table was a message being relayed to attendees of Cook and Eat and other interventions, and was perceived as an exemplar of 'healthy' family life:

> I don't think people think [the programme] is training, it's just an activity that they do...it's a bit of a break from the children 'cause

very few of them have a chance to, to, to prepare food without their children around them [...] then they sit round and eat the food with their children, erm, you know, and, and quite often the children won't have sat round a table...people's living circumstances...you know...we have staff who are kind of encouraging them to, you know, use the appropriate spoons (Mary/Manager/SureStart).

There is a communal quality given over to the public kitchen space Mary describes: a tacit sharing of domestic tasks such as childcare and food preparation is taking place, and eating around the table is seen to provide opportunities for harmonious conversation and problem-solving. There is also the uncoupling of kitchen activity from its context within the home that Floyd (2004: 64) alludes to – the children are cared for elsewhere whilst mum 'gets on' with the cooking, for example. Once again, this reinforces the sense that the programmes are partly seen as nurturing feelings of well-being among the women who attend.

The latter half of the above extract is, however, laden with moralistic undertones and assumptions regarding the 'private' eating practices of some families. An underlying implication is that practitioner input, stealthily implemented via a new formulation of the public gaze, is necessary in order to make up for mothers' (and others'?) failings back in the home. Thus, this space also provides public health workers with new forms of opportunity for the surveillance of family practices. Indeed, successful interventions and resultant feelings of job satisfaction were often articulated with reference to perceived changes in individuals' and families' behaviours, which were associated with definitions of healthy family life. It is the food-related practices of the 'healthy family' that we discuss next.

Healthy family practices

The idea of family is still very strong. It constitutes a key concept by which people understand their lives, and a significant and powerful ideal at the levels of both personal lives and public debate (Ribbens McCarthy et al. 2003: 27).

In their analysis, Jane Ribbens McCarthy and her colleagues argue that it is the 'idea' of family that maintains its inflexibility, rather than the material reality of the dynamics of family life. As we suggested earlier, there has been a pronounced shift in focus towards the 'doing' of family in analytical terms. However, it was clear that almost all our study participants shared an 'ideal' of family life that reflected the normative functions and expectations of the traditional nuclear family, consisting of male breadwinner father and female homemaker mother. This 'ideal' permeated all interview data irrespective of participants' experience of family form (for example, lone parent; extended; reconstituted and so on) or their discussion of family typologies. The practitioners engaged in delivering food-related initiatives in localities. For example, there were a number of images associated with 'healthy family', many of which drew on vivid childhood memories, invested with powerful moral connotations about parenting. A Sure Start staff member from a British Asian family commented:

> We always used to eat together and that was a time where your dad would say or your mum would say, 'What've you been doing at school?', you know...being able to discuss things and I think 'cause we were able to do that, personally I now am able to voice my opinions or my views...that's how I am as an adult now [...] It impacts on how you are as an individual...so I'd say that is really important because obviously there's, there's so much happening in a child's life when they're at school. You need to know whether it's bullying, drugs, all that type of thing. You need to be able to discuss things like that as a family (Senga).

The 'family meal' is here perceived to constitute a time for communication and a place where children's difficulties at school or elsewhere can be confronted, monitored and/or controlled, as well as the means through which future adult identities are formulated. In many accounts, participants' memories also made reference to the impact of gendered routines, at work and in the home, on past and present food practices: *when we used to have a meal [mum] used to shout us all down [...] so in a way it's like a tradition. I've never known anything different* (Janice/Family/married/two children). The dinner table was also then the key site of communication for several of our family interviewees, and in a similar vein to manager and participant narratives, nostalgia played a part in family participants' views about present-day and potential future family eating practices:

> When I got home from work, a meal would always be ready, it might be, I don't know, stew, or it might be a roast dinner, but we always sat down, yeah...well it was me mum and me sister not

necessarily always me dad, because he'd not finished work till late...and that's why I say we want to make sure that we do that with Yale [...] it's family, you know, communication...and especially when the children get older, it's a time to talk about the day, if they've got any problem. I just think you know, 'cause you're all sat, sat down as a family. (Christine/Family/married/one child).

It was the case that the family meal was pursued by several participants as a means of sustaining family togetherness and the continuity of family relationships (Green forthcoming), as children's changing needs and wants (Lawler 1999) and their pursuit of independence began to impact on the dynamics of family life and mother/child relationships:

It's probably the only time that we do actually sort of all have half an hour together 'cause having a teenage girl is sort of, 'I'm going upstairs, I'm listening to me music'...t'little lad, he's 11, and he's sort of, 'I'm going to play football now mum'...and I make sure that like if there's only one time that we come together, it is at a mealtime (Janice/married/two children).

Some childhood memories were painful rather than pleasant, associating food practices with lack of care, feelings of rejection and incidences of violence. This could provide a strong impetus to do things differently in adult life. Paul and Toni for example, a married couple with two children whom we interviewed together, were committed to giving their own children very different childhood experiences from their own. Providing healthy food and eating together around the dining table was the benchmark by which they could measure their 'good' parenting practices:

She [mother] used to make me go out to a farmer's field and pinch sprout and what have you...I hated it. Hated pinching. [Meals] were pretty regular but bit boring...used to sit and eat quietly. There was no conversation, nothing...the most time we ever talked is when they were shouting at me...and hitting me with a blue leather strap, which I can remember (Paul).

I don't want the kids going through what we went through. Eh we want them to be healthy. We don't want then to think, 'I'm hungry I, I got to pinch food', or, 'I'm hungry eh or I'm, oh I'm filling my face'...we do control their diets a lot. We, we don't want them to have the same problems as what we, we've had obviously with the weight gain and stuff like that (Toni).

For some interviewees, on the other hand, the practicalities of daily life were articulated as militating against families being able to eat together. Indeed, it was often the managers and practitioners who acknowledged that balancing work and family commitments led to compromises in their own lives, and departing from the advice that they relayed to their clients:

> I was very much brought up...it was always meat and two veg... and it was the main meal of the day. [....] But when I came back to work full-time [...] I suddenly had to make a decision. I'm getting back from work at five and the kids are home from school, they've already been in the fridge because they are waiting for me to come in and I was not in and therefore I use things that quicken the process. Because we were geared around a time when we all tried to eat at a certain time, so I notice that change in myself...I used to bake but I don't now, I go to Sainsbury's and find something that meets the need and I have to balance out my time (Jess/Manager/Children's Centre).

> Thinking about when I was young, we had like three meals a day, your breakfast, your lunch and your tea. It just doesn't seem to be like that anymore...we've got this snacking culture (Nadine/Manager/Oral Health Promotion).

In the present-day material world, where eating around a table is not always possible, because of time constraints, lack of furniture/space, shift-work, changing family dynamics and so on, families exercised other ways of communicating and being together that they regarded as equally meaningful. Vaughan for instance told us he *used to sit down on't floor or sit on t'settee wi' [the children] and talk to them while they were eating [...] or watch a DVD*. The 'ideal world' perhaps evokes recollections of the *idea* of family, and a yearning for times past, either real or imagined. The pursuit of the family meal thus contains a mythical quality that seemed somewhat at odds with its reality, for example, as Andrea, a partnered mother of four told us, *I want to maintain it, eh, family eating and with us sat round, because it's good and **it's how it should be*** but later added that if she allowed her children to *eat Sunday dinner watching telly, they'd eat it up and I wouldn't have the arguments*. In her discussion of celebrity chef Nigella Lawson, Joanne Hollows (2003a: 193) comments that Lawson draws on 'micro-narratives of matrilineal relations in which both lived and imagined experiences are intertwined with emotions that are a source of comfort in the present'. In our data, nostalgia for a real or imagined past clearly played a part in participants' understandings of the 'healthy family'.

The discussion of our data so far has highlighted how poverty impacts on a family's ability to make healthy choices and how, within healthy eating interventions, particular messages are being relayed that equate the 'ideal' family with healthy eating practices. Women are at the forefront of these messages, either in their delivery or their receipt, and we now explore the relationship between family, food and gender.

Family, food and gender

> *'The decisions made in the supermarket have an impact on the rest of the family'* (Belinda/Manager/PCT).

Public health policy is underpinned by the notion that 'good' parents give their children healthy food. The gender composition of our study cohort (56 women:9 men) highlights how the term 'parent', which is currently utilised across policy documentation and other legislation relating to children, young people and family, masks the fact that the 'parent' in question is usually the mother. It is also the case that the areas of practice and management we were addressing are dominated by women staff numerically (more senior managerial and policy domains remain dominated by men). That women prioritise care for others over themselves is well-documented (Charles and Kerr 1988; DeVault 1991; Dowler and Calvert 1995; Finch and Groves 1983; Hollows 2003a; Murcott 1983; Ribbens McCarthy *et al.* 2003; Sevenhuijsen 1998; Williams 2001). As Christina Hughes (2002: 107) comments regarding gendered caring practices, 'research in this field has made explicit that it is women who undertake and are perceived to be mainly responsible for the physical and emotional work of care giving'. Caring for the family is associated with domestic and intimate relationships – private forms of caring that are enacted by women in the home – for partners; for children; for elderly parents and so on. In this account a woman is expected to put the needs/demands of others in her family before her own needs. This underlies notions of the 'good mother' (Silva 2000; Silva and Smart 1999) and in turn acts as affirmation of the caring female self (Ribbens McCarthy *et al.* 2003). The same patterns extend into the realm of paid work, where women undertake the majority of caring roles – for example, nursing, teaching young children and community-based health work. As Marilyn Poole and Dallas Isaacs (1997: 531) state 'women are seen as the most appropriate carers both at home and in the workplace'. It was to mothers that our manager and practitioner interviewees usually directed their interventions:

> What we are trying to do is to go through the woman...to get to the family and that's why you have to look at it...and say 'who has the responsibility, who is the main person responsible for managing the budget, for doing the shopping?' (Jess/Manager/Children's Centre).

> To give women more confidence about buying, preparing, erm, serving up appropriate food that their family would eat, that's what you'd really love to happen, erm, erm, I think, and, and carry on doing that, you know, have that embedded in, you know, into their lives (Anna/Practitioner/Community Food Worker).

As we outlined earlier, in many of our manager and practitioner accounts, a successful intervention was viewed as one in which a family's eating behaviours were seen to change. There is then a clear purpose to the healthy eating interventions Jess and Anna, as well as other practitioners and managers oversee: women need to be given the confidence to buy and cook appropriately healthy food for their families; these practices need to become part of their everyday lives. These messages were reinforced regardless of the amenities available in the locality where the intervention was implemented.

Our interviews with senior managers also reflected the ways in which current policy discourses tend to address the individual consumer and 'the community' rather more explicitly than the family. For many, 'family' seemed to remain a taken-for-granted term: *we do a lot less work with families as such, but we do work with individuals, and that impacts on families, and obviously the outcomes for those individuals are affected by their families* (Sharon). As a community dietician dealing with overweight and obesity in adults, Sharon's work was focused on one-to-one consultations with clients. In this instance, as in the majority of examples given by our interviewees, the 'individual' she worked with was the mother, who was thus charged with the task of changing her family's eating practices in order to address her own health needs. However, and as Sandra implies below, returning home with a diet plan or other food-related information might not, in some instances, be as effective as a public health worker might wish:

> I know for, em, most women that, whatever culture, that the family will take priority, and rightly so, I'm not saying that's wrong. But from being in a position in the class where they can just really focus in on their work and their thoughts and thinking new thoughts and writing that down and creating things and then going away and possibly wanting to continue with that, then there's tensions back in the home where they have to then cook the meals and see to the kids and have the food on the table for the husband and as I say, that's across the board (Sandra/Manager/Community Development and Health).

Women managers' and practitioners' ways of thinking about feeding their own families were also brought into the public kitchen space and incorporated into their working practices. It was often the case, for example, that memories of 'being mothered' impacted on the way that women approached their work in the community: *my mother is a very caring mother and thought that if you had a lot to eat, that was good, you know...she was looking after me...food was love* (Rita). Rita interpreted her mother's giving of food as love – but there was also an element of moving on in her and many other participants' narratives; of changing food practices from those of her upbringing towards those of the contemporary 'expert' voice. Evidently, through her work and training as a Food Advisor, Rita was changing the way in which she thought about food herself; less food or more of the 'right foods' were interpreted by her as love and care. Feeding the family the 'right' food was a common thread throughout our data and, we suggest, is currently symbolic of women's successful caring practices – of getting motherhood 'right'. This was clear in Linda's account of her own food-related practices in the home:

> I take meals out of the [freezer] it's no different to taking out some of the ready meals, it's just I made it myself and froze it, so really doesn't, it does take a bit extra time, of course it does, but it's worth it, that's my personal...you know what you're feeding your family (Linda).

Most interviewees' accounts demonstrated that women continued to be perceived as responsible for care in relation to food in the family, despite the increase in women's workplace participation. In some accounts, women's paid work outside the home emerged as a site of contestation: *you're in this conflict…I want to stay at home but equally I am being told to be part of the workforce, women have chained themselves to railings to put me where I am today* (Jess). This kind of tension was often expressed through a discourse of women's assumed responsibilities for care:

> I still think that women are still seen as the nurturer and the preparer…of the food and, speaking for myself again, the people that I talk to who are working women with young babies who have to work because they need to maintain their lifestyle, would say, 'I would be very happy to stay at home and to prepare meals' (Rita).

> [My husband's] never, never cooked, never…I've always said to him, much rather him to make me tea one night than buy me anything, you know? 'cause I think it's, it's same with anything, if you've gotta do it all the time…Things always taste better, don't they, when someone else does it…especially like 'cause I work on Thursday and Friday, you see, I mean, I only work till 4 o'clock anyway, but…I then come home and obviously I want to see [my baby] but I still gotta make tea as well (Gail/Family/partnered/one child).

To summarise, interviews with managers, practitioners and family members showed that women continued to be held (and often to hold themselves) responsible for the health and well-being of their families. Although there were a few exceptions, our findings indicated little movement in the gendered division of labour within the home: gendered patterns of care, in relation to families and food, remained intact.

Concluding discussion

In concluding this chapter, we would like to emphasise two main points. First, *our study suggests that current 'healthy eating' interventions are both fragile and ambiguous.* They are fragile because they are not securely staffed or funded; the resources allocated to them simply do not match the level of concern that is expressed publicly in government policy and in media discourses about food and health. They are ambiguous because the practitioners who deliver the various programmes, and the individuals who attend them, have very diverse agendas and expectations. For some in both categories, the main emphasis is not directly on food at all, but on creating or strengthening social networks, particularly for women. There is a relationship between this and the goal of improving diet and health, since 'empowered' women are often assumed by policy-makers and practitioners to be in a better position to overcome disadvantage and to make 'healthy' food choices, for themselves and for their families. But as Lawrence (2008) has pointed out most recently – echoing a long series of earlier studies – patterns of food consumption are overwhelmingly shaped by poverty and social class. Leaving aside for a moment the related issue of education, families who live on benefits or on low incomes, on a long-term basis, do not have the resources to sustain a healthy diet and often live in areas without easy access to good, affordable food. Even if healthy eating interventions were to recruit large numbers of participants with an explicit desire to learn about food and health – and our study does not suggest that this has been happening – families on low incomes cannot readily translate healthy eating information into shopping trolleys filled with fresh fruit and vegetables. Rather, as our respondents made clear, the trolleys are more likely to contain bargain foodstuffs that often fall into 'unhealthy' categories but deliver calories more cheaply than higher-quality items. In addition, changes to family food practices can bring risk and uncertainty; uneaten food, for example, results not only in waste, but also in hungry children. While the practitioners who deliver 'Cook and Eat' classes often acknowledge this context, they are not equipped to change it. We are thus in agreement with Dowler and Caraher (2003: 57) who argue that interventions such as those we have investigated cannot 'address longer-term changes needed in economic structures or food access, and they can pose challenges to social justice in that the realities of life lived on a low income, faced on a daily basis by diverse households, are by-passed in favour of quick solutions'.

Second, *recent healthy eating interventions constitute a form of 'public kitchen', in which women's 'care' practices and parenting practices are under particular scrutiny.* We have noted that current government policies and interventions on food and health are addressed to 'responsible citizens', who are expected to take sensible steps to look after themselves. In practice, the responsible citizen who is made visible through participation in this 'public kitchen' is almost always the mother, charged with introducing, sustaining and sometimes 'displaying' healthy eating routines for herself and for the rest of the household. There is a link here with the notion of 'displaying' family to powerful observers, developed by Finch (2007). The mother who departs from the approved pathway can encounter strong public censure, as the 'junk food mums' in Rawmarsh found in 2006, when they were pilloried in the press for appearing to defy a new school healthy-eating policy by passing burgers and sandwiches through the school fence to their children at lunchtime. A 'healthy family', then, is still one that relies on women's caring labour in substantial and familiar ways, often summed up with reference to childhood memories. Whether these memories are benign or painful, the point of reference is often the idealised 'family meal' around the dining table, made possible by the mother's presence.

In the public kitchen of healthy eating interventions, *family forms* are acknowledged by all parties to be flexible, encompassing reconfigurations, active fathers and increased employment levels among women. Indeed, current government family policy (supported by tax and benefits structures) places a strong emphasis on paid employment as intrinsic to being a 'good parent'. At the same time, dominant policy and practitioner views of healthy *family practices* still emphasise routines and expectations that have women's domestic and emotional labour at their core. Recent 'healthy eating' interventions reflect this gendered emphasis, in their uneasy mix of messages about 'empowerment' for women and nostalgic references to an idealised past. Both professional and lay accounts illustrate the tensions that exist between these implicit models of 'healthy family' and the pressures and complexities of daily life, both for families struggling to make ends meet and for the often harassed professionals who deliver 'healthy eating' programmes.

12
Institutional Dining Rooms: Food Ideologies and the Making of a Person

Oscar Forero, Katie Ellis, Alan Metcalfe and Rebecca Brown

Introduction

While most of the preceding chapters have focused on the domestic setting of family eating, this chapter examines three different contexts where people eat in institutional settings associated with schools, voluntary associations and homeless centres. Examining the food ideologies and practices associated with these institutional environments, we argue, sheds light on the normative assumptions involved in 'feeding the family'.

Institutional Dining Rooms (IDRs) are not only about the provision of food and the arrangements of amenities for their consumption, they are also platforms for the socio-cultural reproduction of food values, as they provide space for creating, re-creating, transforming and reproducing values associated with food provision and consumption. In this chapter it is argued that by documenting the way dining rooms are organised, and by examining the interactions of staff and user-clients, it is possible to better understand what different social actors think of the food provided, what effect they think such foods will have on their health and well-being, and what are the criteria for considering the appropriateness of foods offered. All of these are essential components of 'food ideologies' (Eckestein 1980). This chapter presents a comparative analysis of three different IDR settings in England examining the performances of social actors in each of them, identifying the food ideologies reflected in such settings and performances.

The investigation follows Foucault's perspective that power is not exercised exclusively by the State over a population in a unidirectional way, but that there are multiple specialists and experts advising and intervening in the production and reproduction of the governmentality under which a population is apparently self-governed (Foucault 1979b; Dean 1999). By deconstructing the seemingly routine and unimportant meal practices in different IDRs, and by tracing the fluxes of power involved and their effects on the foodways of user-clients, this investigation attempts to advance the critique of governmentality in IDRs.

In order to operate, IDRs need organisational arrangements, assuring compliance with complex regulations that are said to ensure the safety of user-clients. Sometimes food providers complain of regulations being too strenuous or excessive, but nutritionists and government argue that strong regulatory frameworks are needed in order to safeguard the rights of 'vulnerable' population segments such as school pupils (SMRP 2005), homeless people (Evans and Dowler 1999) and diasporic émigrés (Anderson and Rogaly 2005) – all three groups attending IDR settings included in this comparative study.

Many user-clients of IDRs are considered to be vulnerable or at risk. On the one hand, there are some user-clients who require institutional arrangements to facilitate access and social interaction within the IDRs due to their special needs or disabilities. Other user-clients may be temporarily disabled, recovering from accident or illness, or deemed to be not yet fully capable. This incapacity was levelled not just at the user-clients themselves. In each case, their presence was also connected to imagined families. The reference to 'failing families' is most apparent in those who find themselves in the homeless centre; in the schools, it is considered that some families cannot be entirely trusted to provide appropriate food and/or that others need support to provide such food; while in both the homeless centre and the Ukrainian club the IDRs are places where 'fictive kin' are re-created within 'family-like environments'. Although family is imagined and played out in multiple ways, the creation and re-creation of family always involves 'foodways': the ways food is obtained, prepared, served, consumed and what it means for each individual, for the 'fictive family' and for the group or community as a whole. Recognising the relationship between dining halls and families provides a critical perspective on the changes that are ongoing in food and family-life.

On the other hand, food scientists have argued that a risk situation does not arrive solely because of lack of care on the part of the provider but also as a result of user-clients' behaviour and culture (Redmond and Griffith 2003). Such reasoning is at the core of a long running debate about the responsibility of supermarkets and advertising industry in imprinting or altering children's food habits (Brody *et al.* 1981; Balfour-Jeffrey *et al.* 1982).

The assumption that risk situations in food consumption are mainly set off by user-clients themselves has been instrumental in policy-making. Service providers' expressions of outrage at what they consider unacceptable behaviour (Lupton 1993), make use of risk discourses to emphasise the need to discipline or at least invigilate user-clients. Used in this way, risk discourse seems to echo the 'deserving poor' discourse, which has influenced the policy for feeding the poor in Britain, the United States and other pioneering industrialisation countries (Mead 1997).

There are many expressions of contested ideologies at play when service providers and user-clients (come together and) perform in IDRs. Politicians, civil servants, supermarket chain managers, educators, directors of charities and NGOs, restaurateurs and other stakeholders know that through the provision of food and catering services IDRs not only influence nutritional intake, they also promote products and services, instruct and educate user-clients (DoH 1999). In the case of children and teenagers, although personal agency is recognised, it is argued that peer interaction in spaces such as IDRs influences their food habits (Giddens, 1999) and that such influence has long lasting effects throughout the individuals' lives (Warde 1997; Wills 2002). This chapter advances the debate about the instrumentality of IDRs in governmentality by examining how food ideologies are expressed and negotiated within and in relation to the IDRs observed.

To operate effectively, IDRs need to display a credible discourse about their knowledge of effects of the services provided in the life and well-being of their user-clients. Thus IDR managers need to maintain a system for gathering information about user-clients and, depending upon users' capacity and competence (as defined by government regulations), they need to monitor the activities and behaviour of user-clients as well. Another justification for developing such systems of surveillance is that supervision and monitoring are necessary to advance the project of enabling and empowering user-clients. In fact the Food Standards Agency (FSA) has commissioned Health Protection Scotland (HPS) to deliver the UK Food Surveillance System within a three-year period (September 2008).

IDRs' government bodies need to deal with the issue of demonstrating to varied stakeholders, including civil servants and health and safety officers, that they are effectively directing user-clients to governmental power. However, IDR's government bodies are not simple sociocultural devices of control and discipline; they are enacted to protect the interests of the user-clients. The descriptions provided in this study show how such attempts on the part of IDRs' government bodies are contested, negotiated or transformed through social interaction within IDR spaces in variant ways. This 'governmentality' of IDRs creates space for multiplicity and multi-directionality of power fluxes that travel and circulate through all of the social actors performing within and about it. IDRs are invested with certain causal powers within programmes and projects for the government of users, such power is never total or unidirectional and thus, paraphrasing Huxley (2007: 200), IDRs become 'unstable, heterogeneous, assemblages of technologies of rule'.

The comparative analysis reported in this chapter draws on four projects each of which had its own aims, methodology and timetable. This posed special challenges for analytical work, as all researchers involved needed to be aware of similarities and differences in the collection and generation of data. However, all studies encompassed ethnographic work and privileged reflectivity over simple text mining. Becky Brown explored the homeless centre, Katie Ellis four secondary schools, Oscar Forero the Ukrainian Club and Alan Metcalfe four primary schools. The following section outlines these institutional settings, discusses social actors' performances and reveals contested food ideologies. The last section is composed of recommendations and concluding remarks.

Institutional settings and food ideologies

The primary schools

As the 'Men, Children and Food' Project explored food meanings and practices of children and men, it entailed multiple methods including interviewing approximately ten fathers in each area plus arts activities and photo-elicitation with the children. The project examined four primary schools in three areas: Christopher St. an inner city school, Vale Primary a school in a former coal mining village and Netherhope and Upperhope, two small schools in rural Lancashire. In comparison with the other two areas, Christopher St. was much more mixed in terms of ethnicity, religion, family and household organisation, families' income and education, though about 60 to 70% pupils were British Asian (Pakistani and Bangladeshi). The other two areas were relatively homogeneous in terms of ethnic origin and cultural diversity, the majority of pupils were white and British, but different in relation to class; the second area was generally inhabited by poorer and more working-class families, whilst the third area was composed of wealthier, better educated, middle-class families.

In all of the schools the children had lunch/dinner at about 12–12.30 and they had about 50 minutes lunchtime. They could either eat a hot school meal, bring a packed lunch or a few, mainly in Christopher St., went home. No money was exchanged in the dining hall as all food had, in theory, been paid for already; hence there was no marked distinction between those who were on free school meals and those who were not. The school canteens offered some menu options to children; for instance, they could often choose between two hot meals, a sandwich and a jacket potato. However, differences in each school's facilities and organisational arrangements often limited the menu: this was particularly pertinent at Christopher St., where, with no kitchen, the food was brought in about five minutes before being served, the range appeared more limited, there was no space to lay out salads, jacket potatoes or sandwiches, thus fewer of them were displayed and served.

Only limited choices were made once in the dinner queue as children had already chosen their meal that morning and appropriate numbers had then been cooked or ordered in. While 'dinner ladies' ensured the children ate what they had ordered, some negotiation took place once in the dining halls; e.g. over how to combine the hot food offered, which vegetables to accompany the main dish or which sandwich to have. This differed by school, thus in Netherhope it was not uncommon for children to have half and half – say half curry and rice and a smaller slice of pizza.

There was little discussion between senior management and lunchtime supervisors about how children were expected to behave within the dining hall. Consequently perhaps, there were different ideas and practices. This was most obvious in Vale school where many of the dinner ladies were concerned about food going to waste, about the effects of food (or the lack of it) on children, and what proper manners the pupils ought to learn. In contrast, the head, while not disagreeing with these concerns, spoke about how dinner time was a period of freedom for the children, a time away from the rigours of school discipline. In contrast, lunchtime supervisors would often monitor what children had eaten, preventing those who had not eaten enough from returning their plate and leaving to play, imploring them to try some more. This links to a frustration often felt by them, that they would do this better if they could sit with the children. They often said they could offer better guidance and advice if organisational settings were different and let know their opinion that children weren't really learning how to eat properly. The head teacher, though, was more concerned with overall achievable aims of ensuring children could eat in a reasonable environment and timely fashion, though she too was concerned with manners and eating properly but at a more basic level. Just getting children to sit down to eat with cutlery was a big task as, she claimed, many often did not do this at home.

In Vale and Christopher St. one or two teachers did eat with the children; usually the teachers of the youngest classes. They found this a time where they could talk with and get to know children outside the structures of the classroom. They also believed it to be an effective pedagogic strategy, as the children could model their behaviour, they could monitor how children ate and encourage them at the same time. This could not occur in the two rural schools as space was very limited. Anyway, as the children get older, teachers are less inclined to enter the dining room, only using it as a thoroughfare, as in Vale.

Although surveillance systems were in place, there is little chance in the three larger schools especially for the dinner ladies or anyone else to monitor all children and ensure they eat everything or that they 'eat properly'. Realising this situation, children develop strategies to work the system. Often a cook or server could be seen encouraging children to try some foods, like salad, broccoli or anything they would not choose of their own volition. But in this negotiation servers or cooks often accede to some of the wishes of the children, giving them limited amounts of disliked or unwanted foods, or sometimes more of a preferred item to make up for the refusal of another. Playing on this capacity to negotiate they try, and sometimes succeed, in obtaining only the foods they want. Even then this does not mean they will eat what is on their plates. Once sat down they will then eat as they see fit, sometimes pudding first (although rarely), sometimes nothing but pudding, sometimes only certain components of a meal, such as only the meat or only the vegetables of the meat and veg. They can often get away with eating little of any food if they don't like it or don't like the look of it. Though they may be sent back to try some more, it is difficult for any supervisor to ensure this is done.

Dining rooms in secondary schools

The 'Children as Family Participants' project focused on four secondary schools in diverse areas of South Yorkshire. The schools selected were: a deprived inner city school, an affluent suburban school, a multi-ethnic school and a rural school. The researcher conducted participant observations in children's leisure spaces in each of these schools. Working with one class from year seven in each school, the researcher conducted interviews with pupils in pairs during school time and then conducted further interviews with a selection of the same children in their own homes.

All schools had a set time period for lunch, usually 40 to 60 minutes. In three of the four schools, the lunch break was divided into sittings. These sittings usually rotated over the school term, meaning that everybody had a chance to be first in the dining room and hence choose from the 'best food'. Lunchtime was a noisy affair in all of the secondary schools studied, beginning with the piercing ring of a school bell. Immediately after, children appeared from everywhere, usually running (or at least speed marching when being monitored) to be at the front of the lunch queue. In all four schools physical queuing aids had been erected to keep the children in a straight line and presumably to stop other children from 'pushing in'.

All four schools organised their canteens in a café style format where students were able to purchase food of their choosing from the range available from a hot food hatch, a sandwich bar, pasta bar or salad bar. The 'meal deal' option is designed to be nutritionally balanced to ensure that every meal provides a portion of meat, a form of carbohydrate and a vegetable (i.e. lasagne with vegetables or salad), the 'deal' also includes a pudding and costs £1.70.

There are different forms of surveillance in the dining room, the most obvious being the gaze of the dinner ladies who storm around and holler at young people for eating too slowly or for talking too loudly. This monitoring is financially driven and is focused to ensure efficiency in serving all user-clients during lunchtime and does not involve making sure that young people 'eat properly' or that they eat 'decent food'. Sociable eating did seem to be important to young people, however due to limited seating, staff did not encourage this and instead marched around looking for people to eject should they have finished eating and be using the dining room only to 'chat' to friends.

As dinner ladies have been a ubiquitous presence in these IDRs one may think they would be encouraged to play a greater role in helping to shape young people's future eating habits. This is not the case and dinner ladies do not see it as their role to comment on food choices made by the children in their care. However, in some cases, as we will describe below, coordinated action between staff and teachers has been undertaken for purposes of surveillance and compliance with regulations.

When institutional settings do not encourage coordination or at least clarification of staff and teachers' roles and performances at the IDR space, frictions between them are bound to happen and in all schools there was a tension between teachers and dinner ladies. Most teachers argued that since they are not paid to cover lunchtimes, it was not their responsibility to supervise student behaviour during lunchtime. The dinner ladies argued that they were paid to serve food and not to supervise children, thus it should be the teachers' responsibility to do so.

In the deprived inner city school, teachers had a rota and were required to supervise one lunchtime per week. Rather than making a sociable time for pupils and teachers to communicate with one another, this strategy only served in making lunchtime more stressful as teachers were anxious to wind up their lunch duties in time to start their afternoon classes.

Whilst the formal structure of lunchtime within each of the four schools was similar, the context (including organisation particulars) and environment (including ambient infrastructure) were not, meaning that the 'atmosphere' in the four schools was very different. For instance, in the smallest school (with only 500 pupils) came reduced anonymity. In this school the children seemed younger and were organised and supervised more closely. Children were not allowed outside of the school grounds during lunchtime and therefore in comparison to the other schools, take up of school dinners was the highest.

The affluent suburban school had approximately 1000 pupils. Despite this, it was also the most 'relaxed' of all the schools and children were mostly free to eat where they liked and were not constrained to strict sittings. The lack of enforced structure in this school meant that children did not seem as hurried to get into or to leave the dining room; as a result, and in comparison to the other schools, lunchtime seemed more sociable and peaceful. As food was permitted to leave the dining room, many of the children chose not to eat in the dining hall and instead, many congregated in the school hall sitting on chairs in circles of eight or more. During participant observations it was noted that behaviour was generally good in the absence of visible strict supervision.

The deprived inner city school included in the study had received negative attention locally, and some stakeholders referred to it as 'a failing school'. The reaction of government body has been a move to tough supervision. Children were under tight scrutiny, as both teachers and dinner ladies were on a constant look out for bad behaviour and the police were in attendance at the school most days. Here lunchtime felt rushed and uncomfortable and seemed to be dominated by shouting grownups. CCTV cameras were installed and made visible all around the school. It was probably expected that in this manner surges of violence would be controlled and that perhaps a more suitable environment for teaching and learning will be realised. However the overall effect of such a tight system of surveillance is not yet clear. The CCTV cameras had immediate impact on teachers, staff and students in unexpected ways, i.e. whilst before the CCTV cameras were installed school staff were prompt to react to violence surges, after cameras were installed they were not willing to intervene in breaking up fights, as they could be caught on camera and personally prosecuted. Children on their part felt intimidated and socially coerced and most of them spent lunchtime at the local chip shop instead of in school.

In the multi-ethnic school there had previously been a problem of children leaving school premises at lunchtime and not coming back. To combat this problem the school altered their lunchtime to 20 minute shifts so that children would literally only have time to eat before class started again. To make up for the shortened break time, this school finished earlier than the others.

The 'Children as Family Participants' project started, in the months before 'healthy schools' came into practice. Even so, at the time of the research, the rural school had made their own moves to initiate healthy eating within school. The head teacher, disappointed with the quality of school food provision, took a radical move and took over financial and managerial responsibility for the school kitchens. He then granted the school cook almost absolute control over the food served. With this power invested in her, the school cook was able to tailor her menu to suit children's taste and hence the food at this school was by far the most well received of all the other schools. Underpowered school cooks in the other three schools had to prepare foods regardless of client-users' taste or their own consideration. This policy makes no sense in terms of economics or child nutrition and erodes social capital as school cooks are demoralised by children's reactions to the foods offered.

There were many factors unconsidered when launching the 'healthy schools' agenda, some of them crucial for supporting the development of social capital. The rejection of the new 'healthy' food, which is more time consuming to prepare, left cooks feeling disheartened and undervalued, with many considering leaving the job altogether. Some pupils were similarly critical of the programme:

Child: Are you from Healthy Schools?
Interviewer: No, why do you ask?
Child: I wish you were because the food here's horrible and if you were then you could change it

Whilst some children did not welcome the influx of 'healthy' foods, and one boy expressed *'we might as well be rabbits'*; it should be noted that some children did consider the healthy schools agenda to be beneficial as they acknowledged that 'other' children may need guidance:

> If like you're a little kid [and you get fat] then it's not really your fault because like you don't know what you're eating you'll just eat what you're given you don't realise that if you eat that you'll get fat.

Although accepting the need for guidance, children also reclaim 'agency'. Despite the media frenzy, the surveillance systems and all policies aimed at redirecting children's eating habits, our data suggest that most children in secondary schools simply do not eat the 'healthy balanced meal' from which such policies were erected. Almost all of the young people observed in the four schools observed bought pizza, pasta, sandwiches, cookies or muffins on a daily basis and had no desire to purchase the healthy 'meal deal' offered to them. Importantly for this discussion on children's agency are children's claims of dining rooms not offering real choice. Children stated that although they ate pasta every day, this was not because they enjoyed it, rather that it was the best option amongst a series of other bad options:

> It's always cold and you don't get enough sauce.
> I was kind of confused because everyone said it didn't taste very nice but everyone bought it anyway.

It is sometimes assumed that effective implementation of government policy with respect to the foods offered in schools would make it possible for children to choose healthy foods. However, choices are always context specific, and vary in respect of financial and social capital of the children. Most children interviewed had only a limited daily amount of lunch money, therefore the price of the food was the main deciding factor whilst choosing their meal. So for instance, if children couldn't afford pasta AND sauce, which was £1.30, they often bought pasta without the sauce for 50p, so although a child's food of choice was plain pasta, this choice was heavily constrained by financial implications and did not reflect their true food preference.

The Ukrainian Club in Bradford

The 'Socio Historical Transmission and Food Values' project used ethnohistory (which in this case involved archive research and in-depth interviewing in the study of social and cultural processes), participatory action research (active involvement in the activities of the Ukrainian community in Bradford) and photo-journalism, among others methods. Participants in the project included male and female community members of all generations since the arrival of post-war immigrants until now.

To better understand discourses and performance currently occurring in the 'dining hall' of the Ukrainian Club in Bradford it is necessary to refer briefly to its history. At the end of World War II, Ukrainian soldiers fighting with the Nazis surrendered to the British; controversially, in 1948 they were brought to Britain and released as part of the European Volunteer Worker scheme (Smith *et al.* 1998; Cesarani 2001; Hrycyszyn 2002). By 1951 there were around 34,000 Ukrainians in Britain. The majority of migrants were not fluent in English and had little education. They had limited incomes and usually shared rented accommodation as recalled by Bradford primary settlers (PS: M, WG; SS: B0005, B0016, B0133) . They worked together in the formation of the Association of Ukrainians in Britain (*Soyuz Ukrayintsiv Velikoyi Britaniyi*: SUB). The Bradford SUB branch purchased a former Victorian estate in 1961 where they have remained until today. They constructed a large auditorium, which is where almost all important events of the Ukrainian diasporic community had taken place. The auditorium serves as a dining hall where Wednesdays' lunch currently takes place.

The auditorium design and functionality reflect members' thinking and aspirations at the time. The way they saw it their stay in England was temporary and they would return to an independent Ukraine freed from Soviet influences in a foreseeable future (PS: WGI; SS: B0018). Members of the Bradford SUB were often active in the Captive Nations' Society, the Ukrainian Information Services and other anti-soviet groups (SS: B003, B005, B0016, B0018).[1] Their efforts were directed towards influencing 'international politics' and preparing their families for the return to the 'fatherland' or 'father's country' (SS: B003, B0008, B0016). Women in particular organised the logistics of fund raising events, which usually included art functions and dinners (PS: WGI; SS: B005).

The auditorium may be perfect for delivering political speeches but it is inappropriate for hosting a dancing company or a theatre function. In an interview, the founder of the Bradford born 'Cossack Brothers' argued that such inappropriateness was due to the characteristic stubbornness of 'first generation Ukrainians':

> They won't listen, they have their own ideas and there is no way you can tell them how to do anything and they never go out for

advice to people who should know better or do know better (SS: B0133).

This stubbornness characterising the aging generation of post-war émigrés is something that at times causes anxiety for their children, who currently struggle to convince aging parents and grandparents to accept help and request the government support they are entitled to (PS:WGI). However, the majority of these aging Ukrainians feel that accepting such services would imply renouncing their political ideal of minimal if any State intervention on the life of citizens.

The committee running the Wednesday lunch-club is headed by a second generation Ukrainian woman, who is responsible for budgeting, purchases and payments. Cooking is done by three women, but a man helps with serving and cleaning. The club has a housekeeper, who as part of her payment arrangement must work in the kitchen on Wednesday's lunch. One of the women working in the kitchen is usually a volunteer; the other woman is paid monthly depending on her hours and other functions. There is also a volunteer who runs the Pub at SUB premises, which opens an hour before lunch and closes an hour after lunch. There are usually two volunteers helping serving food as well. All of the volunteers and staff are 'second generation Ukrainians'.

Some patterns in seating and serving arrangements at Wednesday's lunch were realised after the first three participant observation exercises. At about 10.30 all the eldest ladies are served tea and biscuits in the 'family room'; right after tea they begin choir rehearsal. The tea tray is then pushed farther down the corridor to the Pub where other people could also have tea or instant coffee and biscuits. Some of the elderly men go to the games' room situated at the side of the bar; some of them play pool, others play chess at one of the three chess tables and others take a domino set to one of the bar tables to play there.

A volunteer comes to direct the choir rehearsals with the elderly ladies in a small room called 'family room'. One of the women who comes for lunch volunteers to collect lunch payment; she sits right by the back entrance with a money box and a clients' list. To her right sits a group of women, who although first generation Ukrainian are younger than those in the choir. Exactly in the opposite side of the Pub, in the other corner, a group of four or five English women and an Austrian all widowed to Ukrainians (except for one, whose husband is still alive) sit together.

Once the choir finishes rehearsing the elderly women move into the dining hall, as some of them are disabled and others have difficulties walking, they sit at the table closest to the kitchen corridor and the main entrance. The tables at the left corner in front of the stage are generally occupied by couples who sit in groups of four or six per table; in front of them other women sit in groups and further up, closer to the stage, the widowed English ladies sit together. The tables at the right corner in front of the stage are generally occupied by a group of men, surviving founding members of the SUB, who tend to sit together as well.

After clients have been served, staff sit in the family room to have their lunch. Staff talk usually relates to forthcoming events that need to be planned, to news about elderly people going into hospital, to funerals (there were three funerals during the 2007 summer alone); although there is some chitchat as well. A subject mentioned several times was that of clients suggesting that they are doing a favour to staff and volunteers as they would not get government money if it wasn't for them attending Wednesday's lunch. This comment pains the administrator who is continuously struggling to keep a clean balance sheet and maintaining the one pound contribution of clients towards Wednesday's lunch.

Lunch has three courses. The entrance is always soup: lentils, vegetables, potatoes and leeks, minestrone and sometimes the always favourite beetroot soup, considered authentically Ukrainian. The main course varies in the same ways as Pub meals do; it could be sausages and mash potatoes and vegetables; or, ham, potatoes and vegetables. Favourite vegetables are cabbage and fried onions, which are though as of Ukrainian. 'Pasta', 'curries' and 'rice' are never served, as these foods are referred to as foreign by first generation Ukrainians who reject all 'foreign foods'.

In 2001 Bradford had the largest percentage of migrants from outside the European Union living in Yorkshire (CCSR 2006), the majority of them of Asian origin. Thus, it may come as a surprise that first generation Ukrainians reject curry and rice, archetypical Asian foods and highly popular in Bradford. However, the stories in which the Ukrainian community cemented their particularity may help explain first generation's taste. When they first arrived in Britain after the war Ukrainians considered themselves in transit and the majority of them were fierce nationalists and outspoken enemies of communist ideas and non-Christian beliefs. It was very important for them to remain uncontaminated by foreign cultures. Living in another country posed imminent risks for them and their families, more so in the multi-cultural environment of Bradford; thus foods produced, prepared or served by non-white non-Christians were surely looked on with suspicion.

The system of surveillance operating at the IDR SUB space is multi-directional. Clients are never left alone for long in any of the rooms of the club. Elderly and disabled people frequently need assistance and staff keep a watching eye and are prompt to provide assistance when needed. Staff encourage clients to confide in them, treating them with familiarity. Staff are usually well informed on the composition, changes and rites of passage of user-clients' families. User-clients on their part monitor the activities of staff, and feel they have the right to complain or question staff's attitude or behaviour. They would not allow Wednesday's lunch to take place in the dining hall if they felt it was not in their interest or the interest of the community as a whole.

By observing the procedures of affiliation to the SUB, the multi-directional character of this system of surveillance can be corroborated. Illegal immigrants cannot be affiliates as SUB members, but legitimate migrants are not immediately welcomed into the community either. Candidate affiliates need to be perceived as potential reproducers of a particular type of 'Ukrainian family'.

The homeless shelter

In-depth interviewing and participant observation were the favoured methods of data generation in the '(no) Family (no) Food' project, which investigated IDRs at a residential and resettlement hostel for the homeless.

The dining room at the hostel is located on the ground floor to one side of the building; it is accessed directly from the central reception area. Residents are on a full board basis which includes breakfast served between 8am and 9am, where they have a choice of a full 'English' breakfast and/or cereal. Evening meals are served between 4pm and 5pm. There is a choice of two main meals and a desert. Examples of main meals include tuna pasta bake, pies, burgers and mince and onions. Wednesday is healthy option day where there are no chips on the menu. Lots of the younger residents complain about this, while the older residents are much happier with that arrangement. The cook sees the healthier, more nutritious home-cooked meal as part of her attempt to better provide for the residents, who otherwise would only have the unhealthy 'options' to eat.

Weekends are slightly different. Breakfast is at the same time although a continental breakfast is served, and dinner is between 12 and 1pm instead of between 4pm and 5pm. Residents sometimes complain of this arrangement as they have a long gap between dinner on Saturday and breakfast on Sunday.

The dining hall has seven tables seating two to three people around the edge, two tables in the centre seating approximately six people and one extra table seating approximately four people. Seating arrangements are subject to change as the dining hall fills and residents move the table's chairs to enable themselves to sit in friendship groups. Tables are laid with a table cloth, a small vase with artificial flowers and salt and pepper shakers.

The food is served from a hatch at the far side of the dining hall, with a queue forming around the edge. Residents are responsible for collecting their food and returning their plates and cutlery afterwards. However there are two residents, Eric (aged 72) and Harry (aged 78) who are exempted from this duty. Staff find it difficult to explain why these residents are treated differently; but the fact is that they have been at the hostel for many years, have a certain status within the hostel and have been given permission by Social Services to stay there forever. Project workers serve Eric and Harry's food to their table so they do not have to queue. This is especially odd given that it was revealed in their interviews that Eric would much rather collect his and Harry's food because this gives him a sense of independence.

A surveillance system is made visible at the hostel; all parts of the building are covered by comprehensive CCTV, including the dining hall. Behaviour of user-clients and consumption of the foods provided are also visibly monitored by staff.

> Project Worker PW01: …If people are not eating as well, they're then kept an eye on. They're marked off on a sheet. One is to check that people are not coming back again and again. Mainly that's because of money, but also to check that people are actually eating. There has been people coming here and they do not want to eat. But that is their choice. As they are eating somewhere else, that's fine. Because some go out all day and don't come back for 4pm. For example, two pensioners, they get and have their lunch and their sandwiches about 7:30. One of them goes out all day anyway, but spends all day in cafes, so I am sure he is well fed. And then, just to make sure that they are always catered for, basically. If someone is not eating, it is always addressed.

Residents of the same nationality also tend to sit together:

> PW02: a couple of them do. One of the pensioners, one of the ones who does not get served, he always sits at the same spot. Erm…

always right at the far of the end of the dining room. Erm...and then, with in terms of who people sit with, they do tend to sit with the same people, because it is like their own little group, isn't it? That sort of own little gangs of mates and things. So they do tend to sit together.
Interviewer: ok
PW02: like we have got a lot of people at the moment. Erm...I think they are Eritrean they all sit together because they speak the same language. And so yes, they do...And then at one point, a couple of months ago, we had four Iranian people as well; they all used to sit together.
I: did they have known each other before they came here?
PW02: I don't think so, just linked by the language.

Because there is a continual turnover of residents, social cohesion is not easily achievable and although residents may form friendships with each other, these friendships are often fraught with difficulties and are often short lived.

Staff also use the dining room, and sit with the residents whilst eating. However some staff consider their break should be a time to have to themselves and so prefer not to use the dining room as they don't feel they are having a break whilst sitting there. There also seem to be ideological differences in food choice between residents and staff, with the staff preferring not to eat the 'stodge' that is served. When the staff are eating the food, their conversation is infused with ironic remarks suggesting that you have to be desperate to eat the food served.

Differences exist between young residents and older residents and the cook. Whilst the cook and the older residents agree that traditional foods, such 'meat and two veg', and 'mince and onions' are 'proper food', the younger ones just want burgers and chips. The cook is aware of the health risks associated with consuming fried food every day and that is the reason she introduced 'healthy Wednesday' as a time when she won't cook chips. The cook takes pride in her food and would prefer to provide 'good honest home cooking' even if it isn't always popular with all the residents. Tension arises between the two groups when different ideas about what food means and what effects food may have on their bodies are expressed. The cook on her part deploys risk discourse to justify changes in the menu served; by referring to the perceived vulnerability of the homeless who (as made obvious by their condition) may not know what's best for them.

Discussion, conclusions and recommendations

The primary school project findings suggest that despite apparatuses of control and discipline children are able to convey the message that they remain sufficiently free to eat what and how they like, within what is on offer. In this, the project found that children are not merely the subjects of systems of surveillance but that they act in terms of these processes and practices of discipline and control contesting authority in different ways, the eating of food being an obvious example.

The project documented the dining hall as a contested space with multiple social actors drawing on multiple discourses such as nutrition, efficiency, choice and civility, as they seek to affect what is served, how it is served and the manner in which it is eaten. Nutritional, economic efficiency and choice discourses have been incorporated in varied ways into the 'materialities' of the school, from meals served through seating arrangements and crockery to timetables. Yet despite this, there is limited scope, if not reluctance, by schools and government to consider 'school meals' as a pedagogic device for teaching food values and healthy eating, or in incorporating children into the production of food. This is not to say that such a pedagogy has not been an ideal in the past (Vernon 2005), and is something that has been opened up in some ways in recent policies, e.g. the Healthy Schools Initiative (see http://www.healthyschools.gov.uk/) and the Free Healthy School Meals System in Hull.

It also appeared that even though schools oversaw behaviour within the dining halls this could only ever be limited. By and large, children were left to choose what to eat and how to eat it, as if the fact that foods are served and consumed within school premises implies that foodways were considered as part of the pedagogic processes; when in truth this is done in a more incidental and informal way. Such findings seem to corroborate the initial hypothesis that food providers displace responsibilities from themselves to user-clients through risk discourse: risk situations, they assert, are the result of user-clients making bad choices.

The secondary school project also seems to corroborate that changes in discourse rather than effective measurable changes in children's food habits may suffice for school government bodies as proof of healthy food policy implementation. In the dining rooms of the secondary schools studied, all daily menus offered nutritionally balanced options, and implemented a significant reduction of 'unhealthy' options. However the removal of previously popular 'unhealthy' foods such as chips, has not encouraged children to opt for the healthier meal options, instead it has shifted their focus to other familiar foods, like pizza.

The project found that there are important stakeholders who feel undervalued and lacking opportunities to effectively contribute to the improvement of young people's diets; a situation that they consider was perhaps worsened after the launch of the rigid and formalised structure of the Healthy Schools campaign.

The two school projects documented a case in which the CCTV installed in a school had the unwelcome effect of intimidating staff and prompting children to spend their lunch break at the local chip shop. This example serves to illustrate how systems of surveillance in secondary schools are not usually considered as tools that aid the pedagogic processes but mostly as discipline instruments.

The two school projects reveal that there in not a unique food ideology that can be traced and assigned as that of government bodies (school board, managers and head teachers), staff (teachers, dinner ladies and cooks) and user-clients (parents and children) when studying social interaction within and around dining rooms in schools. Contradictory discourses and semantics with respect to schools' dining room spaces were found. Some of the children and teachers seem to conceive IDR's as 'out of reach for authority' or 'a distant place' where children can escape the confines of the school structures; indeed a space of the children's own. Cooks and dinner ladies who are requested to deliver what has been thought of at a distance as healthy meals may have very different ideas. There are also the ideas of managers and administrators including the school government bodies' marginal consideration of 'school meals' as a pedagogic device for influencing food habits. This seems to reflect the techno-efficient rationality that characterises neo-liberal economy: in as much as individuals (children) are offered 'choice', the institution is fulfilling its social responsibility.

The project findings confirm that cooks and dinner ladies are left alone to face user-clients in implementing policy schemes that had no consideration of user experiences or of children's opinions. With little training and no formal authority cooks and dinner ladies have no other option but to rely on 'common sense' and personal experience to navigate their way, which entails conveying their own notions of 'proper food' and 'proper manners'.

The Ukrainian and homeless projects also refer to the use of risk discourse by food providers of IDR, particularly in reference to the vulnerability of user-clients. These discourses differ from those of the school for the obvious reason that it cannot be argued that clients are not fully competent citizens. Instead it is argued that they have lost competence and thus they cannot be completely trusted. It is, however, difficult for homeless and migrant people's service providers to intervene and at the same time argue that user-clients are being offered choice. Unlike children, who commonly use mimesis and trickery as devices to contest authority, adults can completely ignore authority or become very vocal and even physical when they perceive surveillance systems are not to their benefit.

Health risks are said to be one of the main concerns of food providers at homeless centres. But the institutionalisation of healthy eating our evidence suggests, has created tensions between staff and younger residents. Results show that young residents have a different idea from that of staff and older residents regarding the effects food has on their bodies and what eating arrangements mean in terms of social competence. Our data suggest that administrators and staff at the homeless centre consider that some residents are not only at risk, but also in need of developing social skills that eventually may allow some of them to become competent social actors or to re-gain competence. On their part, residents seem to consider that they are just using available resources wisely: some of them are used to eat outside in restaurants and cafés, some use the facilities provided to prepare their own food, while others eat at the IDR only to socialise and network. The project suggests that there are different food ideologies and that their expression sometimes creates tension. It was also revealed that despite the visibly intrusive CCTV monitoring, residents seem to be able to argue strongly and without fear, showing they maintain independent thinking and control of their lives.

The Ukranian project revealed that Wednesday's lunch at the SUB Club has become a weekly ritual through which 'first generation Ukrainians' reaffirm their role as guardians of 'Ukrainian values', and second generation Ukrainians renew their commitment to maintain a sense of Ukrainian community. Wednesday lunch is thus an effective inter-generational form of communication.

Although governmentality is reflected in the way risk assessment, documentation procedures and information checking of possible user-clients is carried out in all activities of SUB including IDR, the project revealed that the apparatuses of command and control, including the surveillance system, were adapted to suit the interests of the community as a whole. The so called 'first generation Ukrainians' are willing subjects of a surveillance system, (requested by government and partly operated by 'second-generation Ukrainians') in as much as they consider it useful for their own project: the maintenance of a distinctive identity in multi-cultural environment. Notwithstanding they lead all SUB Club committees, second generation Ukrainians, are themselves subjects to the surveillance system as well. The system is operational – and discursively operational as well – only because user-clients appropriated it and used it to reproduce their community. The project found that despite divergent food ideologies of different cohorts, the system of surveillance had been adapted to advance the fundamental project of rejecting assimilation to mainstream (food) culture and at the same time adapting to the British way of life.

This comparative study suggests that acknowledging agency is not enough to enact policy; after all, agency is inherent to all social actors. Rather, our evidence suggests that poor forms of participation for policy development, such as consultation, when applied to the issue of food provision have left important actors feeling disempowered, thus effectively eroding socio-cultural capital. One main question that arises from the analysis and for which further investigation is needed is that of how is it possible to create government policy in the food provision that although having sound scientific foundations in relation to diet, nutrition and health, also incorporates the lessons drawn from experienced stakeholders and takes into account the opinions, desires and beliefs of all stakeholders, including user-clients.

In terms of policy development it has been made clear that laws, regulations and guidelines aimed at improving the diet of the British, must take into consideration that there is not a unique food ideology behind people's attitudes towards food; and that even when differences of age, gender, class, religion and ethnic origin are accounted for, none of these population segments can be said to possess a well defined 'food ideology' of their own. This conclusion may seem innocuous but, as shown in this comparative research, policy often attempts to modify food practices regardless of food ideologies, making it more likely that resistance to implementation will occur.

Conclusion
Peter Jackson

In this conclusion we bring together some of the themes that have run through the book and suggest some ways forward in terms of future research directions. As a first step, we would like to suggest that the evidence presented throughout the book confirms our initial premise that food is a powerful lens through which to view recent changes in family life. In this respect, the book has done more than provide an account of recent sociological evidence on 'the family'. Instead, it has used food as a way of opening up the 'black box' of family life, approaching the subject from a variety of disciplinary perspectives and using the subject of food as a way of shedding light on contemporary family practices.[1] Likewise, we conclude, our choice of a practice-based approach to 'doing family' has been vindicated by the evidence presented in the preceding chapters. While the idea of 'family' (and the idealised nuclear family in particular) remains a dominant figure in British society, our research confirms that the form of contemporary families is extremely diverse as are the practices that contribute to the reproduction of everyday family life.

In some respects, our research has confirmed the findings of previous studies regarding the highly gendered nature of 'feeding the family', where women continue to do the majority of routine domestic work (cf. Charles and Kerr 1988; DeVault 1991). In other respects, our research goes further, for example, in documenting the ways in which increasing numbers of men are getting involved in various domestic tasks to the extent that helping with shopping and cooking are now seen as a necessary part of being a 'good dad'. Our work also contributes to existing debates about the everyday moralities of family life, as reflected in the kind of 'moral tales' that Ribbens McCarthy *et al.* (2003) recount in their discussion of modern parenting and step-parenting. Our research extends their argument by asking how far the distinction between 'proper meals' and 'junk food' maps on to the distinction between good and bad families. There are many reasons to challenge such a simple mapping and we note that caring for the family can be expressed through a variety of means including the use of 'convenience' food, freeing time for other domestic tasks and expressions of familial love.[2]

While there are many parallels and continuities with previous research, some issues have changed dramatically since these earlier studies, intensifying further during the course of our research. We refer, for example, to the impact of the current global financial crisis (the 'credit crunch' and its impact on the 'real economy', including the rapidly escalating cost of food). Our research was already under way before the extent of the crisis became fully apparent and we were not able to build a systematic assessment of the financial crisis and its implications into our research design. But it is already clear that food insecurity is now a truly global phenomenon, impacting on many of the families who participated in our research as well as having devastating impacts elsewhere in the world. An awareness of the current economic context also serves to heighten our sense of moral indignation when young mothers are blamed for wasting food or for their lack of cooking or parenting skills, when the underlying causes of dietary inequality and increasing obesity surely lie elsewhere.[3] We might ask, for example, why the morality of food practices is so frequently invoked at the household level while the injustice of global food inequalities and the ethics of major food corporations are not subject to such intense scrutiny and are much less salient in popular discourses around food. In examining changes at the domestic scale of individual households and families, we must not lose sight of the bigger picture of global change including the large-scale forces affecting agri-food markets and the governments whose role it is to regulate those markets.

One way of thinking about the relationship between these processes at different scales is to focus on the way that changes in the marketplace and in the world of work affect what is happening in the domestic context of the home (and *vice versa*). While there are no clear boundaries between public and private spheres, our research does show how the intimate world of family life (including the timing of 'family meals') continues to be shaped in significant ways by the routines and rhythms of the workplace. This is one of the reasons why we are so opposed to the current emphasis in government policy on individual consumer choice. Clearly, consumers need to be given sufficient information to make informed decisions about what to buy and what to eat. But their 'choices' are quite palpably shaped by what is available in their locality, within their price range and within the other resources available to them (including the time to shop and cook). These resources are subject to all kinds of constraints that are not easily represented in the models of rational choice that underpin so much of the rhetoric surrounding 'food choice'. It may, for example, be perfectly rational for working-class mothers to feed 'junk food' to their children as a cheap way of providing sufficient calories to fill them up, especially if they know that healthier food will simply go to waste. A recent article in *The Guardian* (1 October 2008), for example, showed that 100 calories of broccoli costs 51p while 100 calories of frozen chips costs only 2p. For families on low incomes, struggling to feed their children, 'unhealthy' food choices can seem quite rational. Likewise, it is no good providing mothers with advice about the nutritional value of aubergines or asparagus if these foods are not available locally or at a price that people can afford. There is, then, no substitute for local knowledge in understanding the social embedding of 'food choice'. We recognise, however, that it is one thing to assert the need to understand the social embedding of contemporary food practices and another to demonstrate exactly how and why such an understanding can make a difference to policy and practice. Hopefully, the evidence presented in this book goes some way towards making that case as well as providing a spur to future research in this area.

Our research was undertaken as 15 separate projects, organised into three research strands dealing, respectively, with pregnancy and motherhood, childhood and family life, and families and the wider community. The preceding chapters have, we hope, demonstrated the value of the life-course model which provided the intellectual rationale for this tripartite structure. But further work on the relationship between families and food at various points along the life-course would also be possible, looking, in particular, at the changes that occur at critical moments of transition. So, for example, we might ask what changes in dietary practices occur (for parents and children) when young people leave home, when new households are formed through marriage or other forms of partnership, or when couples have their first child?

There is also scope for further comparative work, bringing together the findings of different projects and research strands. We have already demonstrated (particularly in the final chapter) the scope for combining the findings of several different projects on non-domestic food consumption (in school dining halls, homeless shelters and voluntary associations). But we plan to extend this comparative agenda in future work by combining the data from several other projects (on motherhood and childhood, for example). There is also scope for comparative work on the idea of 'moral panics' around food and family in an age which many observers feel to be one of growing consumer anxiety.[4] For example, we might ask why contemporary anxieties are so readily focused on food when it is, arguably, safer and more reliable today than ever before. Why, too, is the alleged decline of the 'family meal' so often regarded as a social evil rather than as a sign of women's liberation from a time-consuming domestic chore? And why do these anxieties focus on food rather than on other aspects of our everyday lives?

Our research has also highlighted the way that families are subject to increasing levels of surveillance, ranging from the attention that is paid to women's dietary health during pregnancy to attempts to reduce the amount of 'binge drinking' among young people, and from the medical practice of foetal scanning to the efforts of health professionals to promote adult exercise and reduce obesity among people of all ages. Surveillance is, of course, an ambivalent strategy, offering increased protection and security to some, while simultaneously serving to discipline and punish others. We suggest that further work on the way that food and families are subject to varying disciplinary regimes and regulatory strategies could lead to significant insights on both issues.

Finally, we feel that there is scope for further research which brings the findings of each project into critical conversation with the results of other projects both within our own programme and with other research programmes. For example, our understanding of the vexed question of 'food choice' (a highly politicised term whose individualisation has been a focus of repeated critique throughout this book) could be improved by comparative research within and beyond the UK, as could our understanding of the relationship between food and 'identity', a term which one commentator recently described as 'degenerate' in its casual usage among social scientists and others who should know better.[5] For identity is always a relational term whose significance is not apparent until we encounter those who we perceive to be different from ourselves. Too often, however, identity is regarded as an 'influence' on food choice with insufficient regard for the relational nature of the term. That we cannot simply read off the culinary consequences of 'ethnic' difference, for example, is nicely illustrated by our research on Ukrainian food practices in Bradford. In this case, the research showed how three generations of Ukrainian families used food in different ways to express a sense of group identity in relation to others: as distinct from them (in pursuit of the political project of national independence); as part of a process of 'integration' (where culinary and other cultural distinctions were played down); and as part of a re-emergent identity (where culinary distinctions were re-emphasised in a context defined in terms of multi-culturalism).

As we hope we have demonstrated, the relationship between food and family makes a compelling focus for research. The topic is of enormous academic, personal, political and popular interest and one volume cannot do justice to the richness of the subject.[6] In bringing together this set of essays, we have challenged the received wisdom in several critical areas of current debate including the alleged decline of the 'family meal', the individualisation of 'food choice' and the relationship between professional advice on 'healthy eating' and the everyday practices of family life.

Notes

Introduction

1. Turkey Twizzlers are a processed food made from reclaimed turkey meat, produced by the Suffolk poultry farmer Bernard Matthews. High in fat and sugar, they came to symbolise the poor quality of food served in British schools before the impact of recent reforms (*BBC News On-line* 23 March 2005).
2. The alleged demise of domestic cooking skills has been associated with the rise of 'convenience' foods. In her study of the meaning of cooking in everyday life, however, Frances Short maintains that powerful claims are frequently made about the 'deskilling' of home cooking based on very limited evidence (2006: 6).
3. We should, of course, be careful to distinguish between family and household. The increasing number of people living on their own refers to their household situation rather than to their family status. As classic sociological studies such as *Family and Kinship in East London* (Young and Willmott 1957) revealed, the physical boundaries of a household tell us very little about the social significance of their occupants' kinship relations.
4. As Finch (2007: 71) argues, the findings of this research on the negotiated character of kin relationships and the blurring of boundaries between kinship and friendship can be extended to heterosexual families as well as applying to same-sex intimacies.
5. Again, the strength of family as an ideal is revealed in the research by Ribbens McCarthy *et al.* (2003) who found that many 'step-families' rejected the label and wished to be referred to simply as a 'family'.
6. Another indication of the growing number of same-sex households is the fact that 18,059 couples formed civil partnerships in the UK in 2006 (National Statistics 2007: 17).
7. Anne Murcott (1986) also refers to the need to open up the 'black box' of food, eating and household relationships.
8. We are grateful to David Morgan who made this observation at the *Changing Families, Changing Food* conference at The British Library on 21 October 2008. At the same event, Anne Murcott drew attention to the remarkable stability of many family practices and routines including the gendering of domestic food work and the persistent power of the idea of family. While 'doing family' is intriguingly variable and complex, she proposes, the *idea* of family as a significant notion endures.
9. See, for example, Ward *et al.* (2008) for a discussion of the impacts and implications of the recent reform of the EU's sugar regime.
10. Kjaernes *et al.* (2007) provide a valuable comparative perspective on trust in food across Europe. Their evidence suggests that national variations in trust are not related in any simple way to levels of food safety or even to the variable incidence of 'food scares'. Instead, they suggest, public trust can only

be explained through a more complex institutional analysis involving the interaction of markets, regulators and consumer groups.
11 The report talked about the need to change our obesogenic environment and predicted that rates of obesity, measured in terms of a body-mass index (BMI) of over 30 kg/m^2, would rise from 28% in 2007 to 40% in 2025.
12 The programme was funded by The Leverhulme Trust (award no. F/00 118/AQ) and ran from 2005 to 2008.
13 Time-use statistics from Germany also question the downward trend in the amount of time families spend eating together with reports of an increase over the last ten years (Frank Trentmann, pers. comm. 7 November 2008).
14 Our research supports the findings of a recent report by the children's charity Barnardo's which found that school children often use eating as a form of 'social camouflage', with their food choices designed to help them fit in with their peers. Making 'healthy' choices sometimes appeared to undermine culturally accepted ways of being a child especially for boys (Ludvigsen and Sharma 2004). See also Burgess and Morrison's (1998) innovative ethnographic work on school meals in the 1990s.

Chapter 2

1 For the purpose of this study, obesity was defined as a Body Mass Index (BMI) ≥ 30.
2 This is not to suggest that variations in relationships and parenthood have not always existed but rather, until recently they have not been considered as *normative* patterns of family life.
3 Some states in the USA have foetal homicide laws and have been successfully pursued in a number of cases where maternal 'negligence' has been proven to contribute to the death of a foetus/baby. Under the European Convention on Human Rights, however, the foetus is not entitled to the protection of criminal law because it is not deemed to have the status of a human being.
4 See, for example: Department of Health (2002c) *Infant feeding 2000: a summary report.* http://www.dh.gov.uk/assetRoot/04/08/13/98/04081398.pdf (accessed July 2008); World Health Organisation and UNICEF (2003) *Global strategy for infant and young child feeding.* Geneva: WHO (accessed July 2008); Royal College of Midwives (2004) *'Infant Feeding. Position Statement No 5.* http://www.rcm.org.uk/info/docs/PS5-Infant-Feeding.doc (accessed July 2008); Department of Health (2005) *Maternal and Infant Nutrition*http://www.dh.gov.uk/ Policy AndGuidance/HealthAndSocialCareTopics/MaternalAndInfantNutrition/fs/en (accessed July 2008).
5 During pregnancy Shauna had gained five stone (approximately 31.75 kg).

Chapter 4

1 On occasions, however, both parents chose to take part and were interviewed.

2 Studies have concerned, for example, families with children with disabilities, and post-divorce families (Ferguson *et al.* 2004; Ferguson *et al.* 2008; Mitchell 2007).
3 Women have been widely recognised as being central to the establishment and maintenance of inter-generational relations in the family: see, for example, Putney and Bengtson (2001); Bridges *et al.* (2007).
4 Byng-Hall (1995) refers to family scripts as 'replicative', 'corrective' or 'improvised'.
5 A chocolate-covered breakfast cereal marketed for children.

Chapter 5

1 The *Men, Children and Food* research team included researchers with backgrounds in geography, psychology, psychotherapy and sociology. Our analyses, therefore, have, developed through inter-disciplinary discussion and seek to contribute to debates within a range of disciplinary contexts.

Chapter 7

1 An earlier version of this chapter was presented at the 'Domesticity' conference, at the Humanities Research Institute, University of Sheffield (January 2007). We are grateful to Anne Murcott for her constructive comments on a previous draft.
2 DeVault expands further on this definition: 'Whatever its particular features, a "family" has a problematic existence: it is a socially constructed group, continually brought into being through the activities of individuals. Repeated activities – and especially routines and rituals like those of family mealtimes – sustain the reality of a family' (1991: 54). Beyond these practical and performative aspects, DeVault also recognises that 'family' refers to an institution and to an idea with strongly normative dimensions.
3 We are aware of Miller and Reilly's (1995) dismissal of the applicability of the concept of 'moral panic' to food safety issues. They argue that the original application of the term lacks historical perspective, over-states the power of state control of the media and pays insufficient attention to the active social struggles that are at play in the definition of so-called moral panics. They also argue that it is hard to identify the food industry as a 'folk devil' since the term was originally applied to 'deviant' or socially marginalised groups. Our use of the term implies none of these things but draws attention to the exaggerated scale of the media response to the alleged decline of the 'family meal' and to the neglect of substantive evidence.
4 In their study of food practices among families in northern England, Charles and Kerr (1988) also found widespread concern about producing 'proper meals', consisting, in this case, of meat (or sometimes fish), potatoes and vegetables.
5 For further information on *The Nation's Diet* programme, see Murcott (1998).
6 If anything, people are spending slightly longer per eating episode at home than 25 years ago, with 87% of eating and drinking at home events lasting

no more than 30 minutes in 1975 compared to 83% in 2000 (Cheng *et al.* 2007: 47).
7 In naming meals, we have followed the terminology of the interview schedule which is mirrored by most of the interviewees. Hence, 'dinner' refers to the mid-day meal and 'tea' to the evening meal. We have, however, retained some examples of different naming practices used by the interviewees so, for example, Ronald refers to the mid-day meal as 'lunch'.
8 It is a central argument of the 'Changing Families, Changing Food' programme that food is a valuable lens through which to observe changes in family life and *vice versa*.

Chapter 8

1 An instance from a regular recipe column titled 'Judy on the Kitchen Front' (*WO*, 2 June 1944: 17), dealing specifically with the likelihood of very angry food refusal under the Second World War rationing policy, undergoes detailed analysis elsewhere (Burridge and Barker, unpublished manuscript).

Chapter 9

1 As I have argued extensively elsewhere with reference to Japanese cases, although the mainstream literature on governance tends to locate the 'family' outside of the governance system, the family plays certain roles through its multi-dimensional reproductive functions. For details, see Takeda (2005a, 2005b).
2 When Dean uses the term ethics, needless to say, the words refers to Foucault's discussion on ethics as a particular code of behaviours practiced by individuals.
3 The ambivalent proximity between the 'Third Way' and neoliberalism has continuously been pointed out both in and outside of the UK since its publication. Giddens has responded to a wide range of criticism in his subsequent publications (Giddens 2000). According to Giddens, 'the "Third Way" is concerned with restructuring social democratic doctrines to respond to the twin revolutions of globalization and the knowledge economy'. While Giddens admits various 'gains' generated from the market, he also notes the importance of the regulatory role played by government. Hence, government now should become a 'facilitator' (cf. Blair and Schröder 2000).
4 The changing form and structure of governing from 'government' to 'governance', in which the territorial state plays particular political functions in a coordinated network with other (domestic, international or transnational) actors, was discussed in the 1990s by scholars like Bob Jessop in controversies regarding the transient role/function of the state in response to the progress of globalisation (Jessop 1997, 1998).
5 Following convention, the family name precedes the given name in Japanese (including my name) unless the British convention is preferred by the author. Long vowels are represented by macrons except in cases where the words are conventionally used without them (for example, 'Tokyo').

6 http://www.jcsa.gr.jp/about/outline.html (accessed on 4 September 2008).
7 The mention of the family as the site of the *Shokuiku* campaign in the 2006 White Paper contains the phrase of 'to realize healthy eating life *on the basis of the perspectives of gender equality*'. In contrast, the 2007 White Paper is silent about gender issues surrounding the organisation of family meals at home.
8 In a different paper, I have discussed how the *Shokuiku* campaign serves to disseminate and promote a sense of 'banal nationalism' through food (Takeda 2008).

Chapter 10

1 In a recent report the WHO (2002) argues that there needs to be a coordinated European health policy that integrates a range of social policies concerning the production, availability, and selling of food to consumers. This report focuses on production rather than where food is consumed.
2 Tamas's father's cooking is not unusual in Hungarian Culture. Traditionally the goulashes and meat stews were prepared by herdsmen who tended the livestock. Recipes are handed down from father to son. It is only more recently that women have started to cook these dishes but the job of tasting and seasoning is left to male householders.

Chapter 12

1 During the 1980s, the Bradford Heritage Recording Unit (BHRU) collected oral histories with 'primary settler', or 'first generation' Ukrainians, as they often described themselves. The recordings are available from Bradford's local library. In this chapter, references to the narratives recorded during the most recent fieldwork (2006–2007) have been coded beginning with PS and references to narratives recorded prior to this research will begin with SS. Copies of the recordings (audio visual material) or transcripts of PS can be supplied by the authors on request.

Conclusion

1 While our research has opened up the 'black box' of family life, confirming its diversity of forms and the multiplicity of practices through which it is reproduced, food has been relatively under-theorised. More could, perhaps, have been done to clarify what constitutes a meal, what practices count as cooking and what distinguishes food from the other substances we ingest.
2 One might also cite the kind of ethnographic evidence presented by Helene Brembeck (2005), regarding the way Swedish families are able to incorporate commercial venues such as McDonald's into their family routines, to question the implied relationship between convenience and care which some theorists present as a simple antinomy, comparable to the opposition between novelty and tradition, health and indulgence, economy and extravagance (Warde 1997).

3 This point was made by Libby Bishop in her concluding remarks at the *Changing Families, Changing Food* conference in London in October 2008 where she expressed a sense of anger and moral outrage at the social injustices that are perpetuated by the current agri-food system including the power of the supermarkets and the inadequacy of current systems of food labelling. In these circumstances, she is surely right to argue that the weight of responsibility placed on individuals (often mothers) is simply disproportionate.

4 Several recent books have alluded to the present-day as an 'age of anxiety' about food including Griffith and Wallace's (1998) collection of essays on the anxious pleasures of cooking and eating, John Coveney's (2000) history of food, morals and meaning, and Suzanne Freidberg's (2004) ethnographic study of French beans and food scares. We are, ourselves, about to begin a new research programme on 'Consumer anxieties about food', funded by the European Research Council.

5 This point was made by Anne Murcott at the *Changing Families, Changing Food* conference in London on 21 October 2008.

6 Further books are in preparation addressing other aspects of our research programme and its links to the research being undertaken elsewhere. They include a volume on *Children, Food and Identity* (edited by Allison James, Anne Trine Kjorholt and Vebjorg Tingstad) and a book on the relationship between family, food and social care (edited by Graham Smith and Paula Nicolson).

References

Acheson, D. (1998) *Independent inquiry into inequalities in health*. Stationery Office: London.
Ākaibu Shuppan (ed.) (2008) *Dētā de yomitoku nihonjin no shokuseikatsu 2008*. Ahkaibu Shuppan: Tokyo.
Alanen, L. (2001) Explorations in generational analysis. In Alanen, L. and Mayall, B. (eds) *Conceptualizing child-adult relations*. Routledge Falmer: London, 11–22.
Allan, G. and Crow, G. (2001) *Families, households and society*. Palgrave Macmillan: Basingstoke.
Allen, I., Bourke Dowling, S. and Rolfe, H. (eds) (1998) *Teenage mothers: decisions and outcomes*. Policy Studies Institute: London.
Anderson, B. and Rogaly, B. (2005) *Forced labour and migration*. Study prepared by COMPAS (Centre on Migration, Policy and Society) in collaboration with the Trades Union Congress: Oxford.
Aonuma, Yōichi (2008) *Shokuryō shokuminchi Nippon*. Shōgakukan: Tokyo.
Apple, R. (1995) Constructing mothers: scientific motherhood in the nineteenth and twentieth centuries. *Social History of Medicine* 8: 161–178.
Armstrong, D. (1995) The rise of surveillance medicine. *Sociology of Health and Illness* 17: 393–404.
Bailey, L. (2001) Gender shows: first-time mothers and embodied selves. *Gender and Society* 15: 110–129.
Balfour-Jeffrey, D., McLellarn R.W. and Fox, D.T. (1982) The development of children's eating habits: the role of television commercials. *Health Education and Behavior* 9: 78–93.
Ballantyne, J.W. (1914) *Expectant motherhood: its supervision and hygiene*. Cassell & Co. Ltd.: London.
Barker, K. (1998) 'A ship upon a stormy sea': the medicalization of pregnancy. *Social Science and Medicine* 47: 1067–1076.
Barling, D. and Lang, T. (2003a) The politics of UK food policy: an overview. *The Political Quarterly* 74: 4–7.
Barling, D. and Lang, T. (2003b) A reluctant food policy? The first five years of food policy under Labour. *The Political Quarterly* 74: 8–18.
Bauer, E. and Thompson, P. (2006) *Jamaican hands across the Atlantic*. Ian Rundle Publishers: Kingston.
Bauman, Z. (2004) *Wasted lives: modernity and its outcasts*. Polity Press: Cambridge.
Bauman, Z. (2005) *Liquid life*. Polity Press: Cambridge.
Baxter, J. (2000) The joys and justice of housework. *Sociology* 34: 609–631.
Beagan, B., Chapman, G.E., D'Sylva, A. and Bassett, B.R. (2008) 'It's just easier for me to do it': rationalizing the family division of foodwork. *Sociology* 42: 653–671.
Beck, U. (1992) *Risk society: towards a new modernity*. Sage: London.
Beck, U. (1999) *World risk society*. Polity Press: Cambridge.

Bell, D. and Valentine, G. (1997) *Consuming geographies: we are where we eat.* Routledge: London.

Bengtson, V., Biblarz, T. and Roberts, R. (2002) *How families still matter.* Cambridge University Press: Cambridge.

Benn, M. (1998) *Madonna and child: towards a new politics of motherhood.* Jonathan Cape: London.

Bennett, P. (1999) Understanding responses to risk: some basic findings. In Bennett, P. and Calman, K. (eds) *Risk communication and public health.* Oxford University Press: New York, 3–19.

Bergmann, K., Bergmann, R., Von Kries, R., Bohm, O., Richter, R., Dudenhausen, J. and Wahn, U. (2003) Early determinants of childhood overweight and adiposity in a birth cohort study: The role of breast-feeding. *International Journal of Obesity* 27: 162–172.

Bernard, J. (1982) *The future of marriage,* Yale University Press: New York.

Bianchi, S.M. (2000) Maternal employment and time with children: dramatic change or surprising continuity? *Demography* 37: 401–414.

Blaine, K. Kamaldeen, S. and Powell, D. (2002) Public perceptions of biotechnology. *Journal of Food Science* 67: 3200–3208.

Blair, A. and Schröder, G. (2000) Europe: the third way/die neue mitte. In Hombach, B. (ed.) *The politics of the new centre.* Polity Press: Cambridge, 159–177.

Blake, M.K. (2007) Formality and friendship: Research ethics review and participatory action research. *ACME: An International E-journal for Critical Geographies* 6: 411–421.

Bolling, K., Grant, C., Hamlyn, B. and Thornton, A. (2007) *Infant feeding 2005. A survey conducted on behalf of The Information Centre for Health and Social Care and the UK health departments by BMRB Social Research.* The Information Centre: London.

Bornat, J. (2003) A second take: revisiting interviews with a different purpose. *Oral History* 31: 47–53.

Boswell-Penc, M. and Boyer, K. (2007) Expressing anxiety? Breast pump usage in American wage workplaces. *Gender, Place and Culture* 14: 551–567.

Boyd Orr, J. (1936) *Food, health and income: report on a survey of adequacy of diet in relation to income.* Macmillan: London.

Brannen, J. (2004) Childhoods across the generations: Stories from women in four-generation English families. *Childhood* 11: 409–428.

Brannen, J., Heptinstall, E. and Bhopal, K. (2000) *Connecting children: carer and family life in later childhood.* Routledge Falmer: London.

Brannen, J. and Nilsen, A. (2006) From fatherhood to fathering: transmission and change among British fathers in four-generation families. *Sociology* 40: 335–352.

Brembeck, H. (2005) Home to McDonald's: upholding the family dinner with the help of McDonald's. *Food, Culture and Society* 8: 215–226.

Bridges, L., Roe, A. and Dunn, J. et al. (2007) Children's perspectives on their relationships with grandparents following reference to parental separation: a longitudinal study. *Social Development* 16: 539–554.

BMA (British Medical Association) (1933) Report of Committee on Nutrition. *British Medical Journal Supplement* 25 Nov: 1–16.

BMA (1939) *Nutrition and the public health.* BMA: London.
Brody, G.H., Stoneman, Z., Lane, T.S. and Sanders, A. (1981) *Television food commercials aimed at children, family grocery shopping, and mother-child interactions.* National Council on Family Relations.
Bugge, A.B. and Almås, R. (2006) Domestic dinner: representations and practices of a proper meal among young suburban mothers. *Journal of Consumer Culture* 6: 203–228.
Bull, J., Mulvihil, C. and Quigley, R. (2003) *Prevention of low birth weight: assessing the effectiveness of smoking cessation and nutritional interventions.* Evidence briefing: Health Development Agency.
Burchell, G. (1996) Liberal government and techniques of the self. In Barry, A., Osborne, T. and Rose, N. (eds) *Foucault and political reason.* Routledge: London 19–36.
Burgess, R. and Morrison, M. (1998) Ethnographies of eating in an urban primary school. In Murcott, A. (ed.) *The nation's diet: the social science of food choice.* Longman: London, 13: 209–228.
Burridge, J.D. (2008) The dilemma of frugality and consumption in British women's magazines 1940–1955. *Social Semiotics* 18: 389–401.
Burridge, J.D. (forthcoming) 'I don't care if it does me good, I like it': constructions of children, health and enjoyment in British women's magazine food advertising. In James, A., Kjorholt, A.T. and Tingstad, V. (eds) *Children, food and identity.* Palgrave: Basingstoke.
Burridge, J.D. and Barker, M.E. (unpublished manuscript) 'The housewife' in a time of austerity: rationing, responsibility and food in British women's magazines 1940–1954.
Busch, L. (2000) The moral economy of grades and standards. *Journal of Rural Studies* 16: 273–283.
Butler, J. (1990) *Gender trouble: feminism and the subversion of identity.* Routledge: New York.
Byng-Hall, J. (1995) *Rewriting family scripts: improvisation and systems change.* Guilford Press: New York.
Cabinet Office (2008a) *Food: an analysis of the issues.* Cabinet Office Strategy Unit: London.
Cabinet Office (2008b) *Food matters: towards a strategy for the 21st century.* Cabinet Office Strategy Unit: London.
Caplan, P. (1997) Approaches to the study of food, health and identity. In Caplan, P. (ed.) *Food, health and identity.* Routledge: London, 1–31.
Caraher, M. and Coveney, J. (2004) Public health nutrition and food policy. *Public Health Nutrition* 7: 591–598.
Carson, J. (2000) Introduction: cultures of relatedness. In Carson, J. (ed.) *Cultures of relatedness.* Cambridge University Press: Cambridge, 1–36.
Carter, P. (1995) *Feminism, breasts and breast-feeding.* Macmillan: Basingstoke.
Cavendish, W. (2008) Healthy weight, healthy lives: a cross-Government strategy for England. http://www.tacd.org/events/meeting9/will_cavendish_strategy.pdf (accessed August 2008). Department of Health: London.
CCSR (Cathie Marsh Centre for Census and Survey Research) 2006. 'The Samples of Anonymised Records'. University of Manchester.
Cesarani, D. (2001) *Justice delayed: how Britain became a refuge for Nazi war criminals* (revised 2nd edition). Phoenix Press: London.

Charles, N. (1995) Food and family ideology. In Jackson, S. and Moores, S. (eds) *The politics of domestic consumption*. Harvester Wheatsheaf: Hemel Hempstead.

Charles, N. and Kerr, M. (1988) *Women, food and families*. Manchester University Press: Manchester

Chavkin, W. (1992) Women and fetus: the social construction of conflict. In Feinmann, C. (ed.) *The criminalization of a woman's body*. Haworth Press: New York, 193–202.

Cheal, M. (2002) *Sociology of family life*. Palgrave Macmillan: London.

Cheng, S-L., Olsen, W., Southerton, D. and Warde, A. (2007) The changing practice of eating: evidence from UK time diaries, 1975 and 2000. *British Journal of Sociology* 58: 39–61.

Chodorow, N. (1999) *The reproduction of mothering: psychoanalysis and the sociology of gender*. University of California Press: California.

Choi, P., Henshaw, C., Baker, S. and Tree, J. (2005) Supermum, superwife, super-everything: performing femininity in the transition to motherhood. *Journal of Reproductive and Infant Psychology* 23: 167–180.

Christensen, P. (2004) The health-promoting family: a conceptual framework for future research. *Social Science and Medicine* 59: 377–387.

Cohen, P.S. (1969) Theories of myth. *Man* 4: 337–353.

Cohen, S. (1972) *Folk devils and moral panics: the creation of the Mods and Rockers*. MacGibbon & Kee: London (third edition, Routledge: London, 2002).

Coltrane, S. (2000) Research on household labor: modeling and measuring the social embeddedness of routine family work *Journal of Marriage and the Family* 62: 1208–1233.

Cook, G. (2001) *The discourse of advertising*. Routledge: London.

Cooter, R. and Fulton, R. (2001) Food matters: food safety research in the UK public sector 1917–1990. *Food Industry Journal* 4: 251–261.

Covello, V.T. and Johnson, B.B. (1987) The social and cultural construction of risk: issues, methods, and case studies. In Johnson, B.B. and Covello, V.T. (eds) *The social and cultural construction of risk*. D. Reidel Publishing Company: Dordrecht, Holland, vii–xiii.

Coveney, J. (2000) *Food, morals and meaning: the pleasure and anxiety of eating*. Routledge: London.

Craven, B. and Johnson, C. (1999). Politics, policy, poisoning and food scares. In Morris, J. and Bate, R. (ed.) *Fearing food: risk, health and environment*. Butterworth Heinemann: Oxford, 141–169.

Curtin, D. (1992) Food/body/person. In Curtin, D. and Heldke, L. (eds) *Cooking, eating, thinking: transformative philosophies of food*. Indiana University Press: Bloomington, IN, 3–22.

Dallison, J. and Lobstein, T. (1995) *Poor expectations: poverty and under nourishment in pregnancy*. NCH Action for Children and the Maternity Alliance.

Daniels, C.R. (1993) *At women's expense: state power and the politics of fetal rights*. Harvard University Press: Cambridge, Massachusetts.

Davis, M. (2005) *The monster at our door: the global threat of avian flu*. Henry Holt: New York.

Dawson, J. and Larke, R. (2004) Japanese retailing through the 1990s: retailers' performance in a decade of slow growth. *British Journal of Management* 15: 73–94.

De Beauvoir, S. (1953) *The second sex*. Jonathon Cape: London.

Dean, M. (1999) *Governmentality: power and rule in modern society*. Sage: London.
Dean, M. (2007) *Governing societies*. Open University Press: Maidenhead.
De Boer, M., McCarthy, M., Brennan, M., Kelly, A.L. and Ritson, C. (2005) Public understanding of food risk issues and food risk messages on the island of Ireland: the views of food safety experts. *Journal of Food Safety* 25: 241–265.
Delphy, C. and Leonard, D. (1992) *Familiar exploitation: a new analysis of marriage in contemporary Western societies*. Polity Press: Cambridge.
Dench, G., Ogg, J. and Thomson, K. (1999) The role of grand-parents. In Jowell, R., Curtis, J., Park, A. and Thomson, K. (eds) *British social attitudes: the 16th report*. Ashgate: Aldershot.
Dermott, E. (2008) *Intimate fatherhood: a sociological analysis*. London: Routledge.
Deutsch, J. (2005) 'Please pass the chicken tits': rethinking men and cooking at the urban firehouse. *Food and Foodways* 13: 91–114.
DeVault, M. (1991) *Feeding the family: the social organisation of caring as gendered work*. University of Chicago Press: Chicago.
Deveaux, M. (1994) Feminism and empowerment: a critical reading of Foucault. *Feminist Studies* 20: 223–247.
Dobson, B., Beardsworth, A., Teresa, K. and Walker, R. (1994) *Eating on a low income*, Social Policy Research 66, Joseph Rowntree Foundation: York.
DoH (Department of Health) (1992) *The health of the nation: a strategy for health in England*. HMSO: London.
DoH (1999) *Saving lives: our healthier nation*. The Stationery Office: London.
DoH (2002a) *Healthy start: proposals for reform of the Welfare Food Scheme*. Department of Health: London.
DoH (2002b) *Scientific review of the Welfare Food Scheme*. http://www.dh.gov.uk/assetRoot/04/08/13/98/04081398.pdf (accessed July 2008).
DoH (2002c) *Infant feeding 2000: a summary report*. Report on Health and Social Subjects 51. The Stationery Office: London.
DoH (2004) *Choosing health: making healthy choices easier*. HMSO: London.
DoH (2008) Weaning. Crown Copyright: London. http://www.dh.gov.uk/en/Publicationsandstatistics/Publications/PublicationsPolicyAndGuidance/DH_4117080 (accessed August 2008). Department of Health: London.
Donzelot, J. (1997) *The policing of families*. Johns Hopkins University Press: Baltimore.
Doran, L. (1997) Energy and nutrient inadequacies in the diets of low-income women who breast-feed. *Journal of the American Dietetic Association* 97: 1283–1287.
Douglas, M. (1972). Deciphering a meal. *Daedalus* 101: 61–81.
Dowler, E. (1997) Budgeting for food on a low income in the UK: the case of lone-parent families. *Food Policy* 22: 405–417.
Dowler, E. (2008) Poverty, food and nutrition. In Strelitz, J. and Lister, R. (eds) *Money matters*. Save the Children: London.
Dowler, E. and Calvert, C. (1995) *Nutrition and diet in lone parent families in London*. Family Policy Studies and The Joseph Rowntree Foundation: London.
Dowler, E. and Caraher, M. (2003) Local food projects: the new philanthropy? *The Political Quarterly* 74: 57–65.
Dryden, C. (1999) *Being married doing gender*. Routledge: London.
D'Souza, L., Renfrew, M., McCormick, F., Dyson, L. Wright, K., Henderson, J. and Thomas, J. (2006) Food-support programmes for low-income and socially disadvantaged childbearing women in developed countries. Systematic review of the evidence, available at: http://www.publichealth.nice.org.uk

Du Gay, P. (2000) Entrepreneurial governance and public management: the anti-bureaucrats. In Clarke, J., Gewirtz, S. and McLaughlin, E. (eds) *New managerialism, new welfare*. Sage: London.

Duncan, S. and Edwards, R. (eds) (1999) *Lone mothers, paid work and gendered moral rationalities*. Macmillan: Basingstoke.

Duncombe, J. and Marsden, D. (1993) Love and intimacy: the gender division of emotion and emotion work. *Sociology* 27: 221–242.

Duncombe, J. and Marsden, D. (1995) Workaholics and whingeing women: the last frontiers of gender inequality. *Sociological Review* 43: 150–169.

Earle, S. (2002) Factors affecting the initiation of breast-feeding: implications for breast-feeding promotion. *Health Promotion International* 17: 205–214.

Ebbs, J.H., Tisdall, F.F. and Scott, W.A. (1941) The influence of prenatal diet on the mother and child. *Journal of Nutrition* 22: 515–526.

Ebihara, Y. (2003) Ko mo oya mo makikonde gakkō kyūshoku o jiku ni shoku kyōiku o susumeru. *Yuimāru* 20: 12–17.

Eckestein, E.F. (1980) *Food, people and nutrition*. Avi Publications: Westport, CT.

Ellaway, A. and Macintyre, S. (2000) Shopping for food in socially constructing localities. *British Food Journal* 102: 52–59.

England, P. and Farkas, G. (1986) *Employment, households and gender: a social, economic and demographic view*. Aldine de Gruyter: Hawthorne, NY.

Equal Opportunities Commission (2006) *Twenty-first century dad*. Equal Opportunities Commission: Manchester.

Erickson, R.J. (2005) Why emotion work matters: sex, gender, and the division of household labor. *Journal of Marriage and Family* 67: 337–351.

Evans, N.S. and Dowler, E.A. (1999) Food, health and eating among single homeless and marginalized people in London. *Journal of Human Nutrition and Dietetics* 12: 179–199.

Everingham, C., Stevenson, D. and Warner-Smith, P. (2007) 'Things are getting better all the time'?: challenging the narrative of women's progress from a generational perspective. *Sociology* 41: 419.

Ewald, F. (2002) The return of Descartes's malicious demon: an outline of a philosophy of precaution. In Baker, T. and Simons, J. (eds) *Embracing risk: the changing culture of insurance and responsibility*. University of Chicago Press: Chicago, 273–301.

Eyck, T.A. (2000) The marginalization of food safety issues: an interpretative approach to mass media coverage. *Journal of Applied Communications* 84: 29–47.

Fergusson, E., Maughan, B. and Golding, J. (2008) Which children receive grandparental care and what effect does it have? *Journal of Child Psychology and Psychiatry and Allied Disciplines* 49: 161–169.

Ferguson, N., Douglas, G. and Lowe, N. (2004) *Grandparenting in divorced families*. Policy Press: Bristol.

Fiddes, N. (1991) *Meat: a natural symbol*. Routledge: London.

Finch, J. (2007) Displaying families. *Sociology* 41: 65–81.

Finch, J. and Groves, D. (1983) *A labour of love*. Routledge and Kegan Paul: London.

Finch, J. and Mason, J. (2000) *Passing it on: kinship and inheritance in England*. Routledge: London.

Floyd, J. (2004) Coming out of the kitchen: texts, contexts and debates *Cultural Geographies* 10: 61–73.

Flynn, A. and Marsden, T. (1992) Food regulation in a period of agriculture retreat: the British experience. *Geoforum* 23: 85–93.

Flynn, A., Marsden, T. and Smith, E. (2003) Food regulation and retailing in a new institutional context. *The Political Quarterly* 74: 38–46.

Flyvbjerg, B. (2006) Five misunderstandings about case-study research. *Qualitative Inquiry* 12: 219–245.

Fog Olwig, K. (2003) Children's places of belonging in immigrant families of Caribbean background. In Fog Olwig, K. and Gulløv, E. (eds) *Children's places: cross-cultural perspectives*. Routledge: London, 217–235.

Folbre, N. (2001) *The invisible heart: economics and family values*. New Press: New York.

FSA (2002) *Food fundamentals: qualitative research report*. Food Standard Agency: London.

FSA (2007) Food competency framework: food skills and knowledge for children and young people aged 7–9, 11–12, 14 and 16+, available at: http://www.food.gov.uk/multimedia/pdfs/foodcompetencydraftria.pdf

FSA (2008) Safety and hygiene. http://www.foodstandards.gov.uk/safereating/

Ford, F.A., Mouratidou, T., Wademan, S.E. and Fraser, R.B. (2008) Effect of the introduction of 'Healthy Start' on dietary behaviour during and after pregnancy: early results from the 'before and after' Sheffield study. *British Journal of Nutrition*, First View article, 10.1017/S00711 450813 5899, Published online by Cambridge University Press 19 Nov 2008.

Foucault, M. (1973) *The birth of the clinic*. Vintage: New York.

Foucault, M. (1979a) *Discipline and punish: the birth of the prison*. Penguin: London.

Foucault, M. (1979b) On governmentality. *Ideology and Consciousness* 6: 5–21.

Fox, B. and Worts, D. (1999) Revisiting the critique of medicalized childbirth: a contribution to the sociology of birth. *Gender and Society* 13: 326–346.

Freidberg, S. (2004) *French beans and food scares: culture and commerce in an anxious age*. Oxford University Press: New York.

Frewer, L.J. (1999) Public risk perceptions and risk communication. In Bennett, P. and Calman, K. (eds) *Risk communication and public health*. Oxford University Press: New York, 20–32.

Frewer, L.J., Shepherd, R. and Sparks, P. (1994) The interrelationship between perceived knowledge, control and risk associated with a range of food-related hazards targeted at the individual, other people and society. *Journal of Food Safety* 14: 19–40.

Friedan, B. (1965) *The feminine mystique*. Penguin: Harmondsworth.

Friedan, B. (1974) *The feminine mystique*. Dell: New York (second edition).

Furedi, F. (2001) *Paranoid parenting: abandon your anxieties and be a good parent*. The Penguin Press: London.

Gavron, H. (1966) *The captive wife: conflicts of housebound mothers*. Routledge and Kegan Paul: London.

General Medical Council (2008) List of Registered Medical Practitioners – Statistics http://www.gmc-uk.org/register/search/stats.asp (accessed August 2008).

Giddens, A. (1998) *The Third Way: the renewal of social democracy*. Polity Press: Cambridge.

Giddens, A. (2000) *Runaway world: how globalization is reshaping our lives*. Routledge: New York.

Gillespie, R. (2000) When no means no: disbelief, disregard and deviance as discourses of voluntary childlessness *Women's Studies International Forum* 23: 223–234.

Gillis, J. (1997) *A world of their own making: a history of myth and ritual in family life*. Oxford University Press: Oxford.
Gordon, R. (2001) *Sheffield and its electoral wards: a review of the index of multiple deprivation 2000*. Sheffield Health Authority.
GOS (2007) *Tackling obesities: future choices*, 2nd ed. Government Office for Science: London.
Green, T. (forthcoming) *When adult children leave home: mothers' perceptions and experiences*. Aldershot: Ashgate.
Griffiths, S. and Wallace, J. (eds) (1998) *Consuming passions: food in the age of anxiety*. Manchester University Press: Manchester.
Gross, N. (2005) The detraditionalization of intimacy reconsidered. *Sociological Theory* 23: 286–311.
Hägerstrand, T. (1982) Diorama, path and project. *Tijdschrift voor Economische en Sociale Geografie* 73: 323–399.
Hanson, C. (2004) *A cultural history of pregnancy: pregnancy, medicine and culture 1750–2000*. Palgrave Macmillan: Basingstoke.
Hareven, T.K. (1982). *Family time and industrial time: the relationship between family and work in a New England industrial community*. Cambridge University Press: Cambridge.
Harnack, L., Story, M., Martinson, B., Neumark-Sztainer, D. and Stang, J. (1998) Guess who's cooking? The role of men in meal planning, shopping, and preparation in U.S. households. *Journal of the American Dietetic Association* 98: 995–1000.
Harris, C. (1987) The individual and society: a processual approach. In Bryman, A., Bytheway, B., Allat, P. and Keil, T. (eds) *Rethinking the life cycle*. Macmillan: Basingstoke.
Harrison, M., Flynn, A. and Marsden, T. (1997) Contested regulatory practice and the implementation of food policy: exploring the local and national interface. *Transactions of the Institute of British Geographers* 22: 473–487.
Hatae, K. (2005) Shokuseikatsu no jiritau o mezasu shokuiku. Shokuryō Nōgyō Seisaku Kenkyū Sentā (ed.) *Shokuryō hakusho shokuseikatsu no genjō to shokuiku no suishin*. Nōsan Gyoson Bunka Kyōkai: Tokyo 107–136.
Hattery, A. (2000) *Women, work, and family: balancing and weaving*. Sage: New York & London.
Heaman, M., Sprague, A. and Stewart, P. (2001) Reducing the problem birth rate: a population health strategy. *Journal of Gynaecological and Neonatal Nursing* 30(1): 20–29.
Heelas, P. and Morris, P. (1992) Enterprise culture: its values and value. In Heelas, P. and Morris, P. (eds) *The values of enterprise culture: the moral debate*. London: Routledge, 1–25.
Heidegger, M. (1962 [1927]) *Being and time*, trans. B. Massumi. University of Minnesota Press: Minneapolis.
Heijmans, B.T., Tobi, E.W., Stein, A.D., Putter, H., Blauw, G.J., Susser, E.S., Slagboom, P.E. and Lumey, L.H. (2008) Persistent epigenetic differences associated with prenatal exposure to famine in humans. *Proceedings of the National Academy of Science* 105: 17046–17049.
Hickman, M. and Crowley, H. (2008) *Immigration and social cohesion in the UK*. Joseph Rowntree Foundation: London.

Hill, M. (1989) The role of social networks in the care of young children. *Children and Society* 3: 195–211.

Hitchman, C., Chrisite, I., Harrison, M. and Lang, T. (2002) *Inconvenience food. The struggle to eat well on a low income*. Demos: London.

Hobsbawm, E. and Ranger, T. (eds) (1992) *The invention of tradition*. Cambridge University Press: Cambridge.

Hochschild, A. (with Anne Machung) (1989) *Second shift: working parents and the revolution at home*. Viking Penguin: New York.

Hockey, J. and James, A. (2003) *Social identities across the life-course*. Palgrave Macmillan: New York.

Holloway, S. (1999) Reproducing motherhood in Laurie, N., Dwyer, C., Holloway, S. and Smith, F. *Geographies of new femininities*. Longman: Harlow, 91–112.

Hollows, J. (2003a) Feeling like a domestic goddess: postfeminism and cooking. *European Journal of Cultural Studies* 6: 179–202.

Hollows, J. (2003b) Oliver's Twist: leisure, labour and domestic masculinity in The Naked Chef. *International Journal of Cultural Studies* 6: 229–248.

Holstein, J. and Gubrium, J. (1997) Active interviewing. In Silverman, D. (ed.) *Qualitative Research: Theory, Method and Practice*. Sage: London.

Hoskins, J. (1998) *Biographical objects: how things tell the stories of people's lives*. Routledge: New York.

Hrycyszyn, M. (2002) *God save me from my friends: a Ukrainian memoir*. Vanguard Press: Cambridge.

Hughes, C. (2002) *Key concepts in feminist theory and research*. Sage: London.

Huxley, M. (2007) Geographies of governmentality. In Crampton, J.W. and Elden, S. (eds) *Space, knowledge and power: Foucault and geography*. Ashgate: Aldershot, 185–204.

Iimori, Nōbuo (2007) *Kōzō kaikaku to sābisu sangyō*. Aoki Shoten: Tokyo.

Inubushi, Y. (2005) Teigen hō no umu de kawaru shoku no risuku. In Shokuryō Nōgyō seisaku kenkyū sentā (ed.) *Shokuryō Hakusho Shokuseikatsu no genjō to shokuiku no suishin*. Nōsan Gyoson Bunka Kyōkai: Tokyo, 69–89.

IPPR (Institute of Public Policy Research) (2008) *Best before: how the UK should respond to the food policy challenge*. Institute of Public Policy Research: London.

Jackson, P., Smith, G. and Olive, S. (2008) Families remembering food: reusing secondary data, 'Changing families, changing food' working paper, available from: www.sheffield.ac.uk/familiesandfood/resources.html.

Jackson, P., Stevenson, N. and Brooks, K. (2001) *Making sense of men's magazines*. Polity Press: Cambridge.

James, A., Curtis, P. and Ellis, K. (forthcoming) Negotiating family, negotiating food: children as family participants? In James, A., Kjørholt, A.T. and Tingstad, K. (eds) Children, food and identity. Palgrave Macmillan: Basingstoke, in press.

Jenkins, R. (1996) *Social identity*. Routledge: London.

Jessop, R. (1997) Capitalism and its future: remarks on regulation, government and governance. *Review of International Political Economy* 4: 561–581.

Jessop, R. (1998) The rise of governance and the risks of failure: the case of economic development. *International Social Sciences Journal* 155: 29–45.

Johnston, L. and Valentine, G. (1995) Wherever I lay my girlfriend, that's my home: the performance and surveillance of lesbian identities in domestic environments. In Bell, D. and Valentine, G. (eds) *Mapping desire: geographies of sexualities*. Routledge: London, 99–113.

Joshi, H. (2002) Production, reproduction and education: women, children and work in contemporary Britain. *Population and Development Review* 28: 445–474.

Julier, A. and Lindenfield, L. (2005) Mapping men onto the menu: masculinities and food. *Food and Foodways* 13: 1–16.

Keane, A. (1997) Too hard to swallow? The palatability of healthy eating. In P. Caplan (ed.) *Food, health and identity*. Routledge: London.

Kemmer, D. (1999) Food preparation and the division of domestic labour among newly married and cohabiting couples. *British Food Journal* 101: 570–579.

King, V. and Elder, G. (1995) American children view their grandparents: linked lives across three rural generations. *Journal of Marriage and the Family* 57: 165–178.

Kjaernes, U., Harvey, M. and Warde, A. (2007) *Trust in food: a comparative and institutional analysis*. Palgrave Macmillan: London.

Knowles, T., Moody, R. and McEachern, M.G. (2007) European food scares and their impact on EU food policy. *British Food Journal* 109: 43–67.

Knox, B. (2000). Consumer perception and understanding of risk from food. *British Medical Bulletin* 56: 97–109.

Kowaleski-Jones, L. and Duncan, G.J. (2002) Effects of participation in the WIC program on birthweight: evidence from the National Longitudinal Survey of Youth. Special Supplemental Nutrition Program for Women, Infants, and Children. *American Journal of Public Health* 92: 799–804.

Kremmer, D., Anderson A.S. and Marshall, D.W. (1998) Living together and eating together: changes in food choice and eating habits during the transition from single to married/cohabiting. *Sociological Review* 46: 48–72.

Lake, A.A. (2006) Could your partner be bad for your health? *Complete Nutrition* 6: 8–11.

Lake, A.A., Hyland, R.M., Mathers, J.C., Rugg-Gunn, A.J., Wood, C.E. and Adamson, A.J. (2006) Food shopping and preparation among the 30-somethings: whose job is it? (The ASH30 study). *British Food Journal* 108: 475–486.

Lamb, M.E. (ed.) (1987) *The father's role: cross cultural perspectives*. Lawrence Erlbaum Associates: London.

Lang, T., Barling, D. and Caraher, M. (2001) Food, social policy and the environment: towards a new model. *Social Policy and Administration* 35: 538–558.

Lang, T. and Rayner, G. (2003) Food and health strategy in the UK: a policy impact analysis. *The Political Quarterly* 74: 66–75.

Laslett, P. (1965 [2000]) *The world we have lost; further explored*. Routledge: London.

Lawler, S. (1999) Children need but mothers only want: the power of 'needs talk' in the constitution of childhood. In Seymour, J. and Bagguley, P. (eds) *Relating intimacies: power and resistance*. Macmillan Press: Basingstoke.

Lawler, S. (2000) *Mothering the self: mothers, daughters, subjects*. Routledge: London.

Lawrence, F. (2008) Britain on a plate. *The Guardian* 1.10.08.

Lee, C. (2000) Psychology of women's health: a critique. In Ussher, J. (ed.) *Women's health: contemporary international perspectives*. British Psychological Society Books: Leicester, 26–39.

Lefebvre, H. (2004) *Rhythmanalysis*, trans. S. Elden and G. Moore. Continuum: London.

Leikas, S., Lindeman, M., Roininen, K. and Lahteenmaki, L. (2007) Food risk perceptions, gender and individual differences in avoidance and approach motivation, intuitive and analytical thinking styles, and anxiety. *Appetite* 48: 232–240.

Lien, M.E. (2004) The politics of food: introduction. In Lien, M.E. and Nerlich, B. (eds) *The politics of food*. Berg: Oxford.

Ling, T. (2000) Unpacking partnership: the case of health care. In Clarke, J., Gewirtz, S. and McLaughlin, E. (eds) *New managerialism, new welfare*. Sage: London.

Lipsky, M. (1980) *Street level bureaucracy*. Russell Sage Foundation: New York.

Lobstein, T. (2002) Food policies: a threat to health? *Proceedings of the Nutrition Society* 61: 579–585.

Lobstein, T. (2008) Child obesity: what can be done and who will do it? *Proceedings of the Nutrition Society* 67: 301–306.

Longhurst, R. (1999) Pregnant bodies, public scrutiny: 'giving' advice to pregnant women. In Teather, E.K. (ed.) *Embodied geographies: spaces, bodies and rites of passage*. Routledge: London, 78–90.

Longhurst, R. (2000) 'Coporeogeographies' of pregnancy: 'bikini babes'. *Environment and Planning D: Society and Space* 18: 453–472.

Longhurst, R. (2005) (Ad)dressing pregnant bodies in New Zealand: clothing, fashion, subjectivities and spatialities. *Gender, Place & Culture* 12: 433–446.

Ludvigsen, A. and Sharma, N. (2004) *Burger boy and sporty girl: children and young people's attitudes towards food in schools*. Barnardo's: Ilford.

Luhmann, N. (1993) *Risk: a sociological theory*, trans. R. Barret. De Guyter: Berlin.

Lupton, D. (1996) *Food, the body and the self*. Sage: London.

Lupton, D. (1999) *Risk*. Routledge: London.

Lupton, D. (1993) Risk as moral danger: the social and political functions of risk discourse in public health. *International Journal of Health Services* 23: 425–435.

Lupton, D. and Barclay, L. (1997) *Constructing fatherhood: discourses and experiences*. Sage: London.

Makelakel, J. (1996) A proper meal: exploring the views of women with families. *Sociologia* 33: 12–22.

Markens, S., Browner, C. and Press, N. (1997) Feeding the foetus: on interrogating the notion of maternal-foetal conflict. *Feminist Studies* 23: 351–372.

Marsden, T., Flynn, A. and Harrison, M. (2000) *Consuming interests: the social provision of foods*. UCL Press: London.

Marsiglio, W., Amato, P., Day, R.D. and Lamb, M.E. (2000) Scholarship on fatherhood in the 1990s and beyond. *Journal of Marriage and the Family* 62: 1173–1191.

Mason, J. (2002) *Qualitative researching*. Sage: London.

Mason, J. (2007). 'Re-using' qualitative data: on the merits of an investigative epistemology. *Sociological Research Online* 12, 3 (http://www.socresonline.org.uk/12/3/3.html).

Matsunaga, W. (2005) *Shokutaku no Anzengaku*. Ieno Hikari Kyōkai: Tokyo.

Maxwell, W. (1980) *So long, see you tomorrow*. Alfred Knopf: New York.

Maye, D., Holloway, L. and Kneafsey, M. (eds) (2007) *Alternative food geographies: representation and practice*. Elsevier: Amsterdam.

McIntosh, W.A. and Zey, M. (1989) Women as gatekeepers of food consumption: a sociological critique. *Food and Foodways* 3: 317–332.

McLeish, J. (2005) *Talking about food – how to give effective healthy eating advice to disadvantaged pregnant women. A practical guide for health professionals.* Maternity Alliance.

Mead, L.M. (ed.) (1997) *The new paternalism: supervisory approaches to poverty.* Brookings Institution Press: Washington, DC.

Mechling, J. (2005) Boy Scouts and the manly art of cooking. *Food and Foodways* 13: 67–89.

Mederer, H.J. (1993) Division of labor in two-earner homes: task accomplishment versus household management as critical variables in perceptions about family work. *Journal of Marriage and the Family* 55: 133–145.

Meredith, S. (2005) *Policing pregnancy; the law and ethics of obstetric conflict.* Ashgate: Aldershot.

Metcalfe, A., Owen, J., Shipton, G. and Dryden, C. (2008) Inside and outside the school: themes and reflections. *Children's Geographies* 6: 403–412.

Miles, S. (2004) Public worry about specific food safety issues. *British Food Journal* 106: 9–22.

Millstone, E. and van Zwanenberg, P. (2002) The evolution of food safety policy-making institutions in the UK, EU and Codex Alimentarius. *Social Policy and Administration* 36: 593–609.

Miller, D. and Reilly, J. (1995) Making an issue of food safety: the media, pressure groups, and the public sphere. In Maurer, D. and Sobal, J. (eds) *Eating agendas.* Aldine: New York, 305–336.

Miller, P. and Rose, N. (2008) *Governing the present: administrating economic, social and personal life.* Polity Press: Cambridge.

Mitchell, J.C. (1983) Case and situation analysis. *Sociological Review* 31: 187–211.

Mitchell, W. (2007) Research review. The role of grandparents in intergenerational support for families with disabled children: a review of the literature. *Child and Family Social Work* 12: 94–101.

Moisio, R., Arnould, E.J. and Price, L.L. (2004) Between mothers and markets: constructing family identity through home-made food. *Journal of Consumer Culture* 4: 361–384.

Morgan, D. (1996) *Family connections: an introduction to family studies.* Polity Press: Cambridge.

Morgan, D. (1999) Risk and family practices: accounting the change and fluidity in family life. In Silva, B. and Smart, C. (eds) *The new family?* Sage: London, 13–30.

Morgan, K., Marsden, T. and Murdoch, J. (2006) *Worlds of food: place, power, and provenance in the food chain.* Oxford University Press: Oxford.

Morin, K.H. (1998) Perinatal outcomes of obese women: a review of the literature. *Journal of Obstetric, Gynecologic and Neonatal Nursing* 27: 431.

Mouratidou, T., Ford, F. and Fraser, R.B. (2006a) Dietary assessment of a population of pregnant women in Sheffield UK. *British Journal of Nutrition* 96: 929–935.

Mouratidou, T., Ford, F. and Fraser, R.B. (2006b) Validation of a food-frequency questionnaire for use in pregnancy. *Public Health Nutrition* 9: 515–522.

Munro, E. (2004) The impact of audit on social work practice. *British Journal of Social Work* 34: 1075–1095.

Murakami, N. (2004) *Sekai no shoku o mamoreruka: shokuhin panikku to kiki kanri.* Heibonsha: Tokyo.

Murcott, A. (1982) On the social significance of the 'cooked dinner' in South Wales. *Social Science Information* 21: 677–696.

Murcott, A. (1983) 'It's a pleasure to cook for him': food, mealtimes and gender in some South Wales households. In Gamarnikow, E., Morgan, D., Purvis, J. and Taylorson, D. (eds) *The public and the private*. Heinemann: London, 78–90.

Murcott, A. (1986) Opening the 'black box': food, eating and household relationships. *Sosioaaliliaaketieteellinen Aikakauslehti* 23: 85–92.

Murcott, A. (1997). Family meals – a thing of the past? In Caplan, P. (ed.) *Food, health and identity*. Routledge: London, 32–49.

Murcott, A. ed. (1998) *The nation's diet: the social science of food choice*. Longman: London.

Murcott, A. (2000) Is it still a pleasure to cook for him? Social changes in the household and the family. *Journal of Consumer Culture* 24: 78–84.

Murphy, E. (1998) Food choices for babies. In Murcott, A. (ed.) *The nation's diet: the social science of food choice*. Addison Wesley Longman: Harlow, 250–266.

Murphy, E.A., Parker, S.A. and Phipps, C. (1999) Motherhood, morality and infant feeding. In Germov, J. and Williams, L. (eds) *A sociology of food and nutrition: the social appetite*. Oxford University Press: Oxford, 242–258.

Naikakufu (2006) *Shokuiku hakusho: heisei 18-nendo ban*. Shadan Hōjin Jiji Gahōsha: Tokyo.

Naikakufu (2007) *Shokuiku hakusho: heisei 19-nendo ban*. Shadan Hōjin Jiji Gahōsha: Tokyo.

Naikakufu Shokuiku Suishinshitsu (2008) 'Shokuji ni kansuru ishiki chōsa hōkokuso'. Available online at http://www8.cao.go.jp/syokuiku/more/research/h19/h19/index.html (accessed on 9 September 2008).

NCT (National Childbirth Trust) (1999) *Literature review on infant feeding*. National Childbirth Trust: London.

NICE (National Institute of Health and Clinical Excellence) (2008). *Guidance to improve the nutrition of pregnant and breastfeeding mothers and children in low-income households*. NICE Public Health Programme Guidance 3. London: NICE, available at http://www.nice.org.uk/nicemedia/pdf/MaternalandChildNutritionDraftGuidance.pdf

National Statistics (2007) *Focus on families* (eds S. Smallwood and B. Wilson). Palgrave Macmillan: Basingstoke.

Nelson, M., Erens, B., Bates, B., Church, S. and Boshier, T. (eds) (2007) Low Income Diet and Nutrition Survey. Volumes 1–3. The Stationery Office: London.

Nethersole, O. (1922) *The People's League of Health: the inception of the League*. Metchim & Son: London.

Neuhaus, J. (1999) The way to a man's heart: gender roles, domestic ideology, and cookbooks in the 1950s. *Journal of Social History* 32: 529–555.

Newman, J. (2000) Beyond the new public management? modernising public services. In Clarke, J., Gewirtz, S. and McLaughlin, E. (eds) *New managerialism, new welfare* Sage: London.

Nicolson, P. (1998) *Post-natal depression: psychology, science and the transition to motherhood*. Routledge: London.

Nixon, W.C.W. (1944) A constructive outlook on pregnancy. *Health Education Journal* 2: 58.

Noble, N., McLennan, D., Wilkinson, K., Whitworth, A., Barnes, H. and Dibben, C. (2008) *The English indices of deprivation 2007*. Social Disadvantage Research

Centre, University of Oxford and University of St Andrews, March 2008. Communities and Local Government: London.

O'Malley, P. (1996) Risk and responsibility. In Barry, A., Osborne, T. and Rose, N. (eds) *Foucault and political reason*. Routledge: London, 189–207.

Oakley, A. (1974) *Housewife*. Penguin: Harmondsworth.

Oakley, A. (1980) *Women confined: Towards a sociology of childbirth*. Martin Robinson: Oxford.

Oakley, A. (1984) *The captured womb: A history of the medical care of pregnant women*. Basil Blackwell: New York.

Oakley, A. (1985) *The sociology of housework*. Basil Blackwell: Oxford.

Oates, C.J. and McDonald, S. (2006) Recycling and the domestic division of labour: is green pink or blue? *Sociology* 40: 417–433.

Ontario Public Health Association (1995) *Food for now and the future: a food and nutrition strategy for Ontario*. Discussion Paper of the Food Security Work Group. Ontario Public Health Association: Toronto.

Osawa, M. (2008) *Fukanōsei no jidai*. Iwanami Shoten: Tokyo.

OST (Office of Science and Technology) (2007) *Tackling obesities: future choices*. Office of Science and Technology: London.

Pain, R., Bailey, C. and Mowl, G. (2001) Infant feeding in North-East England: contested spaces of reproduction. *Area* 33: 261–272.

Parkin, K. (2006) *Food is love: advertising and gender roles in modern America*. University of Philadelphia Press: Philadelphia.

Payson, S. (1994) *Using historical information to identify consumer concerns about food safety*. Technological Bulletin, US Department of Agriculture, 1835: 1–19.

People's League of Health (PLOH) (1942a) Nutrition of expectant and nursing mothers. *British Medical Journal* 2: 77–78.

People's League of Health (1942b) Nutrition of expectant and nursing mothers. *Lancet* 2: 10–12.

People's League of Health (1946) The nutrition of expectant and nursing mothers in relation to maternal and infant mortality and morbidity. *Journal of Obstetrics and Gynaecology of the British Empire* 53: 498–509.

Perks, R. and Thomson, A. (eds) (2006) *The oral history reader*. Routledge: London (second edition).

Perrier, M. (2007) *Performing intensive mothering: the influence of class on 'motherwork' accounts*. Conference presentation: Monitoring parents: Childrearing in the age of 'intensive parenting'. University of Kent at Canterbury.

Petchetsky, R.P. (1987) Foetal images: the power of visual culture in the politics of reproduction. In Stanworth, M. (ed.) *Reproductive technologies: gender, motherhood and medicine*. Polity Press in association with Basil Blackwell: Cambridge, 57–80.

Philip, W., James, T., Nelson, M., Ralph, A. and Leather, S. (1997) Socioeconomic determinants of health: the contribution of nutrition to inequalities in health. *British Medical Journal* 314: 1545–1549.

Phoenix, A., Woollett, A. and Lloyd, E. (eds) (1991) *Motherhood: meanings, practices and ideologies*. London: Sage.

Pidgeon, N.F. and Beattie, J. (1998) The psychology of risk and uncertainty. In Calow, P. (ed.) *Handbook of environmental risk assessment and management*. Blackwell Science Ltd: Oxford, 289–318.

Pillow, W. (2004) *Unfit subjects: educational policy and the teen mother*. Routledge: New York.

Policy Commission on the Future of Food and Farming (2002) *Farming and food: a sustainable future* (The Curry Commission) Cabinet Office: London.

Poole, L. (2000) Health care: new labour's NHS. In Clarke, J., Gewirtz, S. and McLaughlin, E. (eds) *New managerialism, new welfare*. Sage: London.

Poole, M. and Isaacs, D. (1997) Caring: a gendered concept. *Women's Studies International Forum* 20: 529–536.

Presser, H.B. (1994) Employment schedules among dual-earner spouses and the division of household labor by gender. *American Sociological Review* 59: 348–364.

Probyn, E. (1993) Choosing choice: winking images of sexuality in popular culture. In Fisher, S. and Davis, K. (eds) *Negotiating at the margins: gendered discourses of resistance*. Rutgers University Press: New Brunswick.

Putnam, R.D. (2000) *Bowling alone: The collapse and revival of American community*. Simon & Schuster: New York.

Putney, N. and Bengtson, V. (2001) Families, intergenerational relationships and kinkeeping in midlife. In Lachman, M.E. (eds) *Handbook of midlife development*. Wiley: New York, 528–570.

Qvortrup, J. (1994) Introduction. In Qvortrup, J., Bardy, M., Sgritta, G. and Wintersbergen, H. (eds) *Childhood matters: social theory, practice and politics*. Avebury: Aldershot.

Radimer, K.L., Olson, C.M., Green, J C., Campbell, C.C. and Habicht, J.P. (1992) Understanding hunger and developing indicators to assess it in women and children. *Journal of Nutrition Education* 24 Suppl., 36S–45S.

Redmond, E.C. and Griffith, C.J. (2003) Consumer food handling in the home: a review of food safety studies. *Journal of Food Protection* 66: 130–161.

Ribbens McCarthy, J., Edwards, R. and Gillies, V. (2003) *Making families: moral tales of parenting and step-parenting*. Sociology Press: Durham.

Rogers, I., Emmett, P., Baker, D., Golding, J. and the ALSPAC Study Team (1998) Financial difficulties, smoking habits, composition of the diet and birth weight in a population of pregnant women in the South West England. *European Journal of Clinical Nutrition* 52: 251–260.

Roos, G. and Wandel, M. (2005) I eat because I'm hungry, because it's good, and to become full: everyday eating voiced by male carpenters, drivers and engineers in contemporary Oslo. *Food and Foodways* 13: 169–180.

Rosati, S. and Saba, A. (2004). The perception of risks associated with food-related hazards and the perceived reliability of sources of information. *International Journal of Food Science and Technology* 39: 491–500.

Rose, N. (1992) Governing the enterprising self. In Heelas, P. and Morris, P. (eds) *The values of the enterprise culture: the moral debate*. Routledge: London, 141–164.

Rose, N. (1996) Governing 'advanced' liberal democracies. In Barry, A., Osborne, T. and Rose, N. (eds) *Foucault and political reason*. Routledge: London, 37–64.

Rose, N. (1999) *Governing the soul: the shaping of the private self, the second edition*. Free Association Books: London.

Rotenberg, R. (1981). The impact of industrialisation on meal patterns in Vienna, Austria. *Ecology of Food and Nutrition* 11: 25–35.

Rouse, J. (2007) Social practices and normativity. *Philosophy of the Social Sciences* 37: 46–56.

Ruddick, S. (2007) At the horizons of the subject: neo-liberalism, neo-conservatism and the rights of the child, part one. *Gender, Place and Culture* 14: 513–526.
Samuel, R. and Thompson, P. (eds) (1982) *The myths we live by*. Routledge: London.
Sanchez, L. and Thomson, E. (1997) Becoming mothers and fathers: parenthood, gender, and the division of labor. *Gender and Society* 11: 747–772.
Sasaki, H. (2008) Japan's new agriculture trade policy and electoral reform: 'agriculture policy in an offensive posture [seme no nosei]'. *Japanese Journal of Political Science* 9: 121–144.
Schatzki, T.R. (1996) *Social practices: a Wittgensteinian approach to human activity and the social*. Cambridge University Press: Cambridge.
Schatzki, T.R. (2002) *The site of the social*. The Pennsylvania State University Press: University Park, PA.
Schatzki, T.R. (2005) Where times meet. *Cosmos and History: The Journal of Natural and Social Philosophy* 1: 191–212.
Schofield, C., Steward, J. and Wheeler, E. (1989) The diets of pregnant and postpartum women in different social groups in London and Edinburgh: calcium, iron, retinol, ascorbic acid and folic acid. *British Journal of Nutrition* 62: 363–377.
Scrimgeour, G.E. (2006) *Women without children: making decisions about mothering in the life course*. Paper presented at the annual meeting of the American Sociological Association, Montreal Convention Center, Montreal, Quebec, Canada.
Segal, L. (1990) *Slow motion: changing masculinities, changing men*. London: Virago.
Sevenhuijsen, S. (1998) *Citizenship and the ethics of care*. Routledge: London.
Shelton, B.A. and John, D. (1996) The division of household labor. *Annual Review of Sociology* 22: 299–322.
Shibata, A. (2007) *Shokuryō sōdatsu: nihon no shoku ga sekai kara torinokosareru hi*. Nihon Keizai Shinbunsha: Tokyo.
Shibutani, T. (1966). *Improvised news: a sociological study of rumor*. Bobbs-Merrill Co.: Indianaopolis.
Shōgenji, Shin'ichi (2008) *Nōgyo saiken: shinka towareru nihon no nōsei*. Iwanami Shoten: Tokyo.
Short, F. (2006) *Kitchen secrets: the meaning of cooking in everyday life*. Berg: Oxford.
Shove, E. and Pantzar, M. (2005) Consumers, producers and practices: understanding the invention and reinvention of Nordic walking. *Journal of Consumer Culture* 5: 43–64.
Silva, E. (ed.) (1996) *Good enough mothering?: Feminist perspectives on lone motherhood*. Routledge: London.
Silva, E.B. (2000) The cook, the cooker and the gendering of the kitchen. *The Sociological Review* 48: 612–628.
Silva, E.B. and Smart, C. (1999) (eds) *The new family?* Sage: London.
Simonsen, K. (2007) Practice, spatiality and embodied emotions: An outline of a geography of practice. *Human Affairs* 17: 168–181.
Simpson, B., McCarthy, P. and Walker, J. (1995) *Being there: fathers after divorce*. The Nuffield Foundation and the Newcastle Centre for Family Studies.
Slovic, P. (1987) Perception of risk. *Science* 236: 280–285.
Smart, C. (2007) *Personal life*. Polity Press: Cambridge.
Smart, C. and Neale, B. (1999) *Family fragments?* Polity Press: Cambridge.
Smart, C., Neale, B. and Wade, A. (eds) (2001) *The changing experience of childhood: families and divorce*. Polity Press: Cambridge.

Smith, T., Perks, R. and Smith, G. (1998) *Ukraine's forbidden history*. Dewi Lewis: Stockport.
Smith, E., Flynn, A. and Percival, A. (2004) Regulating food risks: rebuilding confidence in Europe's food? *Environment and Planning C: Government and Policy* 22: 543–567.
Smith, G.R. (2007) Beyond individual/collective memory: women's transactive memories of food, family and conflict. *Oral History* 35: 77–90.
Smith, J.A. (ed.) (2003) *Qualitative research: A practical guide to research methods*. Sage: London.
SMRP (School Meals Review Panel) (2005) *Turning the tables, transforming school food*. School Meals Review Panel: London.
Spain, D. and Bianchi, S. (1996) *Balancing act: motherhood, marriage, and employment among American women*. Russell Sage Foundation: New York.
Stapleton, H. (2006) *Doing sex, having the baby: young women and transitions to motherhood*. Unpublished PhD Thesis, University of Sheffield (Department of Sociological Studies).
Star Magazine, 10 March 2008 Pregnant Kerry 'drinks a bottle of wine a night'.
Summers, A. (2003) *The end of equality: work, babies and women's choices in 21st century Australia*. Random House: Australia.
Sutton, D.E. (2001) *Remembrance of repast*. Berg: New York.
Takeda, H. (2005a) *The political economy of reproduction in Japan: between nation-state and everyday life*. Routledge Curzon: London.
Takeda, H. (2005b) Governance through the family in Japan: governing the domestic. In Hook, G.D. (ed.) *Contested governance in Japan*. Routledge Curzon: London, 233–248.
Takeda, H. (2008) Delicious food in a beautiful country: nationhood and nationalism in discourses on food in contemporary Japan. *SEN: Studies in Ethnicity and Nationalism* 8: 5–29.
Takemoto, T. (2008) 'Nihon ni okeru shoku risuku bunseki shuhō dōnyū', a memo sent by the author after an interview (29 April 2008 in Tokyo).
The Times, 26 May (2007) Soon pregnant women will be terrified to breathe.
Thompson, P. (1975) *The Edwardians: the remaking of British society*. Weidenfeld & Nicholson: London (2nd edition, 1992).
Thompson, P. (1978). *The voice of the past: oral history*. Oxford University Press: Oxford (2nd edition, 1988).
Tucker, M., Whaley, S.R. and Sharp, J.S. (2006) Consumer perceptions of food-related risks. *International Journal of Food Science and Technology* 41: 135–146.
Tyler, I. (2008) Chav mum chav scum. *Feminist Media Studies* 8: 17–34.
Ussher, J. (1991) *Women's madness: misogyny or mental illness?* Harvester Wheatsheaf: Brighton.
Ussher, J.M. (2006) *Managing the monstrous feminine: regulating the reproductive body*. Routledge: London and New York.
Van Zwanenberg, P. and Millstone, E. (2003) BSE: a paradigm of policy failure. *Political Quarterly* 74: 27–38.
Verbeke, W., Frewer, L.J., Scholderer, J. and De Brabander, H.F. (2007) Why consumers behave as they do with respect to food safety and risk information. *Analytica Chimica Acta* 586: 2–7.

Ver Ploeg, M. and Ralston, K. (2008) *Food stamps and obesity: what do we know?* US Department of Agriculture, Economic Research Service, EIB-34.

Vernon, J. (2005) The ethics of hunger and the assembly of society: the technopolitics of the school meal in modern Britain. *American Historical Review* 110: 693–725.

Wade, A. (2005) Continuity and change in parent-child relations over three generations. University of Leeds, ESRC Research Grant No: R000239523.

Wainwright, E.M. (2003) Constant medical supervision: locating reproductive bodies in Victorian and Edwardian Dundee. *Health and Place* 9: 163–174.

Ward, N., Donaldson, A. and Lowe, P. (2004) Policy framing and learning the lessons from the UK's foot and mouth disease crisis. *Environment and Planning C: Government and Policy* 22: 291–306.

Ward, N., Jackson, P., Russell, P. and Wilkinson, K. (2008) Productivism, post-productivism and European agricultural reform: the case of sugar. *Sociologia Ruralis* 46: 118–132.

Warde, A. (1997) *Consumption, food and taste: culinary antinomies and commodity culture.* Sage: London.

Warde, A. (2005) Consumption and theories of practice. *Journal of Consumer Culture* 5: 131–153.

Warde, A. and Hetherington, K. (1994) English households and routine food practices: a research note. *Sociological Review* 42: 758–778.

Warde, A. and Martens, L. (2000) *Eating out: social differentiation, consumption and pleasure.* Cambridge University Press: Cambridge.

Weeks, J., Heaphy, B. and Donovan, C. (2001) *Same-sex intimacies.* Routledge: London.

Welfare Foods Order (1968) Part 11 3 (1) Statutory Instruments No. 389.

Welfare Food Regulations (1996), Statutory Instrument 1996 No. 1434 ISBN 0110547993.

Whelan, E.M. and Stare, F.J. (1992). *Panic in the pantry* (2nd edn). Prometheus: Buffalo, N.Y.

Wilk, R. and Hintlian, P. (2005) Cooking on their own: cuisines of manly men. *Food and Foodways* 13: 159–168.

Williams, A.S. (1997) *Women and childbirth in the twentieth century – a history of the National Birthday Trust Fund 1928–1993.* Sutton Publishing: Stroud.

Williams, F. (2001) In and beyond New Labour: towards a new political ethics of care. *Critical Social Policy* 21: 467–493.

Williams, F. (2002) The presence of feminism in the future of welfare. *Economy and Society* 31: 501–519.

Williams, F. (2004) *Rethinking families.* Calouste Gulbenkin Foundation: London.

Wills, W.J. (2002) Well-being during the transition to adulthood: analyses of family life and eating healthily in Great Britain. Unpublished PhD dissertation, University of London.

Winship, J. (1980) *Advertising in women's magazines: 1956–1974.* Centre for Contemporary Cultural Studies: Birmingham.

WHO (World Health Organization) (2002) Food and health in Europe: a new basis for action – summary document. Copenhagen: World Health Organization European Regional Office (available online http://www.euro.who.int/document/e78578.pdf, accessed 31 October 2008).

Yamaguchi, S. (2002) *Gendai shaki no yuragi to risuku.* Shin'yōsha: Tokyo.

Yeatman, H.R. (2003) Food and nutrition policy at the local level: key factors that influence the policy development process. *Critical Public Health* 13: 125–138.

Yoshida, T. (2005) *Tabetemo heiki? BSE to shokuhin hyōji*. Shūeisha: Tokyo.

Young, I.M. (1990) *Throwing like a girl and other essays in feminist psychology and social meaning*. Indiana University Press: Indiana.

Young, M. and Willmott, P. (1957) *Family and kinship in East London*. Routledge & Kegan Paul: London.

Zaninotto, P., Wardle, H., Stamatakis, E., Mindell, J. and Head, J. (2006) *Forecasting obesity to 2010*. Report prepared for the Department of Health. National Centre for Social Research and Royal Free and University College Medical School: London.

Index

Acheson Inquiry (1998), 21
'advanced liberal democracies', 15, 167, 183–4
advertisement/adverts/advertising, 15, 60, 163–4
  analysis of issues, 146, 150–8
  claims made, 159–62
affordable food, 13, 31–2, 212–13, 224
Alanen, L., 79
antenatal clinics/care, 22–3, 24, 25, 29, 45, 46
Asian foods, 238
Association of Ukrainians in Britain (*Soyuz Ukrayintsiv Velikoyi Britaniyi*, SUB) *see* SUB Club
awareness, 12, 64, 74

babies, 19, 22–3, 38
balanced meals/balanced diet, 10, 32–3, 151, 161, 235
  caloric balance, 51
  nutritionally, 232, 242–3
  see also 'healthy eating'
Barling, D., 8, 171, 172
Barnardo's children's charity, 252n.14
Bauman, Z., 169
Beck, U., 94
  Risk Society, 170
behaviour change, 12, 119
behaviour patterns, 128, 166
Bellingham, Linda, 156
Bengtson, V., 253n.3
Betty Crocker Cake Mix, 153
'biopolitics'/biopolitical governing system, 166–7, 170, 183
  see also governance (of family meals)
bird flu, 122, 123, 124–5
Bird's Custard, 156
Bishop, L., 255n.3
'black box' of family life, 5, 246, 251n.7, 255n.7

Blake, M., 15
Blank, L., 14
body management/body management practices, 36, 51–4
Body Mass Index (BMI), 31, 252n.11, 252n.1
Bolton, 137
bottle-feeding, 55, 68–72
Bourdieu, P., 5
Bradford, 12, 139, 235, 236, 238, 249
Brannen, J., 87
breakfast, 111, 113, 141–2, 203, 215, 253n.5
  'family practice', 15–16
  with family, 192, 194–200
  in IDRs, 239
breastfeeding, 10, 20, 28–34, 58, 64–6, 68–72, 74
  and dietary inadequacies, 20–1
  family's support to mothers, 51–3, 55–6
  special nutrition programmes for, 24–7
Brembeck, H., 255n.2
Bridges, L., 253n.3
Britain, 1, 2, 3, 6, 9, 12, 14, 26, 44, 58, 62, 69, 131, 134, 139, 152, 156, 168, 173, 208, 228, 236, 238
British Medical Association (BMA), 25
British Medical Journal, 32
British school meals *see* school meals
British-Asian households/families, 4, 113
Brown, Gordon, 8
Brown, R., 229
Burchell, G., 167
Burgess, R., 252n.14
Byng-Hall, J., 87, 253n.4

calcium, 8, 13, 23, 30
capitalism, 39, 166, 169
Captive Nations' Society, 239
Caraher, M., 173, 224

276

care deficit, 187, 200
carers (of children), 11, 112, 182, 221
caring activities, 150, 196
caring roles (of women), 39–41, 150, 221–3
'celebrity mums', 63–4, 74
Census (2001), 3–4
changing consumption patterns (study, 1975–2000), 135–6
changing families, 3–12, 219–20
Changing Families, Changing Food research programme, 16, 95, 121, 147, 151, 163, 252n.8, 254n.8, 255n.3, 256n.5
changing food practices *see* food practices
Charles, N., 148, 154, 156, 213, 253n.4
'chav mum', 63
Cheng, S-L., 135
child food support schemes, 19
child nutrition, 19, 27, 33, 234
Child Tax Credit, 19
childcare, 45–7, 54, 69–71, 95, 116, 143, 216, 248
childhood memories, 217–18, 225
childhood obesity, 1–2, 35–6, 133, 206
  see also obesity/overweight
childhood, 10, 75–9, 97, 118–28, 215–16, 225
  family life, 2–3, 9, 10, 13–14, 98–115, 136–45, 248–9
  food practices, 116–17, 217–20
  inter-generational relations, 80–92
childrearing *see* childcare
'Children as Family Participants' project, 231–5
children, 3–10, 12, 34, 35, 37–40, 42, 49, 54, 62, 138–42, 201–2, 203–4, 207, 217–18
  advertising aimed at, 152, 153–4, 227
  good eating habits, 42, 182, 194–5, 205, 224–5, 248, 252n.14
  grandparents' relationship with, 80–2, 90–2
  health/nutrition of, 12, 24–8, 46–7, 68, 151, 161, 175, 178–9, 200
  of immigrant families, 44–5
  inter-generational relations, 77–9, 83–8
  involvement of fathers with, 54, 60, 94–7, 109, 112–17, 141–4
  'mothering' of, 150, 218
  outside marriage, 3, 37
  school meals for, 1–2, 11, 193, 229–35, 242–3
'Children, Food and Identity' project, 256n.6
Children's Centres (UK), 206
children's eating practices, 92
China, 8
chip shop/fish and chip shop, 85, 139, 143, 234, 243
choice *see* food choice, 'healthy choices'
'chosen' families, 3, 4, 38, 144–5
chosen relationships, 3, 251n.4
Christensen, P., 207
Churchill, Winston, 26
Citizens' Forums, 8
civil servants, 228–9
civility, 11, 16, 242
cod liver oil, 26
Codex Alimentarius Commission, 118
cohabitation/cohabiting households, 3–4, 36, 37
Cohen, S., 132, 133, 135
commensality, 144
commitment, 3, 10, 14–15, 116, 172, 219, 244
Committee on Medical Aspects of Food and Nutrition Policy (COMA), 27
  Panel on Maternal and Child Nutrition, 26
commodity prices, 7–8, 174–5, 235, 248
Common Agriculture Policy (EU), 6, 172
Community Food Educators (UK), 206
community *see* wider community/wider society
complaints (related to food provisioning), 15, 152–9, 163
  see also food refusal
conflicts/conflictual, 37, 88–9
Consumer Attitudes Survey, 12

consumer choice, 8–9, 11, 210–11, 247–8
consumer-oriented food regulatory system, 181–2, 183
consumption (of food/foodstuffs), 1, 5–6, 30–1, 161, 173–6, 207–10, 248–50
   changing patterns of, 53–4, 135–6, 224–5
   and family food practices, 207–10
   in IDRs, 228–9, 240–2
   national food policy and, 165–7
   patterns of, 53–4, 135–6
   risks associated with food preparation, 119–23, 127–8
   transition in familial environment, 34–7, 45–51
contemporary family life, 4, 77, 84–5, 87–8
   diversity of, 11–12
   intergenerational relations, 13–14
   social practices, 5–6
contested spaces, 16, 242
continuities and discontinuities (in family life), 13, 41–4, 61, 78, 82–8
controlled trials, 23
convenience food, 82, 116, 144, 251n.2
convenience stores/store chains, 181
'Cook and Eat' programmes, 213–16
'cooked dinner'/'proper cooked dinner', 85, 134, 147–8, 156
cooked lunch, 15–16, 196
cookery lessons, 1–2, 84
cooking practices, 84–5, 148
cooking skills, 10–11, 13, 30–3, 34, 49–50, 77, 154, 247, 251n.2
   day-to-day cooking, 41–5
   food and health knowledge, 211
   passed down through generations, 2–3, 83
Corrigan, Richard, 133
'Cossack Brothers', 236–7
counter-tendencies, 6, 135–6
Coveney, J., 173, 255n.4
cow's milk, 22, 27
Croft, Mark, 64
culinary skills/competence, 9, 37, 41, 44–5, 47–50, 149–51, 214, 249–50
   accommodating partner's poor skills, 51
   learning, 213–16
   presenting meals of several courses, 142
   and shop-bought 'ready meals', 52
curry and rice, 230, 238
Curry Commission, 7
Curtin, D., 188
Curtis, P., 13

daily life, 188, 191, 195, 219–20, 225
Daily Mail, The, 77, 205
De Boer, M., 128
De Certeau, M., 5
Dean, M., 167, 169, 254n.2
deficit models, 11–12
Department for Environment, Food and Rural Affairs (DEFRA), 7, 171
Department of Health (DoH), 27
dependent children, 3, 138
deprivation/deprived, the, 19, 20–1, 28–9, 80, 136, 231, 233
'deserving poor' discourse, 228
DeVault, M., 4, 95, 98, 115, 131, 148, 149, 150, 154, 190, 253n.2
Feeding the Family, 4
diabetes, 20, 29, 36, 40, 46, 51
   managing, 36, 52–3, 55–6
   obesity/overweight and, 13
diabetic states *see* diabetes
diet and health study project, 206–13
diets, 1–2, 13, 36–7, 58–61, 72, 127, 151, 174–5, 179, 206, 221–3, 245
   for children, 46–7
   in Edwardian era, 138, 140–1
   home cooked traditional, 85–8
   and inequalities, 210–12
   nutrition and healthy eating, 33–4, 203–4
   pregnant women/mothers, 62–8
   risks in, 122–5, 183–4, 188–9
   for women, 13–14, 20–8, 31–3, 249
   for young people's, 243, 248
dietary advice, 2, 24, 25, 34
dietary intakes, 23, 24, 28, 30–1, 32, 34, 151

dietary practices/patterns, 1, 2–3, 20–1, 174, 183, 248
  see also eating patterns; food habits
dining table, the, 55–6, 111, 114
  affording a, 215–16
  eating together/Sunday lunch, 42–3, 55–6, 133–4, 218, 225
'dinner ladies', 230–3, 243
disabled, the, 227, 237–8, 239
discursive construction (of generation), 14, 79, 92
divorce, 3, 4, 37, 60, 81, 253n.2
Dobson, B., 210
'docile bodies', 68, 73
'doing' family, 3–6, 14, 78–9, 85–8, 92, 131–2, 188, 246, 251n.8
domestic kitchen, 96, 214
domestic labour, division of, 13, 37, 38–9, 41–4, 46–50, 93–6, 115–17, 147–8
domestic responsibilities, 10, 144
domestic roles/divisions *see* domestic labour, division of
domestic space, 15, 96
domestic tasks, 14, 55, 95, 160, 216, 246–7
  see also household chores/tasks
domestic work, 41–4, 52–4
  see also domestic labour, division of; household chores/tasks
domesticity, 38–9, 134, 139, 142–4
Donzelot, J., 166, 167
Douglas, Mary, 200
Dowler, E., 224
dried milk/dried cow's milk, 13, 22
Dryden, C., 14
dual-career households, 188, 191, 202
Dundee, 138
Dutch 'Hunger Winter', 34

E. coli, 7, 171, 176
'eat properly', 230–1, 232
eating events, 10–11, 135–6, 188
eating habits, 2, 117, 121, 125, 175, 182, 210, 232, 235
eating outside the home *see* eating together
eating patterns, 20–1, 28, 32, 34, 81–2, 210–11, 224–5
  see also dietary practices/patterns; eating habits; food habits
eating routines *see* eating patterns
eating together, 4, 14, 85, 113–15, 144, 200
  around a dining table, 42–3, 55–6, 218–20, 252
  eating out, 10, 135–6
  see also family eating practices
Ebbs, J.H., 24
'ecocultural approach'/'ecocultural' perspective (to/on family practices), 207
Economic and Social Research Council (ESRC), 134
  The Nation's Diet (research programme, 1992–1998), 134
Economist, The, 8
Edwardian eating practices (study), 136–40
'Edwardians On-Line' (digital archive), 137
elderly, the, 238, 239
Ellaway, A., 174
'embodied knowledge', 10, 67
'emerging economies', 7
'emotion work', 39
emotional labour, 224
emotional management (of the family), 146, 155–64
  food provisioning, 147–51
  producing 'love' and avoiding complaints, 152–4
employment *see* paid employment
'empowered' women, 61, 68, 73–4, 224, 225
'enabled consumers', 175–6, 179, 183
energy intakes, 30, 31
enterprise, 15, 167–70, 183
environmental influences, 33–4
epigenetics/epigenetic processes, 33–4
ethnicity, 4, 5, 9, 21, 28, 29, 38, 137, 229, 80, 137, 245, 249–50
  of research populations, 73–4, 97, 229, 231, 234
  social inclusion of, 207–8
Europe, 6, 7, 69, 135, 176, 251n.10
European Convention on Human Rights, 252n.3

European Research Council, 256n.4
European Union (EU), 172
  Common Agriculture Policy, 6, 172
European Volunteer Worker scheme, 236
'everyday cooks', 106, 111–12
everyday life, 5, 68, 166, 179, 190, 191, 207, 251n.2
Ewald, F., 170
existential time, 188, 190, 192, 194–196, 202
Expanded Food and Nutrition Education Program (EFNEP), 24–5
'experiential time', 15–16
'extended families', 4, 80–1, 113, 143

Fair Trade, 6, 136
families and food, relationship between, 1–8, 12–13, 14, 15, 96, 137, 223, 248
  decline of 'the family meal', 14
  gendered division of labour, 223
  home-produced foods, 43
  men's understandings of food, 96
'Families Remembering Food' project, 137–44
Family and Kinship in East London, 251n.3
family and kinship, 3–4, 37, 115, 227
  biological ties and social relationships, 13–14, 78–9, 91
  changing notions of, 37–9
  friendship, 251n.4
  see also fictive kin/'fictive family'
family cohesion, 42, 55, 202, 204
family context, 5–6, 35, 39, 78–91, 151
family eating practices, 45, 73, 74, 85, 87, 92, 135–6, 217–20, 203, 216, 217
  Britain, 134–44
  fathers' point of view of, 89–114
  food hygiene, 175–6
  healthy diet, 205–6, 211–13, 220, 221–3
  less than 'perfect' meals, 45–50, 85
  traditional, 81–2, 86–8
  see also eating together

family eating *see* family eating practices
family feeding practices *see* family feeding
family feeding, 13, 35–6, 55–6, 192, 195
family food practices *see* food practices
family food scripts/family scripts, 83–5, 87–8, 91, 253n.4
family formation, 13, 35–7, 45–56
  division of domestic labour in, 41–4
  new family structures, 38–9
  see also family structures
family forms, 11, 13–14, 80, 95, 131, 206, 225
  see also household composition
family groupings, 36, 38
family health, 13, 36, 46, 55–6, 207
Family Income Supplements (FIS), 26
family life, 1–16, 38, 44, 82–6, 113–17, 206–10, 252n.2
  'black box' of, 255n.7
  in dual-career households, 191–200
  in Edwardian Britain, 131, 136–45
  and food-related scripts/activities, 87–92, 118–20, 147–50, 188–90, 227, 246–50, 254n.8
  health and, 55–6
  and household composition, 77–81
  household divisions of labour in, 93–112
  interiority of, 39–45
  negotiation of, 115–17
  re-creation of, 227–8
  see also contemporary family life
'family meals', 2, 10–16, 48–50, 96, 111–12, 125–6
  'healthy balance', 42–5
  nationally specific constructions of, 192–201
  regulation of, 165–7, 171–6, 184
  social institution, 3–14, 16, 46, 131–5, 188–90, 202–4
  decline of, 14–15, 110, 136–45
  time for communication, 113–17, 217–19
  see also governance (of family meals)

family members, 10, 13, 15, 39, 70, 78, 134–6, 140, 153, 162–4, 192, 203–4, 206, 213, 223
  domestic routines of, 141–4, 148, 195
  and ecocultural approach, 207–10
  food preferences and tastes of, 10–12, 85–8, 149–51
  food-related roles of, 44–50, 106–13, 158–9, 188–9
family participants (in studies/projects), 211, 217–23
family practices, 5–6, 44, 55–6, 79, 183, 190, 206, 216–20, 225
  disciplinary perspectives, 246–7
  'ecocultural approach', 207–10
  improving diets, 188–9
  special meanings of meals, 15–16, 182
  surveillance of, 216
family relations/family relationships, 5, 78
  food continuities, 82–4
  food discontinuities, 85–7
  generational order within, 88–90
family settings, 36, 41, 54
family structures, 4, 37–9, 162
  see also family forms
family unity, 156–7, 161, 163
Farkas, G., 106
farming/farming and industrial practices, 6–8, 14, 22, 178
  decline of, 171, 172
  risks associated with, 120–2, 127
fatalism (related to food risks), 14, 121, 125, 127–8
fatherhood, 93–117
fathering, 94–5, 116
'Fathers Direct' (pressure group), 94
fathers, 14, 93–105, 115–17, 225, 229
  and childcare, 54
  cooking for the family, 49–50, 106–12
  eating with the family, 113–14, 142
  and household chores, 41–5, 143–4
  feedback (on preparation of food), 148, 163
  giving of care, 149–52
  pleasing of men, 153–9

reception of food, 160–2
feeding the family, 5, 10, 116–17, 176, 191–2, 226
  and emotional management, 146–64
  and gendered practice, 10, 15, 94, 96, 121–2, 142–4, 176, 184, 246–7
  and 'right' food, 222–3
female identity, 39, 42, 52
female partners, 10, 37, 45, 190–2
feminists/feminism, 38–41, 58, 162
  household and family, 93–4
  pregnancy and motherhood, 58
  responsibility for food provision, 160
'fictive kin'/'fictive family', 3–6, 227
Finch, J., 5, 78, 224, 251n.4
'first generation Ukrainians', 236–7, 238, 244–5
  see also 'second generation Ukrainians'
Floyd, J., 216
Flynn, A., 172
'foetal person', 61–8
'foetal rights', 73
folate, 13, 30
folic acid, 20, 27, 30–1
'folk devils', 132, 133
food advice/food advice bureaux, 2–3, 25–6, 28
food and family life, 93–117
food and gender, 220–3
'food as love', 222–3, 146–64
food budgets, 25, 32
'food choice', 3, 127–8, 213
  and IDRs, 232, 241
  improvement by comparative research, 249–50
  individualisation of, 8–9, 15
  'junk food', 248
  nutritional quality of meals and, 25, 120, 224–5
  shopping and selecting food, 122
food consumption, 119
food discourse, 12, 50, 165–7
food engagements, 202, 203
food frequency questionnaire (FFQ), 30

food governance system, 175–6, 180–2
  see also governance (of family meals)
food habits, 25–6, 119–21, 128, 242–5
  altering children's, 227–8
  continuities and changes in, 41–4
  see also eating habits
food hygiene, 119, 128, 175–6
food ideologies, 16, 226–8, 244–5
  and food values, 241–2
  implementing policy schemes, 243–5
  institutional settings and, 229–40
food labelling, 7, 175, 255n.3
'food miles', 6
food outlets, 21, 99
food patterns see eating habits; eating patterns; food habits
food poisoning, 127, 176
food policy/national food policy, 1, 8, 21, 165–7, 170–1, 206, 242–5
  in Japan, 176–82
  in UK, 171–5
food poverty, 19–22, 173–4
food practices, 5, 92, 94–6, 188–90, 247, 249–50, 253n.4
  changes in, 6–12, 248
  and different class backgrounds, 144–5
  family
    fathers' accounts of, 98–115
    grandmother's cooking, 84–5
    sharing the cooking, 109–11
  generational, 88–91
  and parents' childhoods, 86–7
  social embedding of, 8–9, 12
food preferences, 10, 37, 53, 235
food preparation, 46–7, 87–8, 119, 128, 148, 216
  help from men/partner, 50–3, 116–17
  food hygiene in, 119
food prices, 8, 21, 99, 173
food production, 14, 25, 44, 47, 127, 176–7
food providers, 227, 242, 243–4
'Food Provision and the Media' project, 147–62

food provisioning see 'provisioning' (of food)
food quality, 99, 251n.1
food refusal, 147, 149, 254n.1
  see also complaints (related to food provisioning)
food regulatory system/process, 15, 173, 176–83
food retailers/food retailing, 6, 15, 171, 172–6, 181–4, 212–13
  see also retailer-led governance system (of food)
food risk perceptions, 119, 127–8
Food Safety Commission (Japan), 183
food safety risk see food safety/food security
food safety/food security, 8, 14, 118–28, 165–6, 172–3, 251n.10, 255n.3
  assessment of risk, 127–8
  lifestyle versus technological risks, 122
  national policy on, 177–83
  parental attitudes to, 118–21, 128
  transitional risk in, 123–4
  trivialising, 126–7
food scares, 121–2
food shopping, 45, 99–105, 174
Food Standards Agency (FSA), 1, 7, 8–9, 14, 118, 228
  '5-a-day' target, 1, 12
  Low Income Diet and Nutrition Survey, 32
food supplements/food supplementation, 22–4, 31, 25–6
food supply, 6–8, 21, 119–21, 128, 165
food support benefits, 12–13, 19, 22–34
  schemes, 22–8
  for women of childbearing age, 20–1
food support schemes see food support benefits
food values, 226, 242
  see also food ideologies

food, lens of, 1–4, 7–16, 77–8, 246, 254n.8
  changes in family life, 5–6, 57–8
  wider societal changes, 74
food, reception of, 148–9, 159–64
food, sociology of, 145–50, 152–64
food-related activities/work, 13, 14, 35, 85–8, 95, 188–9
food-related practices, 36, 79, 216, 222–3
food-related risks, 14, 178–9
  see also food safety/food security
food-related roles, 44–5, 49–50, 95
food-related tasks/responsibilities, 47, 93–4
foodstuffs, 64, 181–2, 213–14, 224
  prices of, 174–6
  transitional nature of food risks, 123–5
'foodways', 227, 242
foodwork, 10, 34–6, 55, 116
  and maternal repertoire, 45–9
  men's involvement in, 41–4, 52, 95–6, 98–115
Foot-and-Mouth Disease (FMD) crisis (2001), 7
Ford, F., 12, 13
Forero, O., 16
Foresight programme (UK government), 8, 20
  Tackling Obesities (report), 8
formula cow's milk see cow's milk
formula feeding, 68–9, 73–4
  see also bottle-feeding
Foucauldian approach/notions/framework, 16, 58, 62, 65–8, 73
Fox, R., 13
Fraser, R., 12, 13
Free Healthy School Meals System (Hull), 242
Freidberg, S., 255n.4
fresh fruit and vegetables, 1, 12, 27, 224

GATT Uruguay Round, 172
  Agreement on Agriculture (AoA), 172

gay and lesbian couples/families, 4, 38
  see also same-sex partnerships/households
gender divisions, 39–40, 146, 163
  see also gender norms/gendered norms
gender norms/gendered norms, 38, 45, 47–51, 65, 73–4
  see also gendered division of labour
gender roles, 55, 134–6, 144–5
  division of domestic labour, 115–17
  organising food-related practices, 35–9
gendered division of labour, 115, 223
gendered norms see gender norms/gendered norms
gendered patterns/gendered patterning, 116, 131, 206, 223
gendered practices see feeding the family
generational frame, 79, 82, 92
generational identities, 91–2
generational relationships, 43, 80–91
genetically modified foods, 6, 172, 178
genomes, 33–4
geographical contexts, 201, 202, 203
gestational weight gain, 24, 34
Giddens, A., 254n.3
Gillis, J., 5
Glasgow, 137
globalisation, 6, 7–8, 167, 170, 254n.3
  biopolitical governing, points of transition, 167–70
  neoliberal reform agenda, 178
'good dad', 14, 246–7
  see also fatherhood
good manners, 11
'good mother'/good motherhood, 63–4, 68–9, 72–3, 220–1
governance (of family meals), 6, 65, 165–7, 177–82, 254n.1, n.4
  deficiencies in, 175–6
  food policies and, 171–4
  see also 'biopolitics'/biopolitical governing system; neoliberal governance
governing strategies, 15, 167, 183–4

government campaigns, 35, 73
government initiatives, 8–9, 12
  see also Healthy Start (HS)
government policies, 7–8, 16, 94, 210, 214–16, 223, 224–5, 235, 245, 247–8
  food and health, 224–5
  and individual consumer choice, 247–8
governmentality, 16, 58, 169, 226–7, 228–9
grandparents/grandparental generation, 79–82, 87–8, 89
  accepting government support, 237
  spoiling of children, 90–2
Great Britain, 26
Green, T., 15
Griffiths, S., 255n.4
Gross, N., 83
Guardian, The, 248
Guildford, 137

Hägerstrand, T., 189
Hanson, C., 63
Harrison, M., 172
Hazard Analysis and Critical Control Points (HAACP), 7
health inequalities, 19
health interventions, 206, 211–12
health policies, 40, 208–9, 220, 255n.1
health professionals, 13, 15–16, 27–8, 31, 32–4, 63, 249
Health Protection Scotland (HPS), 228
health risks, 120, 241, 244
health visitors *see* health professionals
health-related consequences, 13, 35
'healthy choices', 8–9, 16, 208–10, 220, 252n.14
'healthy eating', 3, 11–12, 209–10, 212–13
  '5-a-day' target, 1–2
  caring, 203
  children's eating patterns, 20–1
  family practice implications for, 188–9
  food hygiene and, 175–6
  interventions, 214–16, 220–1, 223–5
  parenting, 16
  Shokuiku campaign, 177–9, 181–2
healthy eating interventions
  see 'healthy eating'
'healthy family'/healthy families, 15–16, 203, 205–25
  diets and, 210–13
  and food, 206–9
  see also well-being
healthy foods, 13, 31–3, 209, 211, 213–14, 215, 221, 224
  and children, 47, 248
  food safety and, 119–21
  and 'good' parenting practices, 218–20
  policy implementation in schools, 242–3
  time consuming preparation of, 234–5
Healthy Schools Initiative, 242
Healthy Start (HS), 10, 12–13, 175
  low-income pregnant women, 19–34
  Sheffield 'before and after study', 28–33
'healthy Wednesday' *see* Wednesday lunch-club
Heinz Ravioli, 153
heterosexual couples, 3, 35
heterosexual families, 3, 251n.4
Hetherington, K., 109
Hiroko, Takeda, 15
historical and sociological evidence (of family mealtimes and family eating), 10, 14–15, 135–6, 246
historical evidence (of changing role of food), 14
Hobsbawm, E., 132
Hollows, J., 95, 220
home cooking/home cooked, 52, 83–8, 239, 241, 251n.3
homeless centres *see* homeless shelters
homeless shelters, 16, 239–41
homemakers, 45, 148, 217
household chores/tasks, 38, 41, 48–50, 140, 141–4, 249
  see also domestic labour, division of

household composition, 13–14, 77, 97–8, 100–3, 195–6
  see also family forms
household labour, division of see households
households, 3, 4–6, 32, 52, 115–17, 224
  dual-career, 188
  decline of the 'family meal', 131–5
  division of labour in, 45–50
  female headed, 138–44
  food organisation in, 35–44, 51–6
  global change and, 247–8
  in Hungary and UK, 190–204
  inter-generational contact between, 80–2
  men's contribution to, 95–6
  family food practices, 98–114
'househusbands', 105, 110–13
Hughes, C., 220
human rights, 21
human time, 189, 190
Hungary, 12, 15, 188, 190–200, 201
hunger, 21, 34, 43, 48
Huxley, M., 229
hygiene see food hygiene

IDRs see institutional dining rooms
imagined families see 'fictive kin'/'fictive family'
immigrants/immigrant families, 12, 44, 132, 236, 239
Income Support, 19
income-based Jobseeker's Allowance, 19
Independent Inquiry into Inequalities in Health, 19
Independent on Sunday, The, 136
  'Sunday Lunch Campaign', 133
Index of Multiple Deprivation, 29
India/Indians, 8, 44
individual responsibility (for food choices), 15–16, 207–8, 211–13
individualisation (of food choices/diets), 3, 37, 41, 121, 124, 149, 167, 168, 169–70, 174–6, 208, 211
  biopolitical arrangements, 183
  eating together as a family, 113–14
  and food discourse, 166–7, 247–50

and lifestyle risks, 123, 126
low-income households and, 32–3
and preferences, 45, 55–6, 172
and responsibility for food choices, 15, 208
social embedding of food practices, 8–9, 41
women in pregnancy, 57–8
industrialised food production, 14
inequalities, 11, 21, 74, 206, 210–13
  health/dietary, 19, 247
  household divisions of labour, 93–6
infant feeding practices/activities, 32, 34, 54–5
institutional dining rooms (IDRs)/halls, 16, 226–8, 229, 232, 235–8, 244–5
  homeless shelters, 239–41
  schools, 229–34
institutional settings, 3–4, 173, 174, 226–4, 237–41
  see also homeless shelters
'intensive parenting', 38, 65–8
  see also parenting/parenting practices
inter-generational relations/inter-generational relationships, 13–14, 36–7, 43, 58–61, 77–9, 80–2, 86–7
  generational order within the family, 88–91
  meaning-constituted tradition, 83–5
inter-generationality see inter-generational relations/inter-generational relationships
interpretative phenomenological analysis (IPA), 98
Ipsos-Reid (international market research company), 118
iron, 13, 23, 30
Isaacs, D., 221

jacket potatoes, 85, 230
James, A., 236
Japan, 12, 15, 165–84
Jessop Wing (of Royal Hallamshire Hospital), 29
Jessop, R., 254n.4
Jobseeker's Allowance, 19

Joint Council of Midwifery (1939), 22
Joseph Rowntree Foundation, 210
Joshi, H., 94
'junk food', 247, 248
'junk food mums', 2, 225

Katona, Kerry (TV star), 63–4
Keenan, J., 13
Keighley, 137
Kerr, M., 148, 154, 156, 213, 253n.4
kitchen, the, 14, 41–5, 96, 107–8, 110, 206, 213–15, 230, 237–8
  in Edwardian era, 139–40, 142
  fathers contribution to, 106–15
  female accountability in, 150–1
  schools, 230–5
  see also public kitchen
Kjaernes, U., 251n.10
Koizumi, Prime Minister Junichiro, 177, 178

Labour Government (UK), 171–2
labour of love see emotional management (of the family)
Ladies Home Journal, 146, 150
Lancet, The, 23
Lang, T., 8, 172
Lawrence, F., 224
Lawson, Nigella, 220
Lea & Perrins, 153
learned family behaviours, 14, 121, 126–8
leftovers, 194–5, 199, 202
Leikas, S., 127, 128
Leverhulme Trust, The, 16, 252n.12
life-course, 2, 12–13, 78, 136, 191, 248
  eating cultures, 84–5
  food practices of parents' childhoods, 86–8, 92
lifestyle hazards see lifestyles
lifestyles, 27–8, 46–7, 60–2, 68, 161, 205
  food consumption, 72, 119, 177, 179, 182
  hazards, 119, 122–3
  'insidious social control' of, 58
  revolution in, 32–3
Ling, T., 208

Listeria, 7
Liverpool, 137
London, 4, 23, 26, 59, 137, 255n.3
lone parent families/one-parent families, 3, 4, 38, 80, 116
long-term habits, 14, 121, 126–7
low birth weight, 20, 25
Low Income Diet and Nutrition Survey, 32
low-income groups, 19, 32
low-income post-natal women/low-income mothers, 20, 21, 31
low-income pregnant women, 12–13
  food support benefits to, 19–34
  WFS, volume-based food supplement, 27–8
low-income women see low-income post-natal women/low-income mothers
Luhmann, N., 170
lunchtime/lunch boxes, 2, 11, 194, 199, 225
  children and, 225, 229–30, 232–4
  main meal, 201–2
  at work, 203
Lupton, Deborah, 187

Macintyre, S., 174
malnourishment/malnutrition/undernourished, 20–2, 31, 33
manners see good manners
Markens, S., 61, 67
'market failures', 174–5
married couples, 3, 60, 97–8, 218
Marsden, T., 172, 173
masculinities, 96, 156
Mason, J., 5
'materialities', 189, 190, 242
maternal bodies, 13, 57–60, 73–4
  infant feeding practices and, 68–72
  public surveillance and control of, 61–7
maternal mortality, 22–3
maternal nutrition, 32, 53
Maternity Alliance, 32
Matthews, Bernard, 251n.1
McDonald's, 255n.2

McFadden, Brian, 64
'meal deal', 232, 235
meal preparation, 35, 43–4, 45, 51–3, 95, 115
mealtimes, 10–11, 53, 113–15, 138–42, 144, 145, 187–204, 253n.2
　accommodating baby's needs, 53–4
　Edwardian practices of, 136–7
　and related chores, 98
　social significance of, 134–5
media, 8, 58, 60–1, 64, 125–6, 211
　articulation of 'moral panic' by, 132–3, 253n.3
　and celebrities, 63, 205
　and children's eating habits, 235
　discourses about food and health, 223–4
　family meal campaigns, 10, 14–15
　motherhood and pregnancy, 58, 64, 73–4
　nutrition research findings, 33
　reporting of food scares/risks, 14, 120–4, 128, 176–7
　school meals campaigns, 11
media discourses, 211, 223–4
Medical Officers of Health, 22
medicalisation (of pregnancy), 10, 13, 58, 61, 64–74
'Men, Children and Food' study, 96, 115–17, 254n.1
　fathers' involvement in family food practices, 98–114
men's voices, 14, 93, 96
menu, 230, 234, 239, 241, 242
middle-class families, 12
Miller, D., 253n.3
Ministry of Agriculture, Fisheries and Food, 7
Mitchell, C., 138
Moisio, R., 86
　'sense of coherence' in family life, 86–7
Montreal Diet Dispensary (MDD) programme, 25
'moral panic', 14–15, 131–3, 135, 144, 249, 253n.3

Morgan, D., 5, 6, 78, 85, 251n.8
Morrison, M., 252n.14
mortality rates, 22
mother-daughter dyads, 43
motherhood, 2, 13, 30–8, 42–5, 51, 248
　and caring practices, 222–3
　changes over time in, 57–63
　employment and, 39, 41, 46
　ideals and norms of, 73–4
　and infant feeding practices, 68–72
　medicalisation of, 64–74
　transition to, 46–50, 55
　voluntary childlessness, 40
　see also mothering; pregnancy; pregnant women
mothering, 39–40, 45, 47, 150
　see also motherhood
mother-in-law, 156
Murcott, A., 93, 95, 96, 107, 117, 134, 135, 144, 147, 148, 149, 156, 200, 251nn.7–8, 253n.1, 256n.5
　'cooked dinner', 134
　'It's a Pleasure to Cook for Him' (paper), 117
'my mother' generation, 60–5, 69–72
'My Mother, My Self' project, 59–72
'my self' generation, 60, 69–71
myths (of the family meal), 14, 15–16, 131, 142–5, 206, 219–20
　commonalities in, 140–1
　current debates on, 133–5
　food-related scripts and, 87
　longer-term trends, 136–9
　moral panics, 132

'nanny state', 62, 183–4
National 'Change4Life' programme, 32
National Birthday Trust Fund (NBTF), 22–3
national diet see food policy/national food policy
national food policy see food policy/national food policy
National Institute for Health and Clinical Excellence (NICE), 33

neoliberalism/neoliberal governance, 58, 62–8, 74, 167, 177–9, 243, 254n.3
  globalisation and, 167
  and responsibilisation, 168
  shortcomings in food policy, 173–6
  technology of, 167, 183–4
  upgrading national governing system, 167, 170
  see also 'biopolitics'/biopolitical governing system; governance (of family meals)
Neuhaus, Jessamyn, 149
neural tube defects, 30–1
new baby, 51, 53
'new' foods, 48, 85, 179, 183–4
Nilsen, A., 94
  'fatherhood to fathering', 94
'(no) Family (no) Food' project, 239–45
non-heterosexual couples see 'chosen' families
normative pressure, 183–4
Northern Ireland, 4
nourishment/malnutrition/undernourished, 20–2, 31–4
Novelli, Jean-Christophe, 133
nuclear family, 5–6, 11, 43, 88, 162
  archetypal/traditional, 3–4, 217
  'spoiling' children, 89–91
  and vegetarianism, 88
nutrition, 11, 16, 21–3, 29, 206, 248
  and food enjoyment, 119
  government regulation of, 227–9
  and healthy eating and cooking, 178–9, 210–16, 232, 245
  interventions, 32, 34
  media representations/coverage of, 33, 119–20, 161–2
  pregnant and post-natal women, 12–13, 28–9, 51–4
  research, 32, 33
  in school meals, 1, 242–4
  surveillance, 21, 57, 74
  training, 32–4
  for women and children, 19–20, 24–5, 26–7, 31–2, 166–7, 234–5
nutritional initiatives, 1–2
nutritional standards, 1–2, 53

nutritional status, 19, 20–1, 27, 33
nutritionists, 206, 227

O'Malley, P., 168
obesity/overweight, 1, 13, 19–21, 247–8, 249–50, 252n.11
  care deficit and, 187–8
  high prevalence in UK, 31–2
  lifestyle issues and, 120
  'obesity epidemic', 120, 122
  political concerns over/policy efforts, 179, 189–90, 221–3
  see also childhood obesity
'objective time', 15–16, 188, 190
Oliver, Jamie, 1, 2, 96
Ontario Public Health Association, 21
Orr, Boyd, 25
Oxford, 137
Oxo gravy cubes, 156

packed lunches, 2, 230
paid employment, 42, 43, 47, 49, 109, 111, 140, 145, 225
paid work/unpaid work, 43–5, 95, 131, 221, 223
Pakistanis, 44
parenthood, 35–7, 41–5, 55, 252n.2
  approach to food safety, 118–28
  household labour, 39–40
parenting styles, 38, 55
parenting/parenting practices, 16, 55, 109–11, 137, 206, 218, 246–7
  and family food practices, 42, 206, 218–20, 224–5
  'fatherhood to fathering', 94–5
  'intensive' style of, 38–9, 65
  moral connotations about, 217–20
  'paranoid parenting', 72–3
Parkin, K., 146, 150, 152, 154, 156
  Food as Love (2006), 146
pasta, 8, 51, 84–5, 105, 232, 235, 238, 239
Patient Administration System (PAS), 29
patriarchal societies, 40–1, 96
Patten, Marguerite, 153
Paxo Stuffing, 153
People's League of Health (PLOH), 23

peri-conceptional supplements, 31
personhood, 188, 207–8
Peyton, Oliver, 133
pizza, 105, 114, 197–8, 230, 235, 243
point of delivery, 11, 208, 220
policy and practice, 11, 206, 248
Poole, M., 221
post-natal women, 13, 20, 22, 28, 29, 30
poverty, 11, 28, 138
  optimal nutrition, 210–11, 220
  patterns of food consumption, 224
practices/social practices
  'doing' family, 3–6, 14, 78–9, 85–8, 92, 131–2, 188, 246, 251n.8
  family eating practices, 15–16, 45–50, 73, 74, 81–2, 85, 86–8, 89–114, 134–6, 175–6, 203, 205–6, 211–13, 216, 217–20, 221–3
  family practices, 5–6, 44, 55–6, 79, 182, 183, 188–9, 190, 206–10, 216–20, 225, 246–7
  food practices, 6–12, 84–7, 88–92, 94–6, 98–115, 144–5, 188–90, 217, 245–50, 253n.4
  parenting/parenting practices, 16, 38–9, 42, 55, 65, 72–3, 94–5, 109–11, 137, 206, 217–20, 224–5, 246–7
  see also cooking practices
pregnancy outcomes, 19, 20
'pregnancy police', 40, 57–60, 69–70
  moral geographies of motherhood, 71–2
  public surveillance and control, 61–8
pregnancy, 2, 28–9, 40–1, 60–3, 74, 248
  diet/nutrition in, 19–28, 30–9, 40–50, 55–6, 249
  'healthy living' during, 10
  medicalisation of, 57–9, 64–74
  planning of, 60–1
  post-natal period, 42, 51–4
  see also motherhood; pregnant women

pregnant women, 12–13, 29–31, 68–71, 73–4
  food support benefits to, 19–28
  'insidious social control', 57–8
  public surveillance and control of, 58, 61–7
prejudices, 11, 15–16, 206
pressure groups, 94–6, 173–6
primary schools, 96–8, 192, 229–31
'proper meal', 42, 95
'provisioning' (of food), 94, 115, 191–2, 195, 199–200
public consciousness, 200
public debate, 14, 132
  current debates, 133–6
public health nutrition, 23
public kitchen, 96, 213–16, 222–5
  see also kitchen, the
public policy, 8, 21, 171
Putney, N., 253n.3

Qvortrup, J., 78

Ranger, T., 132
'ready meals', 52, 84–5
Reckwitz, A., 5
Reilly, J., 253n.3
responsibilisation (of food governance), 168–70
retailer-led governance system (of food), 6, 21, 212–13
  in Japanese food policy, 176–82
  restoring consumer trust in food, 7–8
  role in UK food system, 15, 171–5
  see also food retailers
Ribbens McCarthy, J., 216, 246, 251n.5
'right foods', 99–106, 222–3
risk see food safety/food security
  health risks, 120, 241, 244
  technological food hazard/risks, 119–21, 127
  see also food safety/food security
Rogers, I., 20
Rose, N., 169
routines and rhythms, 15–16, 247–8
Royal Hallamshire Hospital, Sheffield, 29

Salford, 137
salmonella contamination, 6–7, 122, 123, 171, 176
salt consumption/intake, 1, 175
same-sex couples *see* 'chosen' families; same-sex partnerships/households; same-sex partnerships
same-sex family units *see* same-sex partnerships
same-sex partnerships/households, 3, 4, 37–8, 251n.6
  see also gay and lesbian couples/families
Samuel, R., 132
  'the myths we live by', 132
Schatzki, T.R., 189
school lunch *see* school meals
school meals, 1–2, 11, 193
  free, 22, 230
  objectives of, 242, 243
'scientific motherhood', 63–72
'second generation Ukrainians', 237, 244–5
  see also 'first generation Ukrainians'
Second World War/World War II, 4, 23, 28, 34, 162, 254n.1
  changes in family living arrangements, 6–8
  rationing and food support benefits, 22
secondary schools, 1, 2, 229, 231–5, 242–3
self-governance, 6, 65–8, 73–4, 167, 227
separation, 3, 4, 37, 81
Seven-Eleven Japan, 181
Sheffield, 12, 28, 29, 30, 120
  National 'Change4Life' programme, 32–3
Shibutani, T., 132
Shokuiku/Shokuiku campaign, 177, 178, 179, 181–2, 255nn.7–8
shopping, 14, 30, 45–50, 96, 115, 120, 173, 174, 213, 224
  eating habits, 121
  food scares/risks, 122–4

reliance on male partners for, 51, 93, 98–105, 116–17, 197, 246
Short, Frances, 251n.2
single-parent families *see* lone parent families/one-parent families
Smart, C., 82
snacking/snacks, 10, 135, 138, 194
social actors, 16, 78, 226, 229, 242, 244–5
social barriers, 12, 70
social class/classes, 14–15, 66, 79, 97, 121, 137, 144, 224
social cohesion, 200, 241
social differentiation *see* inequalities
social embedding, 8–9, 12, 248
social groups, 72, 73, 167, 174–5
social ills, 132–3, 187–8
social institutions, 3–6, 39, 131–2, 138, 144, 166
social interaction/life, 91, 132, 227, 229, 243
social networks, 3, 5, 71, 135–6, 207, 224
social organisation, 131, 147–8
social practices, 5–6, 15–16, 152, 187
  creation and recreation of families, 188–90
  weekly 'Sunday lunch', 144–5
  see also practices/social practices
social relationships, 14, 91–2, 187–90
social security, 21, 26, 179
Social Services, 240
social significance (of cooked meals/'family meals'), 15–16, 134, 251n.3
social support, 20, 25
socialisation/socialising, 11, 13, 41–5, 54, 56, 151, 244
'Socio Historical Transmission and Food Values' project, 239–45
socio-economic status, 20–1, 32–3, 69, 142–5
Soho Hospital for Women, London, 26
South Wales, 133
South Yorkshire, 2, 80, 121, 231
spatio-temporal contexts (of food activities), 188–9

Index 291

Special Supplemental Nutrition Programme for Women, Infants and Children (WIC), 24, 31
stakeholders (of institutional dining rooms), 228–9, 233–4, 243–5
Stapleton, H., 13
Star Magazine, 63–4
state-individual relationship, 166–7, 170
step-families/stepfamilies, 3–4, 38, 104, 246–7, 251n.5
study couples, 45
SUB Club, 236, 237–9, 244
subjectivity (in food choices), 15, 151, 166, 168–71, 182–3
Sunday Dinner, 107, 108, 114
Sunday lunch, 42–3, 112, 133–4, 144, 202, 203–4
supermarkets/supermarket chains, 6, 99, 105, 180–1, 211
 accessibility to, 174
 and children's food habits, 227
 pre-prepared ingredients and meals from, 116
 shopping economy in, 21, 104, 211
Supplementary Benefit (SB), 26
surveillance/social surveillance, 10, 13, 21, 57–61, 69–74, 182, 231–9, 244–5, 249–50
 government, 176–82
 in homeless shelters, 240–3
 in IDRs, 228–9
 of infant feeding practices, 68–72
 'insidious social control', 57–61
 neoliberal governance and, 62–7
 private kitchen practices, 213–15
 in schools, 231–4, 243
Sutton, D.E., 195

technological food hazards/risks, 119–21, 127
 see also lifestyles
Thatcherite Britain, 168
Thompson, Jonathan, 133

Thompson, P., 4, 132, 133, 136, 137, 138
 The Edwardians (1975), 136
 'the myths we live by', 132
 The Voice of the Past (1978), 136
Time *see* human time
 existential time, 188, 190, 192, 194–196, 202
 'experiential time', 15–16
 'objective time', 15–16
Times On-line, The, 2
Toronto supplementation study, 24
tradition, 12, 15, 83, 84, 86, 132, 195–6, 255n.2
Sunday lunch, 133
traditional family, 87–8, 187–90
'traditional' food, 83–4, 86, 87, 89–90, 196, 241, 255n.2
transnational families, 4
treats/treat foods, 10, 48, 90–1, 197–8
Turkey Twizzlers, 1, 251n.1

UK Food Surveillance System, 228
UK food system, 15, 171–5
UK, 4, 6, 7, 15, 19, 20, 25, 27, 28, 30, 31, 34, 35, 54, 62, 64, 77, 118, 122, 123, 125, 165–84, 188, 190–200, 201, 205, 206, 208, 228, 249, 251n.6, 254n.3
Ukrainian club (Bradford), 227, 235–9
Ukrainian community, 12, 238, 244
'Ukrainian family', 239
Ukrainian Information Services, 239
undernourished *see* malnourishment/malnutrition/ undernourished
unhealthy diets, 32, 179
United States, 73
University of Sheffield, 121
user-clients (of institutional dining rooms), 228–45

vegetables, 86–8, 177, 139, 194, 200–1, 238
  '5-a-day' target for, 1–2, 12
  element of 'cooked dinner'/'proper meals', 156, 230, 231, 232, 253n.4
  healthy eating and, 224
  HS scheme vouchers for, 27–8, 30
  in low socio-economic groups/households, 21, 32
vegetarianism, 87–8, 177
vitamin C, 13, 23, 30
vitamins, 23, 26, 27, 34
voluntary associations/organisations, 16, 182, 226
vouchers (Healthy Start), 12–13, 19, 24, 27–8, 32
'vulnerable' groups, 24, 27, 32, 37, 124, 183, 227
  homeless, 241
  lower social groups, 174–5
  mothers, 22, 55
  population segments, 227
  user-clients of IDRs, 227, 243

wage earners, 41, 45, 49
Wainwright, E.M., 63
Wallace, J., 255n.4
Warde, A., 109, 135, 146, 149, 153, 160, 161, 162, 251n.9
Wednesday lunch-club, 236–9, 241, 244
Weeks, J., 3
Welfare Food Scheme (WFS) (1940), 22–3, 26–8, 30–1

well-being, 13, 25, 38, 207–8, 214, 223, 226, 228
  see also 'healthy family'/healthy families
Western Europe, 167
White Papers, 8, 19, 178, 181, 182, 208, 255n.1
  Choosing Health: Making Healthier Choice Easier (2004), 8, 19
Williams, F., 208
Winship, J., 150, 160
Woman and Home (WH), 146, 151, 152, 162
Woman's Own (WO), 14, 146, 150, 151, 152, 153, 161, 162
women's diet, 13, 249
women's role (in the family), 12, 187
working lives, 15–16, 139–42
working-class families, 26, 53–5, 137–8, 140, 141, 248
  childcare in, 69–71, 248
  pre-natal care for, 63–4
workplaces, 39–40, 46, 58, 69, 223, 247
World Bank, 8
World Health Organisation (WHO), 188, 255n.1
World Trade Organisation (WTO), 172, 177
World War II *see* Second World War/World War II

Yorkshire family, 194–200
young mothers, 10, 134, 247